It Ended Badly

It Ended Badly

*Thirteen of the
Worst Breakups
in History*

Jennifer Wright

Henry Holt and Company
New York

Henry Holt and Company, LLC
Publishers since 1866
175 Fifth Avenue
New York, New York 10010
www.henryholt.com

Henry Holt® and ® are registered trademarks of Henry Holt and Company, LLC.

Distributed in Canada by Raincoast Book Distribution Limited.

Library of Congress Cataloging-in-Publication Data is available.

ISBN: 978-1-62779-286-8

Henry Holt books are available for special promotions and premiums.
For details contact: Director, Special Markets.

First Edition 2015

Designed by Meryl Sussman Levavi

Printed in the United States of America

1   3   5   7   9   10   8   6   4   2

*To Abe, Andy, Brennan, Chris, Colin, Dana, Davey,
Gustavo, Jared, Jason, Lex, Liam, Morgan, Nate,
Opus, Peter, Roby, Tim, and Tom*

From whom I learned some things

And to Mary James (Grandma)

From whom I learned a lot of things

In the end, only three things matter: how much you loved, how gently you lived, and how gracefully you let go of things not meant for you.

—Buddha

♡

We are never ever ever ever getting back together. Like, ever.

—Taylor Swift

Contents

It Ended Badly

Introduction

*I*f you are lying in bed right now, a pint of ice cream in one hand, a bottle of Scotch in the other, and this book clenched between your teeth (one tooth is missing from last night's bar fight), with tears streaming down your face over how much you loved, loved, loved your ex, let me commend you on how well you are coping. You could be doing so much worse. *So* much worse. You could be beheading your ex or castrating strangers or starting an exciting new life with a sex doll. *YOU ARE A HERO.* Your restraint exceeds that of the Dalai Lama, who is the happiest, most loving person I can think of. He can't even date, probably because if he did there would inevitably be tabloid stories of a drunk Dalai Lama speed-dialing his ex forty times in a row.

God knows I have done that. The most embarrassing moments of my life have all been spurred by breakups. I know there are people who handle romantic disappointment by talking calmly to their therapists, taking some time to grieve quietly, and reemerging grateful for what they have learned. Sometimes I pretend to be one of those people, but in reality I am someone who handles breakups by taking Klonopin, sleeping for sixteen hours at a time, and writing long, honest, *heartfelt* e-mails to my ex. And then some texts to make sure my messages arrived.

I have also been known to listlessly dump a pint of Ben & Jerry's Cookie Dough ice cream into a pan to see if it will bake into a giant cookie rather than going to the store for more cookies. It will, by the way, so that's not really embarrassing so much as it is a fun baking tip.

We know there's nothing better than love. Even a Ben & Jerry's Cookie Dough ice-cream cookie, while a close second, is not as good. (I have, admittedly, never tried heroin.) You don't even have to *believe* in love for this statement to be true. Love isn't Santa Claus. It is real emotion that results in altered brain chemistry. This seems obvious because anyone who has ever loved knows there is no pleasure greater. When I think of the things in life that I most enjoy—wintry mornings cozy in bed, old movies, good food and wine with friends, and the first cup of coffee in the morning—I am so aware of how much better all of these are when shared with someone you love. Loving someone who loves you back is perhaps the only time we feel completely safe and joyful and kinder. It's like coming in from the rain, arriving someplace safe and warm.

When love stops, it feels like being outside in a hurricane. (Unlike heroin, I have been out in a hurricane for almost a full minute; a cool personal fact about how I'm a survivor.)

And just as most people experience love, most suffer the heartbreak of breakups. A mathematician much smarter than me, using assumptions on the number of people in the world and how many breakups are average, very conservatively estimated that half a million people suffer a breakup every day. These breakups usually happen after about six months of dating. Evolutionary biologists found that people experiencing heartbreak have brain scans that mirror those of cocaine addicts in withdrawal. We do not handle breakups well. Humans are unbelievably resilient creatures in the face of most of the world's horrors. We are brave in battle, heroic in the face of disease, and really just terrific on the whole until someone breaks up with us. And then we absolutely *implode*.

That such a state of love can be attained and then lost seems *insane*. No wonder we behave insensibly—the best feeling in the world has vanished. This is the perfect time to go crazy.

We often crash in ways that horrify ourselves. Later, when we look back, we often obsess about stupid, angry, or, in retrospect, just plain weird things we did. Perhaps you were very bad at your job for a while or showed some irrational behavior like throwing things—crumpled-up letters, old CDs, tiny animal figurines— against a wall. Or you might have been more creative. Why did you think making a heart-shaped mosaic of chopped-up tie pieces would bring anyone back? That never won anybody back! I firmly believe that one day the ladies of Icona Pop will think about how they threw their ex's belongings into a bag and kicked it down the stairs and will reflect, "Maybe that was not my finest moment." In that hideous afterglow, we are all left wondering if we are the worst person ever. Heartbreak has the potential to make everyone a worse version of themselves. When my friends do that, I hold their hands tenderly and tell them, "You're not the worst. Norman Mailer is the worst. Norman Mailer is always the worst."

Norman Mailer actually is the worst, but we'll get to that later in this book.

If your breakup makes you behave like a tormented, crazed shell of your former self, you are not alone. Some of the most notable, most talented people in the world have gone absolutely nuts in the face of romantic disappointment. Edith Wharton. Oskar Kokoschka. Oscar Wilde. Awesome men and women who have left profound artistic legacies for the world have crumbled in the face of heartbreak. The notorious people of history—who have left so-so legacies—go even crazier. Think how Henry VIII just started lopping off heads. Anna Ivanovna locked people in an ice palace. Things got weird.

There is a great scene in the classic movie *The Lion in Winter* (1968) where a group of men are waiting to be killed. One says that he is determined to die nobly, and a second replies, "You chivalric fool, as if the way one fell down mattered." The first responds, "When the fall is all there is, it matters." There are many situations in life—certainly breakups—when we're not going to get what we want, regardless of how we behave. We can choose whether to fall badly, like Nero, Henry VIII, Norman Mailer, and many others in this book. Or we can try to fall well, like Anne Boleyn and Oscar Wilde, and to handle our suffering with poise and elegance.

Most of us fall somewhere in between.

You may think that everything was sublimely romantic in past eras, and knights pledged themselves to ladies forever, and Mr. Darcy was always riding about on a horse ready to marry someone. That's never been the case. History isn't the present, but it's not *that* different and certainly not any better.

The disappointments surrounding love today were experienced just as much, and often with more terrifying consequences, by humans in the past. In any era, love and heartbreak preoccupy everyone who is not a saint or a psychopath. Love and its after-effects are the main preoccupation of good people, bad people, most all people. You know, maybe even psychopaths are affected, because look at Emperor Nero. Or take the Borgias, who were known mostly for poisoning their enemies. And orgies. Lucrezia Borgia did not plot political overthrows at night, lying in her bed. She went to sleep preoccupied with worry that she was going to run into her ex-husband and it was going to be *so weird.*

There's no time in history where people have not experienced heartbreak. If anything, it used to happen more because there were no television distractions. (TV is great. Don't let anyone tell you different. It is the only thing stopping wealthy, idle people from forcing underlings to dress up as chickens and pretend to lay eggs in their foyers—another real thing that happened.)

But aside from realizing that a breakup can badly affect any-one and everyone throughout history—and some of these stories are weird, weirder than Anna Ivanovna's wildest dreams—there is another, more reassuring message to take away from these tales. Heartbreak is almost never the defining moment of one's life. Almost no one is remembered simply for their outlandish breakup behavior (and in the case of Norman Mailer this is *frustratingly* true). When you look up Oskar Kokoschka, he is acknowledged, according to the Belvedere Palace and Museum in Vienna, as "a seminal pioneer of Expressionism." He is not referenced as "that guy who built a giant sex doll shaped exactly like his ex-girlfriend." No one actually remembers the doll. I mean, I do, and you will, so I guess I'm ruining that for him, but until this moment most people forgot about Oskar's sex doll. Oscar Wilde, on the other hand, is so beloved that a barrier had to be erected in front of his grave because people kissed it too much (and most of those affec-tionate souls were probably more familiar with *The Importance of Being Earnest* or *The Picture of Dorian Gray* than "The Ballad of Reading Gaol"). Edith Wharton doesn't quite rival Jane Austen as a "lady writer young women idolize," but give her another hundred years. So while our breakups can feel terrifying and all-encompassing and the major event of our lives as they are happening—they gener-ally aren't the crowning moment.

People go on. They lead good lives. They do great things.

There are happy endings.

Experiencing great love with someone new and better is a kind of happy ending that happens *all the time*. And there can be other growth from breakups. Sometimes they are necessary to help us accomplish what we need to do and to transform us into who we need to be. Eleanor of Aquitaine had to experience romantic dis-appointment to break free of suppressing herself as just a wife and mother. Edith Wharton needed loss to write some of her most enduring and touching works. As great as happiness is, knowing loss often helps us connect with and comfort others.

Undoubtedly, love is a dangerous and potentially fatal game. But what alternative do we have? It's the only sport in town. Without its pursuit, what would we do? We might build more aqueducts and have more scientific cures, but what for? Those accomplishments exist so we can have more years to brew coffee with our partners in the morning.

So we go on from breakups. We pick ourselves up whichever way we fall. We mend ourselves as best we can, and the breaks make us more interesting. We appreciate love more the next time we find it. We are heroic survivors, stronger and wiser and better.

Except for some of the people in these stories.

1. Nero

Poppaea

You know what's amazing? That we become upset when a politician cheats on his wife. Remember President Bill Clinton? Or would you like to discuss other of our country's leaders? And every time we, as a society, react with distress and disappointment, my heart sings a little. It rejoices because people actually behave extremely well now. That sense of collective indignation would not have happened had we lived in ancient Rome. To those living under the reign of Emperor Nero, the idea of a high-ranking political figure getting into trouble because they had sex with another willing adult would be *hilarious*.

That is because ancient Rome was a world full of nightmares, where every romance became a horror movie ending in poisoning, murder, suicide, and, in Nero's case, what may be the most terrifying rebound in history.

Maybe you could blame a tiny bit of Emperor Nero's difficulties with relationships on his parents. Most people learn about relationships from their parents—how to keep love alive and overcome

Nero has one of those busts that you immediately want to punch in the face.

differences and all of those good things, but also in some cases how to break up without killing each other. Sadly, the humane approach was not something Emperor Nero was taught by his mother, Agrippina the Younger.

There are many accounts about her horrible activities, but this one story sums up her villainess-on-a-soap-opera persona. First you have to understand that, in addition to being the mother of Emperor Nero and the sister of Emperor Caligula, Agrippina was married to Emperor Claudius. I bet you remember him. You picked up this book, so you strike me as the kind of person who studied a dead language and watched the *I, Claudius* television miniseries with a container of your favorite Ben & Jerry's ice cream resting in your lap.

(In college I studied ancient Greek, Late Night Snack is my favorite flavor, and I'll be coming to your house next week for a BBC movie night. I am really looking forward to it!)

But if you need a refresher: Claudius was the fourth emperor of Rome. He is probably best remembered for his numerous tics including a stammer and a limp. He was also thought to be partially deaf. The historian Suetonius wrote, "His knees were weak and gave way under him and his head shook. He stammered and his speech was confused. He slobbered and his nose ran when he was excited." Suetonius also said that his mother, Antonia, often called him "a monster of a man, not finished but merely begun by

Dame Nature." If she accused anyone of dullness, she used to say that he was "a bigger fool than her son Claudius."

She was wrong. In reality, Claudius was a smart man who needed a hanky.

Seriously. None of his tics had any influence on Claudius's very considerable intellect. Those quirks caused people to assume he was mentally delayed, though. That was great. If you are transported back to ancient Roman high society, begin with this pretense. If you show any trace of intellect, ambition, or popularity, whoever is in power will more than likely decide you are an enemy trying to usurp them and will kill you. Acting like a simpleton is your best bet for survival. To stay alive in ancient Rome, you should operate the way you would if you suddenly discovered all of your friends were in the Mafia.

So Claudius was fortunate, because his tics caused everyone to dismiss him. While his relatives were killing one another, they simply overlooked him. Except for a consulship that he shared with his nephew Caligula in 37 CE, Claudius didn't really enter public life until age forty-nine in 41 CE. He was then crowned emperor following the assassination of Caligula, in which he may or may not have been involved. Supposedly the people loved him. Following the assassination, according to Suetonius, "the populace, who stood about the [senate] hall, called for one ruler and expressly named Claudius. He allowed the armed assembly of the soldiers to swear allegiance to him, and promised each man fifteen thousand sesterces; being the first of the Caesars who resorted to bribery to secure the fidelity of the troops."

See? Smart.

He then revealed himself to be extremely competent and intelligent, and had a brilliant reign, greatly expanding the Roman Empire, even as far as Britain. His only real misstep might have been marrying Agrippina and adopting Nero.

Almost all historians agree that in 54 CE Agrippina poisoned a dish of Claudius's mushrooms. This is referenced in many comedies of the time; there are tons of mushroom jokes. In his *Epigrams* Martial directs the comment "May you eat such a mushroom as Claudius ate!" to an unlikable character. All of the jokes are identical; they're all just "go eat a mushroom and die." Today, you can really only use that line to insult your four friends who studied ancient Greek and Latin (who are also invited to our BBC drama night), but maybe it will give them a chuckle.

Perhaps because of all those bad jokes, people remember the mushrooms today. What is often forgotten is that, according to the historian Tacitus, Claudius attempted to use a feather to induce vomiting. Remember, Claudius was a smart man, and doubtless thought if he had been truly poisoned, he could tickle his throat and vomit up the poison. Great planning, right? Really clever.

Agrippina poisoned the feather.

At least that's my favorite version of the story about how Claudius died. There's some dispute. Suetonius claimed that Agrippina fed Claudius a second helping of poison in a bowl of gruel that she said would soothe his stomach. That just never strikes me as being as elegant as the feather. The point is, though, that she not only poisoned her husband but poisoned him twice.

If you are feeling really bad for the emperor right now, know that Claudius had executed his third wife, Valeria Messalina (Agrippina was the fourth), and her lover. Supposedly Valeria married her lover, Gaius Silius, while Claudius was away on vacation. She celebrated with an enormous wedding and a public banquet—never a smart thing to do, under any circumstances, if you are already married. (And especially risky today, with Twitter and Instagram.) Claudius also ordered the deaths of all the wedding guests. Allegedly when he was informed at dinner that his orders had been carried out and they'd all been killed, he just calmly asked for more wine.

Remember, these tales are only intended to set up the story of Emperor Nero's breakup. His parents had nothing on him.

Have I mentioned that ancient Rome was a mind-bogglingly bloody place? Many people mistakenly believe that Rome was somehow a more civilized place to live than, say, medieval Europe. Granted, the Middle Ages were a terrifying time. Scholars from the period were more or less in agreement that it was a time when everyone who did anything deserved to die. In the eleventh century Saint Peter Damian ruled that a Venetian princess deserved to die of a wasting disease because she ate her food with a fork. There was a lot of talk around that time about whether or not forks were tools of Satan. (Answer: maybe. I guess we'll never know.)

Compared to that deadly religious fervor, ancient Rome, with its indoor plumbing and togas and organized system of government, seems pretty cool. If people think that it was violent at all, they kind of confine that vision to gladiatorial arenas and just imagine Russell Crowe killing people. And as every single middle school Latin or history teacher will point out, *gladiatorial matches did not necessarily end in death.*

Do you know what those teachers do not tell us? That gladiatorial matches ended in death most of the time and not just for the gladiators. That sometimes audience members—just people who'd shown up for a good time to see the fights!—would be pulled into the arena and thrown to wild animals. Extra death!

Romans loved finding creative and unexpected ways to kill people. The Roman punishment for patricide was to blindfold the offender, beat him repeatedly with rods, and then toss him into a sack. An ape, a snake, a dog, and a rooster would also be put in the sack, and then it would be sewn up. The idea was that those animals would not be friends. But, you know, it didn't really matter because then the bag would be thrown into a river. Even if you had some sort of Kumbaya moment where you were able to simultaneously charm an ape, a snake, a dog, and a rooster (in this situation you are not only a time traveler but also Dr. Doolittle), you would drown anyway.

So I don't know why history teachers try to make ancient Rome

sound civilized. If the city-state had a motto, it would be ABSO-
LUTELY NO ONE HERE DIES OF NATURAL CAUSES. There is a very
bad movie called *The Purge* (2013), starring Ethan Hawke, whose
illogical premise—and tagline!—is FOR ONE NIGHT OF THE YEAR,
ALL CRIME IS LEGAL. That was seemingly the generally accepted
operating system in 50 CE Rome—365 days a year.

Accordingly, if a Roman couple broke up and one or both of
them killed the other, that would not even merit a footnote. It
would be surprising if that did *not* happen. And yet it was completely unnecessary—divorce was common in ancient Rome. I have
only mentioned Nero's mom and dad in this story:

- To provide fun facts for you to bring up the next time anyone anywhere praises ancient Rome as the first great civilized nation. You are going to *crush* seventh-grade history
  teachers.
- To offer some insight into the severity of Nero's reaction to
  his own breakup with Poppaea. Which was *terrible*.

If you know anything about Emperor Nero, it's that he was
insane and supposedly played the fiddle while Rome burned. He
was mad. That part is true, and we'll get to that. He didn't actually
fiddle, though! According to the historian Dio, he climbed to the
roof of the palace, dressed up in professional singer garb, and sang
verses about the burning of Ilium (Troy). Which is not an improve-
ment, really, now that I think about it.

Nero inherited his mother's love of pageantry and ruthless-
ness, and had none of his stepfather's understated intellect. At
every key moment in his life, he expressed his desire to be a poet
or a musician. He was not very good at either, as far as we know,
but it's possible that had his mother not been pushing him to be
emperor, he would have had a reasonably happy, sane life, perhaps
killing only one or two or three people. So, a normal number for
the time.

Agrippina had been campaigning for Nero to be emperor since he was age nine, when she told everyone that he slept surrounded by snakes. He didn't. That was just something she told people, like some parents say their kid aced the SATs. All of those people are lying, maybe. I don't know. I did not ace the SATs and am not a sleuth.

Nero had the kind of disposition where he saw himself performing on a grand stage all the time. And he wanted a partner. He was married to Claudius's daughter, Octavia, in 53 CE. Agrippina arranged the marriage because she thought it would lend an appearance of legitimacy to his reign—that is to say, he should be emperor because he was not only adopted by Claudius but also married to his daughter.

Octavia was, according to Tacitus, a virtuous Roman wife. I imagine she had some problems being married into the family that murdered her father, but she took it in stride—as a virtuous Roman wife who did not want to die. Nero did not desire her and responded to her virtue by periodically trying to strangle her.

But that is not the bad breakup in this story.

The bad breakup involved Nero's love affair with Poppaea Sabina, which began in 58 CE. Poppaea Sabina supposedly possessed every virtue someone like Nero could want. In other words, Tacitus claimed she "possessed

This picture does not do remote justice to how much Poppaea looked like Christina Hendricks. Just imagine Christina Hendricks.

every virtue but goodness." He also wrote, "From her mother the loveliest woman of the day, she inherited distinction and beauty. Her wealth, too, was equal to her birth. She was clever and pleasant to talk to. She seemed respectable. But her life was depraved." A fun fact: according to Suetonius, her beauty secret was donkey milk and gladiator jism.

The philosopher and dramatist Seneca also compares her to Octavia in his play *Octavia* thusly:

NERO: I have a consort whom her rank and beauty make worthy of my bed; Venus would yield to her, Venus and loyal Juno and armed Minerva.

SENECA: Virtue and loyalty and the pure heart—these things should please a husband, these alone. The glories of the soul live to eternity. The flower of beauty fades from day to day.

NERO: God had united every high perfection in her: the Fates created her for me.

Nero liked her a lot! If you believe Seneca, Poppaea was super-hot (this seems true, based on a posthumous depiction of her where she closely resembled the actress Christina Hendricks), and Nero decided that meant he was her soul mate.

By the time Nero began his romance with Poppaea, she had already been married twice. The first marriage was to Rufrius Crispinus in 44 CE. Rufrius had been commander of Emperor Claudius's Praetorian Guard until Agrippina had him banished in 51 CE, suspecting that he had too much affection for the recently murdered Valeria. Agrippina did not have him killed. Weird! He was killed, of course, but that was later, in 65 CE, by Nero. He was *sixty-six years old*, which is, I think, as long as anyone could ever hope to be alive in Rome.

Following her first husband's banishment, Poppaea was married to Otho, a close friend of Emperor Nero's. She had likely been

Otho's mistress while still married to Rufrius, which probably accounts for a sliver of that dig about her depraved behavior. There's some conflict in accounts over this relationship. Tacitus writes in his *Historiae*:

> Otho's had been a neglected boyhood and a riotous youth, and he had made himself agreeable to Nero by emulating his profligacy. For this reason the emperor had entrusted to him, being the confidant of his amours, Poppaea Sabina, the imperial favorite, until he could rid himself of his wife Octavia. Soon suspecting him with regard to this same Poppaea, he sent him out of the way to the province of Lusitania, ostensibly to be its governor.

If that's the case—and the biographer Plutarch presents a similar account in *Life of Galba*—then Nero wanted Poppaea for himself and married her off to Otho assuming that Otho would be too preoccupied with his many other women to focus on just one. Mistake! Otho fell in love with Poppaea. Nero was not allowed in their house and was reduced to begging outside to see Poppaea.

Then the accounts differ. Suetonius's *Life of Otho* claims that Poppaea reciprocated Otho's feelings, so much so that she turned Nero away. Meanwhile, Dio maintains that she cleverly used Nero's jealousy of her husband in order to have Otho banished and reinforce Nero's desire for her. And the Wikipedia page claims that "Otho introduced his beautiful wife to the Emperor upon Poppaea's insistence," which would seem to indicate even more plotting was afoot on her part.

All of these theories result in the same outcome. Otho was banished to Lusitania in 58 CE, and Poppaea was free to marry again. Agrippina was not all that keen on Nero breaking things off with Octavia in favor of Poppaea. According to Tacitus in *Annals*, Poppaea knew this.

[Nero's] passion for Poppaea daily grew more ardent. As the woman had no hope of marriage for herself or of Octavia's divorce while Agrippina lived, she would reproach the emperor with incessant vituperation and sometimes call him in jest a mere ward who was under the rule of others, and was so far from having empire that he had not even his liberty. "Why," she asked, "was her marriage put off? Was it, forsooth, her beauty and her ancestors, with their triumphal honors, that failed to please, or her being a mother, and her sincere heart? No; the fear was that as a wife at least she would divulge the wrongs of the Senate, and the wrath of the people at the arrogance and rapacity of his mother."

You know how it is. Your boyfriend keeps taking his mother's advice on everything, his mom hates you, you tell him to stop being a mama's boy and imply that his mother is a . . . not nice lady . . . and your boyfriend promptly proves his devotion by murdering his mother.

Or maybe that was a thing that happened only this one time.

Interestingly, Tacitus notes that no one really saw that murder coming. Except for you, I bet, because you know how these people operate. I know what you're thinking. You're thinking, *He is reaching for a vial of poison.* That is correct! Suetonius claimed that Nero did try to poison Agrippina three times, and each time she took an antidote and survived. Because Agrippina won all the poisoning prizes. You do not spit into the wind, you do not kid a kidder, and you do not poison Agrippina.

Open aggression was thought to be too risky. Nero was not going to stab his mother in broad daylight. So the prefect of the Misenum fleet, Anicetus (who hated Agrippina), suggested that they construct a collapsible ceiling over Agrippina's bed. The idea was that it would cave in and crush her. I have no clue how they were going to build this secretly above her bed. It was not a great plan and was scrapped. The idea, though, led to the notion of

creating a ship designed to be unseaworthy, so that it would col-
lapse as soon as it was in open water and Agrippina would drown.
That seemed more promising than stealthily constructing a collapsible bedroom.

Nero invited Agrippina out to meet him at an island, promising reconciliation. He kissed her eyes and her breasts (things might
have been different in the past, but that detail is still odd, always
odd, odd forever). According to Dio, Nero sent Agrippina away saying, "For you I live, through you I rule."

Would a woman as canny as Agrippina have suspected anything? Almost as soon as she was out to sea, the boat's canopy, which
had been weighted with lead, collapsed—just as a ceiling might!
The ship capsized. Agrippina and her friend Acceronia Polla were
thrown into the water. Agrippina, despite supposedly having consumed a massive amount of wine and having a wounded shoulder,
began swimming to shore. Meanwhile, Polla screamed that she
herself was Agrippina and was the mother of the emperor and
needed help, whereupon the crew beat Polla to death with oars.
Which is just as well because otherwise surely Agrippina would
have had her killed for impersonation.

Agrippina was now convinced Nero was trying to murder her,
but she pretended to be ignorant of his plan. She sent a message
to him saying that there had been an accidental sinking of her
ship, and that while she was certain he wanted to visit her, he should
wait until she was recovered. But Nero sent hired assassins to her
house. Anicetus was told not to fail again. He broke into Agrippina's home with a team of men and declared that, on the orders of
the emperor, he was there to murder her. Agrippina insisted that
her son would never order such a thing. In response, a henchman
clubbed her in the head. Agrippina's last words were "Smite my
womb!"

Nero came to the house later and meticulously examined
Agrippina's limbs. He carefully critiqued each and, upon finishing,
announced that for the first time he was aware of how beautiful

his mother was. For years afterward, Nero said that he was pursued by Agrippina's angry ghost and that he heard sounds of lamentation whenever he visited her grave. His subjects didn't take well to matricide. Shortly after the murder a baby was left in the Forum, with a tag bearing the note "I will not rear you up lest you slay your mother."

A real live baby, just abandoned in a public place to make a political point. It was a hell of a town.

Conditions were equally bad for poor Octavia, who definitely wasn't the leading lady Nero envisioned in his great love story. He ultimately divorced her and, when the people continued to like her—presumably because I cannot find any indication that she ever murdered anyone, which seems to make her better than anyone else in that hellscape—banished her to an island. There was public outcry over that—groups marched down the streets shouting, "Bring back Octavia"—which disturbed Nero. So he had her suffocated in a vapor bath.

Nero purportedly was troubled by dreams in which he dragged Octavia to her watery grave afterward. So even if you have no moral compass, I suppose the lesson is don't kill people because you might have night terrors.

You know who did not feel bad about any of this? Poppaea. Which maybe lends some legitimacy to the claim that she had been plotting to become empress all along. When Octavia was executed, she finally claimed that title.

Was it all worth it? Were Nero and Poppaea happy together? They were not.

They had one daughter, whom Nero welcomed, according to Tacitus, "with something more than mortal joy." Unfortunately, she died soon after her birth, and, after deifying her, Nero returned to his normal ways. Dio writes:

He secretly sent out men who pretended to be drunk or engaged in other kinds of mischief, and caused them at first to set fire to one or two or even several buildings in different parts of the city, so that people were at their wits' end, not being able to find any beginning of the trouble nor to put an end to it, though they constantly were aware of many strange sights and sounds.

So he was setting his own city on fire for fun, which is not a cool thing to do. He blamed the fire of 64 CE on the Christians and executed them so horribly that it's still remembered in the Bible as a time of "great tribulation, such as was not seen since the beginning of the world to this time, no, nor ever shall be." That's largely because Nero was a terrifying sadist. According to Tacitus:

> Mockery of every sort was added to their deaths. Covered with the skins of beasts, they were torn by dogs and perished, or were nailed to crosses, or were doomed to the flames and burnt, to serve as a nightly illumination, when daylight had expired. Nero offered his gardens for the spectacle, and was exhibiting a show in the circus, while he mingled with the people in the dress of a charioteer or stood aloft on a car. Hence, even for criminals who deserved extreme and exemplary punishment, there arose a feeling of compassion; for it was not, as it seemed, for the public good, but to glut one man's cruelty, that they were being destroyed.

By now Nero was losing popularity because he was a deranged fiend. However, more relevant in terms of his marriage was Dio's account that

> [Nero and his comrades] would also enter the brothels and without let or hindrance have intercourse with any of the women who were seated there, among whom were the most beautiful and distinguished in the city, both slaves and free, courtesans and virgins and married women; and these were

not merely of the common people but also of the very noblest families, both girls and grown women. Every man had the privilege of enjoying whichever one he wished, as the women were not allowed to refuse anyone.

Poppaea had her own tabloid-version-of-Marie-Antoinette excesses, though none that seem particularly evil. The mules that drew her carriage wore horseshoes made of gold, and she had five hundred donkeys milked every day so she could bathe in the milk. While her lusty nature is alluded to, I don't know that she was foolish enough to be unfaithful to Nero, and if she was, we most likely would have found accounts of her infidelities. Besides, being unfaithful to anyone who turns people into human lanterns just seems like such a catastrophically bad idea.

As behaviors of murdering, city-burning emperors go, I don't find rape that shocking. But Poppaea Sabina, as you might expect, was less than thrilled that Nero and his friends were hanging out in brothels all the time. It honestly seems a little naive of her to think that her husband was going to be faithful because . . . well, because Nero had no redeeming qualities I can see, absolutely none— he was a *monster*. But Nero's sexual indiscretions became a source of great discord between them.

Finally, one night, after Nero had been at the races, Poppaea, who was pregnant at the time, began yelling at him. And so he jumped up and down on her belly until she was dead. Nero felt bad about this. He ordered that rather than being consumed by fire, her body should be stuffed with fragrances and embalmed, which is . . . nice, I guess? He exalted her virtues while giving her eulogy. Later, when performing in classical dramas, Nero would wear a mask depicting his dead wife for all female roles.

He also grieved the end of their relationship by murdering her son. Suetonius writes in *The Life of Nero*: "Rufrius Crispinus [the younger], a mere boy, his stepson and the child of Poppaea, he ordered to be drowned by the child's own slaves while he was fishing, but it was said that he used to play at being a general and an emperor." Well, if the kid played at being emperor while he was fishing, I suppose you've got to do what you've got to do.

Then Nero went on a nifty little spree where he killed everyone close to him. Suetonius elaborates:

> He banished his nurse's son Tuscus, because when procurator in Egypt, he had bathed in some baths which were built for a visit of Nero's. He drove his tutor Seneca to suicide, although when the old man often pleaded to be allowed to retire and offered to give up his estates, he had sworn most solemnly that he did wrong to suspect him and that he would rather die than harm him. He sent poison to Burrus, prefect of the Guard, in place of a throat medicine which he had promised him. The old and wealthy freedmen who had helped him first to his adoption and later to the throne, and aided him by their advice, he killed by poison, administered partly in their food and partly in their drink.

These are not logical murders. If these murders showed up in an episode of television's *Law and Order*, you would initially guess that Nero definitely did not commit the crime because he had no motive. (Nero would be played by a celebrity guest to help viewers suspect that he *did* kill them all.) But this is where the breakup with Poppaea goes from being horrible but still a little bit normal for the times to exceedingly bizarre.

Nero had a slave named Sporus who seemingly resembled Poppaea, to the very vague extent that a prepubescent boy can resemble ancient Rome's answer to Christina Hendricks. At the very least, we know that he was young and beautiful. Now, homosexual liaisons were frowned upon at this time in ancient Rome. While that definitely did not deter Nero, it might have played into the decision to castrate Sporus before marrying him.

You read that correctly. Nero rebounded in 67 CE by castrating an underage slave boy who looked like his ex-wife and using him as a stand-in for her. I know that at this point you are thinking, *Yeah, castration, well, you know, ancient Rome, that was just a thing there,* but, no, remarkably it was not. Castration was illegal in ancient Rome. You could purchase eunuchs from other countries, but one of the privileges of being a *Roman* slave was that your genitals would be spared.

Nero changed Sporus's name to Sabina and made him dress up as Poppaea, appearing in public wearing her regalia. Sporus was also supposed to be referred to by the crowds as "Lady" or "Empress." Suetonius writes that the couple could be seen "riding in a litter, he took him to the assizes and marts of Greece, and later at Rome through the Street of the Images, fondly kissing him from time to time."

Nero offered enormous sums of money to anyone who could surgically change Sporus from a man into a woman. I don't want to spoil anything about medicine for you, but the technology to do that didn't exist in 60-ish CE. It is very fortunate that nobody gave Nero a particularly compelling medical pitch. Surely there were madmen who *thought* they could do it, and Nero was not good at making decisions. There's a good chance Sporus could have been tortured more than he already was.

Poor Sporus. I think he is the only innocent person in this story. The historian Edward Champlin estimates that he was probably not twenty years old when he died in 69 CE. And he certainly doesn't seem to have been pleased about the situation— or to have experienced whatever sort of Stockholm syndrome would cause someone to love their captor in these circumstances. It seems very purposeful and bold that he gave Nero a New Year's gift of a ring depicting the Rape of Proserpina. The story tells the tale of a beautiful young goddess abducted and dragged into hell by the king of the underworld. It's not really a suitable gift for someone you love, a piece of jewelry explicitly calling them the devil. There are still Christians who think that Emperor

Nero was the physical embodiment of the devil. I don't believe that, because I think the devil would be a lot more likable, Rolling Stones–style. No one, with the exception of his murdered mom, seemed to like Nero all that much.

By the late 60s Nero's sexual perversions had become so bizarre that he used to enjoy dressing up as an animal in a cage, and then upon being released, running out and biting the genitals of shackled prisoners. Suetonius describes his behavior as follows:

> He so prostituted his own chastity that after defiling almost every part of his body, he at last devised a kind of game, in which, covered with the skin of some wild animal, he was let loose from a cage and attacked the private parts of men and women, who were bound to stakes, and when he had sated his mad lust, were dispatched.

Really, no one's genitals were safe during Nero's reign, despite what Romans had come to expect.

Dio writes about an incident that resulted in a joke that has endured for centuries, though pretty much exclusively in the portion of the library that classics majors occupy. Maybe it will give you a giggle, though.

> While Nero had Sporus, the eunuch, as a wife, one of his associates in Rome, who had made a study of philosophy, on being asked whether the marriage and cohabitation in question met with his approval, replied: "You do well, Caesar, to seek the company of such wives. Would that your father had had the same ambition and had lived with a similar consort!"— indicating that if this had been the case, Nero would not have been born, and the state would now be free of great evils.

Provinces rose up in rebellion because, in addition to being a terrible human being, Nero was not great at managing finances.

The provinces were vastly overtaxed, which led to open revolt. But that is tedious fiscal policy, and this is not a boring government book. In any event, Nero's resignation was demanded, and he was eventually abandoned by the Praetorian Guard to the furious crowds in his palace and shortly after he committed suicide. His last words were "what an artist dies in me."

The last words of most of his victims are, unsurprisingly, unknown.

Nero had wanted Sporus to die alongside him—and perhaps in this moment he recalled that Seneca's wife attempted to commit suicide alongside him *because Seneca was a really nice guy whom Nero killed*—but Sporus fled. I want to say that was pretty ballsy of him, but that is just too dark a joke. It's worse than a mushroom joke. I will say that it was sincerely brave.

I wish that I could tell you things worked out OK for Sporus. I'd like to say that Sporus met someone nice who helped him, slowly, overcome the profound psychological damage he must have experienced over the course of his relationship with Nero and who maybe, eventually, made him feel as if he could be safe and love again. Or I'd like to say that Sporus led a contented, solitary life somewhere in the country, reading lots of books and cultivating meaningful relationships with pets. That seems to be the next best thing or, depending on how you feel about relationships at the moment, maybe an even better outcome.

That is not what happened.

Almost immediately after Nero's death in 68 CE, Sporus came under the care of Nymphidius Sabinus, who had been prefect of the Praetorian Guard under the rule of Nero—and had been the architect of his abandonment to the murderous crowds. We mustn't hold that against him. I'm OK with military leaders rebelling under insane and corrupt rulers, and it's the kind of decision that makes me hope Nymphidius might have been saner than his predecessor. But he was only kind of better, at least as far as Sporus was concerned. In what I can only imagine was an attempt to maintain some consistency as he tried to declare himself emperor, he took Sporus as a wife and continued calling him Poppaea.

Nymphidius was killed almost immediately. At that point Sporus was married to Otho. Yes. *That* Otho. The one who was married to the real Poppaea. Otho declared himself emperor, but that only lasted three months until he was murdered. At which point Sporus was passed on to the new emperor Vitellius, who was as obsessed with cruel amusements as Nero. He wanted Sporus to play the role of Proserpina during a halftime show at a gladiatorial game, during which Sporus would be raped.

Suicide is never the answer, and things do get better, always, except here. Ancient Rome was a place where life never got better, ever. So in a decision that I think very few people could hold against him, Sporus took his own life. This is tragic because Sporus might be the only person in this period of ancient Rome who is actually likable. Well, Octavia also seems A-OK.

There is a Chinese curse (at least according to John F. Kennedy) that runs, "May you live in interesting times." Every character in this story had the misfortune to live in extremely interesting times. We are very privileged to live in such sedate times that we become genuinely indignant at the prospect of two consenting— though otherwise committed—people having pleasurable sex. We're very lucky.

And what is the message of this story? In addition to making it clear that we live in very good times, this puts being in a certain type of breakup situation in perspective. There are times when we feel we are trapped in a relationship with someone who is clearly terrible for us. But we can leave! We are all blessed with the ability to walk out of bad relationships. We are not Sporus. Thank God, we're not Sporus. And no matter how badly you might have behaved, you're certainly not Nero.

2. Eleanor of Aquitaine

Henry II

The stories of medieval history are seldom fairy tales. They should be because when people begin "Once upon a time . . ." they are generally thinking of an era around 1100. They envision wicked stepmothers then but also handsome princes ready to save beautiful maidens from harm. And castles and fairy godmothers. To anyone who thinks the medieval ages were like that: Disney lies. There's a joke that, today, if you lose your shoe at a party dancing around midnight, we know it is because you are drunk. But if you lost your shoe at a party in 1100, there is a chance someone hacked your foot off and took your shoe, and maybe you are dead. And if you were imprisoned in a tower, you were not a fair, magical maiden letting down her hair; you were probably under actual armed siege like Eleanor of Aquitaine, queen to two kings and the mother of kings (not the mother of dragons—though if anyone could have been, it would have been her).

It would be nice if Eleanor of Aquitaine had a fantastic, happy life, instead of a fairy-tale-gone-wrong existence, because she was *spectacular.* When we think of noble knights and ladies-in-waiting and Robin Hood, we are referencing a world she had a large hand in creating.

How can you begin to describe Eleanor? The first image that always comes to my mind is of her—in her early twenties—when she rode with her ladies-in-waiting in the Second Crusade. She was married to Louis VII, the king of France, at the time. She was supposedly extraordinarily beautiful, with blond—or possibly auburn—hair and blue or gray eyes. Even today, in the course of research for her trilogy of novels about Eleanor, Elizabeth Chadwick encountered modern male historians "drooling over her curvaceous figure." All of this may be speculative, and it's hard to get a precise read on what people who lived a thousand years ago

Eleanor of Aquitaine, super-babe.

looked like, but, hell, it's fun to think that Eleanor was extremely beautiful, so let's go with it. Rumor says that she and her women dressed as Amazons, with spears and armor, and rode bare-breasted into battle. In *The Lion in Winter* (the best movie ever) Eleanor says, "I damn near died of windburn, but the troops were *dazzled.*"

They must have been.

Honestly, if any pop starlet today charged into any dispute— a riot! A protest! A traffic jam! A minor scuffle at Denny's! Anything!—half naked and waving a spear, we'd still be dazzled. We're mightily impressed when Rihanna goes topless on Instagram in violation of its no-boobs-allowed policy and she does not have so much as a penknife. Not even Rihanna is as edgy and daring as Eleanor was nine hundred years ago.

Dazzling as she might have been, it was her time on the crusade that ultimately brought about the demise of Eleanor's marriage to Louis. Not because she was riding around on horseback with a spear *like some Greek goddess,* but because the couple differed on whether the crusade's objective should be to recapture the town of Edessa (as Eleanor and her uncle Raymond wanted to) or to reach Jerusalem. When Louis demanded that she follow him to Jerusalem, Eleanor demanded an annulment. He did eventually persuade her to accompany him, but the expedition failed, as Eleanor predicted, and they returned to France on separate ships.

The pope tried to convince them not to annul the marriage. I assume Eleanor stared at him skeptically and sort of rolled her eyes the entire time because the marriage did indeed end in 1152, when Eleanor claimed that it was unholy to be married to a man who was her third cousin, as Louis was. The marriage might have been more difficult to terminate had Eleanor produced a male heir instead of two daughters with Louis. Which is not to say that she did not have a significant impact on the country during her time as queen of France. When not on crusade, Eleanor had been a force to be reckoned with at Louis's court. She introduced the idea of courtly behavior; she even staged trials where ladies would sit and judge knights as they recited love poems. The fairy tale/Arthurian mythology/Renaissance fair notion many of us share when we think about royal courts is in part due to her influence. From Louis she learned Aristotelian logic, and the couple supposedly had many happy talks and debates in the palace garden.

Louis was, seemingly, a delightful, down-to-earth person. He once described the gold and treasures possessed by foreign kings to the Welsh writer/courtier/archdeacon (triple threat!) Walter Map and then claimed that he himself had only "bread, wine and contentment." If you think Louis sounds like a nice person to go on a picnic with, you are not wrong! But you can also read into that statement that he didn't quite have Eleanor's ambition or her love of the worldly. Louis's pious nature—he sang in the church choir, fasted, dressed monkishly, and refrained from luxuries—never really paired well with Eleanor's vivacious personality. And he was frankly never as bright as her, though his emotional IQ may have been off the charts. The historian William of Newburgh summed it up when he said of Louis, "He was a man of warm devotion to God and of great gentleness to his subjects and of notable reverence for the clergy, but he was rather more simple-minded than is becoming to a prince."

Louis wasn't smart, but he was nice and had a delightful beard, and that's almost as good.

That is such a superbly polite way to call someone in a position of power an idiot. But Louis was nice. He was a really good guy. Eleanor left the marriage with the lands she had inherited from her father—namely the Aquitaine and Poitou regions—with the expectation that she would retire to Poitiers (the capital of Poitou), where she would be conveniently close to visit Louis and her daughters. Then the king would be free to marry a younger woman and have more children. Meanwhile, at age thirty—relatively old for the time—Eleanor might live out the rest of her life quietly, with the freedom to rule her court as she saw fit and presumably practice some nifty needlework.

Eleanor wasn't into that.

Eight weeks after leaving Louis of France, Eleanor married King Henry II of England. He was twenty years old at the time and known more for his ambition and energy than any other qualities. Though he was said to be good-looking, he was stocky, paunchy, and slobbily dressed, with wild red hair and bloodshot eyes. He supposedly had a face that resembled a lion's. There was even a rumor that he was descended from the devil, gossip that his

King Henry II—no beard or niceness; super smart.

family encouraged. At first glance he wasn't at all Eleanor's type, by which I mean he wouldn't have won the courtly love poetry contest.

You know what he did win? Battles.

Though Henry II was only the son of the Count of Anjou, from an early age he was determined not just to be king of England but to reclaim all of the territories that had been held by his grandfather, Henry I. (His mother was Henry I's eldest daughter.) When he was fourteen he set off to battle with his first mercenary army, landing in England from Normandy, where Henry had spent his childhood. Although his invasion caused some uproar, it failed. When Henry couldn't pay the troops—because he was *fourteen*—he asked King Stephen of England, who was his mother's cousin, for the money. King Stephen not only paid but took young Henry under his wing. The whole "he secretly raised a mercenary army" thing was apparently considered charming in his family.

And his skills in battle improved as time went on. Spoiler if this was a book about war, which it is not: by 1172, when Henry was thirty-nine, he ruled all of England, half of Ireland, half of France, and most of Wales. So he accomplished what he had set out to do at age fourteen, which is more than most of us can say. (If I had become the person I wanted to be at fourteen, I would be a vampire with veterinary skills.)

His ideas also set the foundation for English common law, under which a jury would investigate claims against the accused (though trial by ordeal or combat persisted until 1215). Henry also decreed that the eldest son in a family inherited land, and he made it possible for subjects to sell their lands. Doing so allowed for social mobility. These were good decrees, setting principles by which England operated for the next thousand years. Henry, unlike Louis, was not more simple than befits a king.

Eleanor was a good judge of character, and I'm willing to bet that as much as she enjoyed poetry and philosophy, ultimately she always cared more about power. She wasn't going to end up married to another husband who, like Louis, didn't know how to win. Still, she might never have ended up with Henry if, immediately after her annulment, as she was returning to Poitiers, Henry's younger brother, Geoffrey, hadn't attempted to abduct her. Geoffrey hoped to marry her to gain access to Eleanor's lands. His ambush failed. After arriving safely in Poitiers, Eleanor decided if she was going to be chased by English nobles, she would rather be pursued by the one who would be king. She sent a note to Henry to come and marry her himself. He rode immediately to Poitiers.

In *A History of Britain,* Simon Schama claims, "Barely eight weeks after Eleanor's divorce in May 1152, Henry stood at the altar beside this considerably older woman whom all contemporary accounts describe as a dark-eyed beauty, disconcertingly articulate, strong-minded and even jocular and not at all the modestly veiled damsel in the tower."

It all sounds very romantic, and it made Louis absolutely *furious.* Relations between France and England never really recovered. But who cared? Henry and Eleanor were together, they were probably the most dynamic couple in Europe of the century, and by 1154 they were crowned king and queen of England at Westminster.

Sometimes, when extraordinary personalities come together, things go very, very well.

Those couples are not in this book.

Other times, extraordinary personalities get together, and then they destroy each other. This is what happens here.

Life went well, until it didn't. And by well, I mean children! Male children! Eleanor bore Henry eight children, five of whom were boys, which meant there were plenty of heirs. No simple "heir and a spare" stuff for Eleanor—she overachieved. If you need to know why this is good news, you can skip ahead to chapter 4 and read about Henry VIII.

Despite the fact that Henry must have been attracted to Eleanor, he cheated on her rampantly. Was Eleanor OK with that? Maybe. It seems as if she overlooked this behavior, at least when he was involved with peasant women, who couldn't be expected to resist the king and who weren't any special threat to her family. She spent much of her time seemingly trying to be a good wife. For the first decade of her marriage to Henry, in addition to advising him on strategy and policy, she was occupied with planning her children's marriages and orchestrating extremely elaborate birthday parties for them. There were a whole lot of pan flutists to hire for those parties.

Reading about Eleanor being domestic is a bit like imagining a former Fortune 500 CEO moving to the suburbs and overcompensating by baking six hundred cupcakes. (This is a plot point from the 2004 *Stepford Wives* movie that I just stole. It holds up, though.)

It worked for a while. But then the marriage fell apart when Henry met a very young, seemingly unextraordinary (but nice? Probably nice!) woman named Rosamund Clifford. She was the daughter of Walter de Clifford, who occupied a castle along the Welsh border, an area Henry had reason to visit in 1163 as he was trying to pacify Wales from some uprising (again, not a war book). She quickly became Henry's mistress, which wouldn't have been surprising. Again, Henry seduced a great many women. What was surprising was that she remained Henry's mistress until 1174. Eleven years is a long time to keep someone around as your mistress. She supposedly had unambiguously golden hair and a sweet disposition. The seventeenth-century historian Thomas Hearne wrote that Henry was devoted to her "not only on account of her exquisite beauty but for the sweetness of her temper."

Certain writers give the impression that Rosamund was the kind of gentle, obliging woman that men love, whereas Eleanor was obviously terrifying, what with her elaborate parties and all of those pan flutes.

Let us stop right here and think about this. Sometimes, when people write about the past they are in actuality projecting their personal experiences and views of the world to those times. We are doing that here, obviously. A lot. Perhaps so did Thomas Hearne and other Victorians who assumed Rosamund must have been a girlish, wilting flower of a woman, since those were virtues that men seemed to cherish during their own time. This notion that Rosamund was sweet and timid and Eleanor was domineering and unlovable comes up a lot in Victorian English writings.

But look, that's not necessarily the way it was. First of all, the assumption that being strong and passionate and accomplished will make you an unlovable woman simply isn't true. Most men are not sitting around saying, "My main turn-on is definitely incompetence." Eleanor was loved, and downright worshipped, by a lot of men. Troubadours from Poitiers used to brag about their brilliant duchess, who could read and write. The fact that she wasn't able to inspire devotion in Henry doesn't mean that women need to focus on being sweet or gentle instead of being smart and brave in order to land a man.

Moreover, we know essentially nothing about Rosamund Clifford. It's easy to assume that since Eleanor seemed very strong and Henry did not seem to love her especially, Rosamund was attractive because she was Eleanor's opposite. That's a pretty big leap of logic. Maybe Henry loved her because she was a pleasant, retiring blossom, or maybe he loved her because she could burp the alphabet. Maybe he loved her because she had webbed toes and he was into that. We have no idea! There is amazingly little actual historical knowledge about Rosamund. We only know that she was seemingly willing to live alone in a hunting lodge surrounded by a hedge maze. (The only other famous hedge maze I know of is in the 1980 film *The Shining*.)

The rumor goes that Henry housed Rosamund, a woman who had some traits of some sort, at the Woodstock hunting lodge. He built an enormous maze outside it to hide her from Eleanor's prying eyes. It's often referred to as Rosamund's bower. John Aubrey, in 1686, described it thusly:

> *Yea, Rosamond, fair Rosamond,*
>   *Her name was called so,*
> *To whom dame Elinor our Queene*
>   *Was known a deadly foe,*
> *The King therefore for her defence*
>   *Against the furious Queene*
> *At Woodstocke builded such a Bower*
>   *The like was never seen.*
>
> *Most curiously that Bower was built*
>   *Of stone and timber strong.*
> *An hundered and fifty dores*
>   *Did to this Bower belong,*
> *And they so cunningly contriv'd*
>   *With turnings round about*
> *That none but with a clew of thread*
>   *Could enter in or out.*

It's weird how Aubrey types had all these questions: Why was the queen so upset? Was she just wicked? Why didn't she like Rosamund? Is Eleanor simply mean? Rosamund is fun, have you seen her burp the alphabet while doing her webbed-foot somersaults?

But it's absolutely not that outlandish that Eleanor would be the foe of a woman with whom her husband was having an affair.

And, you know, if you want to keep the world and its rumors out, maybe *don't build a giant hedge maze around your mistress.* That's actually a colossal arrow pointing to her—an arrow made out of foliage. In such a case it would probably be better to pretend she was just a family friend or use any of the approximately two million excuses that would be less conspicuous than erecting a huge bower right around her.

Unsurprisingly, Henry's bower-of-secrecy strategy proved ineffective. Stories about Rosamund spread wildly. Gerald of Wales, the tabloid newspaperman of the twelfth century, knew all about the affair and wrote an attack on Rosamund and Henry that claimed "[Henry] who had long been a secret adulterer now flaunted his paramour for all to see, not that Rose of the World, as some vain and foolish people called her, but that Rose of Unchastity."

Now, Gerald of Wales's works also contain other spurious allegations like the one that Eleanor slept with Henry's father:

> Count Geoffrey of Anjou when he was seneschal of France took advantage of Queen Eleanor; for which reason he often warned his son Henry, telling him above all not to touch her, they say, both because she was his lord's wife, and because he had known her himself . . . [Henry] presumed to sleep adulterously with the said queen of France, taking her from his own lord and marrying her himself. How could anything fortunate, I ask, emerge from these copulations?

Did Eleanor sleep with Henry's father? Maybe. But Gerald of Wales basically just liked talking shit about people. Eleanor might be able to dismiss stories about Rosamund as appealing only to gossips (come sit over by me, Gerald), but by the late 1160s she was staying in Poitiers away from Henry and his love bower most of the time. There, at her "court of love," she engaged in theoretical debates. One focused on whether love could flourish within a marriage. It was decided that it could not. She educated the young men who flocked there—to joust, to write poems, and to fall in love—on how to pay proper tribute to women. Eleanor also staged amazing debates about equality between the genders in which her position was not that men and women were equal, but rather that women were vastly superior. The court was idyllic, if that is possible in a fairly barbaric time.

However, even residing at Poitiers, Eleanor couldn't fail to hear the increasing volume of the rumors. It was certainly worse because she knew they were true. In 1166 she had been enraged at the news that Henry had begun to house Rosamund in Eleanor's own apartments, and so she furiously withdrew to a different castle. And you can only imagine how painful the affair must have been for a woman like Eleanor, whose major achievement was introducing the idea of chivalrous love to the courts of France and England. At one time Eleanor was also known for being one of the most beautiful women in Europe; this was the woman of whom the troubadour Bernard de Ventadorn sang, "You have been the first among my joys and you shall be the last, so long as there is life in me." For a person who was once so admired, hearing her husband's young mistress called "the rose of the world" in any context must have been hurtful. And while she had a younger and virile husband, Eleanor was herself entering her midforties. During the twelfth century that meant she was inching into serious old age.

Rosamund's presence also, likely more importantly to the queen, meant Eleanor was distanced from Henry's power. As Marion Meade writes in her biography *Eleanor of Aquitaine*:

In large part [Eleanor's] discontentment stemmed from the gradual waning of her influence. Whatever else Eleanor may have loved, she loved to rule best . . . Slowly, irrefutably, Henry had edged Eleanor further and further from the high place where he sat, and now, to add a gratuitous insult, he publicly honored a concubine, installing her in a palace where the queen had been undisputed mistress. Other queens might sit by helplessly and watch themselves relegated to a secondary role, but Eleanor had the resources to spare herself that humiliation.

The legend goes that Eleanor killed Rosamund. According to some stories, Eleanor followed a skein of silver thread that had trailed behind Rosamund, lost from her beautiful needlework case, into the bower guarding her lodgings. Once she made it to the center of the maze, Eleanor overpowered the single brave, but apparently really inept, knight guarding Rosamund. She then gave her rival the choice to die by dagger or by poison. Rosamund chose poison.

Marion Meade remarks that in choosing poison Rosamund was "as brave as she was fair," though personally, I would choose poison as well. The dagger thing seems really painful.

If Eleanor of Aquitaine posed that question to you, what would you choose? Would you ask what kind of poison first? Do you think you could quickly concoct an antidote? What if, in this scenario, you were a time traveler? Could you probably argue Eleanor out of

Rosamund's gown does a great job of hiding the weird webbed feet I've decided she has.

the whole killing thing if you were a talented debater *and* time traveler? Discuss.

At least Rosamund was a pretty corpse. The historian Elizabeth Jenkins mentions a ballad from the period that runs:

And when that death through every limb
Had shown its greatest spite
Her chiefest foes did plain confess
She was a glorious sight.

So that's nice.

If you are also thinking, *That story sounds suspiciously like something out of a fairy tale, not real life,* you are almost certainly correct. Charles Dickens disputes it in *A Child's History of England* in the nineteenth century:

There was a fair Rosamond, and she was (I dare say) the loveliest girl in all the world, and the king was certainly very fond of her, and the bad Queen Eleanor was certainly made jealous. But I am afraid—I say afraid, because I like the story so much—that there was no bower, no labyrinth, no silken clue, no dagger, no poison. I am afraid Fair Rosamond retired to a nunnery near Oxford, and died there, peaceably.

Unlike Dickens, that coward, I am not afraid of scary stories. I don't try to blot them out with "the truth." In fact, if you like the whole "Eleanor was a wicked queen who poisoned fair Rosamund" story, there is even an especially gruesome fourteenth-century version where Eleanor first strips Rosamund naked, sets her on fire, places toads on her presumably burned breasts, and then bleeds her to death in a bathtub, laughing all the while. That must have required a lot of maneuvering. I don't know how the toads played into it. Maybe there was some symbolism that I am missing. Or maybe it's just good to work frogs into stories because it's that kind of offbeat detail that readers will remember. (If I had a pet frog, I would name it Queen Eleanor.)

No matter. Rosamund did die. She went to a nunnery, where she died, in 1176 possibly, from (according to my make-believe sources) very slow-acting poison that took many years to complete its effects—or from natural causes. Her body was housed in a beautiful shrine until 1191, when a bishop pointed out that she couldn't be buried on church ground because she was a concubine. She was moved to the nuns' house, where her grave could be visited. Her gravestone reads, HERE IN THE TOMB LIES THE ROSE OF THE WORLD, NOT A PURE ROSE; SHE WHO USED TO SMELL SWEET, STILL SMELLS—BUT NOT SWEET. Reading this, I can't believe that she was the sweet, gentle, timid flower that some historians describe. Anyone who inspired that tombstone inscription must have had a pretty dark sense of humor. Her tomb remained at the shrine until the Reformation in the sixteenth century, when the scholar John Leland wrote that it had been dug up, and "when it was opened a very sweet smell came out of it."

And so Rosamund is largely forgotten by history, but Eleanor—who may not have done the weird toad, horror-movie acts that the ballads depict—never forgave Henry for the affair. If you are familiar with the book and/or movie *Gone Girl* (2014), you may think the main character's reaction to her husband's adultery is way out of line. She has absolutely nothing on the queen.

Eleanor had lands and connections and the loyalty of her sons. If Henry was not going to allow her to be an equal partner in his rule, she decided it might be best to govern alone. So she enlisted her three sons—Henry the Younger, Geoffrey, and Richard—to join her in open revolt against their father.

Convincing them wasn't a hard task. While Eleanor had doted on her sons, Henry had been a fairly neglectful father given to fits of anger. Marion Meade recounts some great stories about how much they disliked their dad. Geoffrey claimed that discontent was natural among their family. "Don't you know that it is our nature to quarrel, our heritage that none of us should love the other?" Geoffrey may have just been kind of along for the ride on the revolt, but Richard, who perhaps loved his mother best, claimed of his father's side of the family, "From the devil they came, to the devil they will go."

For those who remember the story of Robin Hood, the Richard mentioned here is Richard the Lionheart. Robin Hood and his band of (merry) men are waiting for this good king to return from his imprisonment abroad, and, in some versions, Richard later saves Maid Marian from execution. Cool fact!

Even Henry the Younger, who was known for his graciousness, at least in public, didn't like his father all that much. He once sat at a dinner where King Henry served him boar. King Henry remarked, "It is surely unusual to see a king wait upon the table." To which Henry the Younger snapped, "But it is not unusual to find the son of a count waiting on the son of a king," reminding Henry of his low birth.

The twelfth century was just full of insults.

The rebellion was led by Henry the Younger, understandably, as he was the eldest son. The notion was that he would be king, while Eleanor would rule the Aquitaine with Richard, who, honestly, everyone knew was her favorite. In 1173 the trio enlisted support from the court of King Louis. With his help, they were able to raise an army.

For all the talk of bad exes in this book, it's really one of the nicest things in the world when you can go to someone you were once in a relationship with for reassurance or emotional support or to wage war against your philandering new husband. Louis was just so nice. How was he so nice? Well, admittedly, he also *really* hated Henry since Henry married his ex-wife, who was supposed to stay single forever.

It was only then, after she got an army together, that Henry started begging Eleanor to come back to him. Through the archbishop of Rouen he sent her the following message:

Pious queen, most illustrious queen, before matters come to a worse end, return with your sons to your husband, whom you are bound to obey and with whom you are forced to live; return lest he mistrust you or your sons. Most surely we know that he will in every way possible show you his love and grant you the assurance of perfect safety. Bid your sons, we beg you, to be obedient and devoted to their father, who for their sakes has undergone so many difficulties, run so many dangers, and undertaken so many labors.

Eleanor never responded because she had blocked Henry's number. Besides, she'd already overruled the pope in her last marriage. No one could expect her to take an archbishop seriously.

In spite of Louis's support, the rebellion ultimately failed. Eleanor had attempted to go to King Louis's castle disguised as a man. She was eventually apprehended, likely by four barons from Poitiers, who had seemingly not paid very careful attention to the stories about being loyal to ladies. They later received considerable sums of money from Henry.

Upon her capture, Henry locked Eleanor away in a tower in Chinon, like a fair maiden in a fairy tale. She was to be imprisoned in a variety of locales for the next fifteen years.

You might wonder, *Wait. Why didn't Henry kill her?* That is, considering the horror show that is history, an extremely valid and very puzzling question.

Eleanor hated being alone. She loved society. Being trapped in a castle would have been a nightmare for her. People point out that maybe Henry was doling out a fate worse than death by imprisoning her. But Henry didn't necessarily even want to imprison her; he suggested that she retire to an abbey, not as a normal nun but as an abbess, who would be in charge of the nunnery. There, she could occupy her time managing its operation with a group of women, many of whom had elected to become nuns because they wanted to live independent from men. That actually seems like something Eleanor would enjoy. But she refused that offer, perhaps because she liked men and sex and love and the power that existed in a masculine realm. She might also have been forced to surrender to the church all her possessions, including her considerable landholdings, which I expect she would never do willingly.

Again, though, Henry could have killed her. Rulers did kill their wives, especially if they were well past childbearing age. No one would have held it against him after she committed treason.

But he didn't.

OK, there were lands, she was the mother of his sons (and daughters), she was politically well connected, and all of those things have to be considered. Those would be valid reasons not to kill someone. So at this point you might guess, *He probably liked her.* That seems about right.

When Eleanor realized her marriage was essentially over, she could have handled the situation in an extremely gracious way, like Anne Boleyn, wife to a future Henry of England. That might have made her much more lovable in the eyes of some Victorian scholars I could name. But her brazenness and stubborn resistance seem more true to the young girl who rode like an Amazon into battle. In her rebellion, Henry saw exactly who Eleanor was—not just a wife who could offer him territory and politically savvy counsel and good child care, but a formidable adversary against a man who was one of the greatest leaders of the century. It was as though, after many years of trying to be a good wife, Eleanor finally reverted to being her true self.

He must have thought that was pretty cool.

Sometimes, we allow our partners to see us clearly only after we're no longer with them. Given the constraints of a relationship—the desire to appear nice or sexy or cool or organized or intellectual or whatever we think the other party views a good partner as—we don't show them how bold and fearless and powerful and strange we can be.

Eleanor had more in common with Henry than she had ever

revealed before. Waging war was something they both *loved*. His success in battle was probably what had attracted her to him in the first place. During her marriage, though, Eleanor was too busy trying to organize those birthday parties like a good twelfth-century wife to ever mention it. This revelation doesn't mean that Henry fell in love with her again. After Rosamund, he began an affair with a girl named Alais Capet, who—and this was especially needling to Eleanor—the queen had partly raised.

It's a shame that showing our full range of emotions doesn't necessarily make us lovable, which is perhaps why we're sometimes afraid to show them. But Henry certainly respected Eleanor in a way he never had before. He never let her out of the tower, though. Even when Henry the Younger died in 1183 and with his last words begged his father to set Eleanor free, Henry refused, perhaps (correctly?) believing that if she were left unguarded she would wage another civil war against him.

But after Henry the Younger's death, the king allowed Eleanor to travel with an escort around some of her lands and to visit her children. Her allowance for clothes and wine increased considerably. And in 1184 he allowed her to spend Christmas with him and their sons. During that time he asked her to approve some of his governmental choices regarding divvying up the kingdom. Eleanor refused to agree to any of his suggestions.

Before Henry II's death, there was a dispute over who would inherit the lands that Eleanor had brought to the marriage. Henry decided that all of them would revert to Eleanor upon his death. By then he must have known she would take a keen interest in ruling them. Immediately after the king's death in 1189, Richard rode to his mother's tower to see that she was released. This is probably as close as this story gets to a fairy tale—the bold, good, young king riding to free the woman locked in the tower. When he arrived, he found she had already claimed her freedom and met him on the grounds.

That year, when she was sixty-seven years old, Eleanor saw

Richard crowned king of England. When Richard went off on the Third Crusade, she chose not to join him, even if she might have liked the adventure. Instead, she ruled England on his behalf. (And then she rode to Germany to negotiate his release when he was kidnapped. This is a part of the story Robin Hood overlooks.)

She finally ruled without a man, which I think is what she always wanted. There was absolutely no ambiguity about who was in charge because Eleanor signed all her letters "Eleanor, by the Grace of God, Queen of the English, Duchess of the Normans."

And, until she died at eighty-one, she lived, as much as a person can, happily ever after.

3. Lucrezia Borgia

Giovanni Sforza

A major takeaway of this book is that it is a false notion to think of the past as being a happier time than the present. Earlier periods may have had their charms, but most of history was much worse than today, filled with senseless violence and disease and premature death. People probably experienced significantly less happiness in their lives than they would have if they were born now.

Not the Borgias, though.

I love the Borgias. It's definitely not politically correct, and I feel kind of conflicted about it, but what the heck, I'm going to let myself. I love Pope Alexander VI (born Rodrigo Lanzol Borgia), and I love his daughter, Lucrezia. This murderous fifteenth-century papal family really knew how to poison people, but, more than that, they knew how to have fun. Hugh Hefner wishes he were that Borgia pope.

Alexander VI partied the way nobody else in history had ever partied or ever will again. In his twenties, when he was a cardinal, he was reprimanded by Pope Pius II for throwing parties where he invited all of the most beautiful women in the city with their "husbands, brothers and fathers" excluded. Pius claimed that the only reason for doing this was so that Alexander's "lust might be all the more unrestrained."

That was a totally correct supposition.

Nobody seemed especially upset about it, though, other than Pius. You would think that the fact that Alexander was known for having unbelievably decadent sex parties would stop him from becoming pope, but no, it did not, because he handsomely bribed his way into office.

When he became pope in 1492, the parties only grew wilder. When guests approached the papal palace, they were greeted by entirely naked men and women, made to resemble statues. There was a particularly memorable party in 1501, held there and organized by the pope's son, Cesare. In his *Diary* chronicler Johann Burchard describes the event:

> On the evening of the last day of October, 1501, Cesare Borgia arranged a banquet in his chambers in the Vatican with "fifty honest prostitutes," called courtesans, who danced after dinner with the attendants and others who were present, at first in their garments, then naked. After dinner the candelabra with the burning candles were taken from the tables and placed on the floor, and chestnuts were strewn around, which the naked courtesans picked up, creeping on hands and knees between the chandeliers, while the Pope, Cesare, and his sister Lucrezia looked on. Finally, prizes were announced for those who could perform the act most often with the courtesans, such as tunics of silk, shoes, barrets, and other things.

Everything about that event is just so exceedingly odd. The crawling-for-chestnuts aspect seems rather arbitrary—did they pick up the chestnuts with their nether regions? Maybe. It's also fun to think about how the prizes were distributed; I kind of wonder if people knew enough to try to prep beforehand, though I don't know how you'd prepare for that contest. There appear to have been a lot of winners. I may have read too much about "scary sex in history," but this might have been an entertaining evening. By that I do not so much mean "Let's crawl naked around candelabras at my place next week, after the BBC viewing," as "No one died! And I bet that silk tunic was beautiful! That's cool! It's nice that lots of people got prizes!"

The sex stories about the Borgias rarely sound terrifying, and on the whole I feel orgies with consenting individuals are a less horrible abuse of power than every other exploitation by rulers in this book. I bet Silvio Berlusconi would agree with me.

The weirdest part of the evening might be that his daughter Lucrezia was in attendance. But then, the pope always had a close relationship with his four children—Cesare, Lucrezia, Giovanni, and Gioffre—and a surprisingly progressive outlook on what Lucrezia could be exposed to. Their mother was Alexander's mistress, Rosa Vannozza dei Cattanei, who, interestingly, was the daughter of one of his other mistresses. According to the historian William Manchester in *A World Lit Only by Fire,* Alexander is supposed to have seen Rosa naked while he was having sex with her mother and immediately switched partners. This is real actual history. Just popes having naked chestnut parties with the kids borne by one of their many mistresses' teenage daughters.

While together for a number of years, Alexander and Rosa ultimately parted, seemingly in a very civilized, friendly fashion. He continued to assist her financially after their breakup. He stayed close to all of his children, though it's possible that Lucrezia was his favorite. She was an accomplished poet and apparently a very good writer. In 1816, when he read her work, Lord Byron claimed she wrote "the prettiest love letters in the world . . . I shall go repeatedly to read the epistles over and over . . . they are short but very simple, sweet and to the purpose." Byron is not someone who would just say that to be nice about a woman who was dead and therefore unable to have sex with him. She could read Greek and Latin, as well as speak Italian, French, and Spanish (Byron also mentioned that there were some Spanish verses by her), all in a time when very few women were even literate.

She was also famously beautiful. According to a contemporary, Niccolò Cagnolo of Parma: "Her face is rather long, the nose well cut, hair golden, eyes of no special color. Her mouth is rather large, the teeth brilliantly white, her neck is slender and fair, the bust admirably proportioned." Which doesn't sound that flattering, but white teeth are probably a lot more common now than they were then.

Her crowning glory, though, was her long, wavy blond hair, of which Lorenzo Pucci the cardinal wrote: "It reached down to her feet; never have I seen such beautiful hair. She wore a headdress of fine linen and over it a sort of net light as air with gold threads woven in it." She supposedly bleached it by lying in the sun, though she may have also used an early hair dye that required two pounds of alum, six ounces of black sulfur, and four ounces of honey. (Have you heard the excuse that someone can't do something or go somewhere because they "have to wash their hair"? That excuse originated with Lucrezia Borgia.) All this hair fixation was worth it, though, because her hair has a history all its own. A lock of it, which she originally sent to a lover, is still on display in the Biblioteca Ambrosiana in Milan, as if it were a relic from a saint. Byron stole some strands (or, at least, he said he was going to) when he saw it because, well, that seems like the kind of thing he would do. Walter Landor, the nineteenth-century poet, even wrote the following poem about her hair:

> BORGIA, thou once wert almost too august
> And high for adoration; now thou'rt dust;
> All that remains of thee these plaits unfold,
> Calm hair meandering in pellucid gold.

She was, and it's perhaps unsurprising considering her father's proclivities, also known for her sexual escapades. Lucrezia Borgia was apparently pretty cool with handing out door prizes to whoever had the most orgasms at an orgy. In a time when women were expected to be chaste, the fact that she seemed to take lovers and enjoy lovemaking is notable. However, some of the rumors—in particular that she had incestuous relationships with her brother Cesare and her father—are likely greatly exaggerated.

Lucrezia is nip slipping you while holding up some flowers, and it's amazing this picture isn't the cover of a cool person's music album yet.

We'll get to these rumors, which play a part in the spectacular disintegration of her first marriage.

In 1493 Lucrezia Borgia was married to Giovanni Sforza. The Sforza family was an influential dynasty in Renaissance Italy and the ruling family in Milan. During this period being a pope wasn't largely a ceremonial office. You didn't just offer mass, wash people's feet once a year, and bless the wives of foreign heads of state. Alexander would never have wanted to be pope if that was all it entailed. He was the sixteenth-century equivalent of a louche playboy hanging out on a yacht somewhere. Instead, at the time, being pope conferred a considerable amount of political power, and the office could be compared, very loosely, to being the ruler of Rome. If Alexander wanted to strengthen his ties to

Giovanni Sforza's fur coat hides his dumb heart.

Milan, marrying Lucrezia to Giovanni was an excellent way to go about it.

It wasn't a love match. But then, marriages between powerful families rarely were. Lucrezia was thirteen, and Giovanni was in his mid-twenties. Their contract stipulated that she would remain in Rome for the next year preparing for the actual wedding, which she did, in a palace with the pope's mistress, Giulia Farnese, conveniently located near the papal palace. Giulia oversaw the event, which occurred on the twelfth of June in 1493 because astrologers had told the Sforzas that it was a favorable date. (This was the first cause of dispute between the pope and the Sforzas; Alexander may have been from the late fifteenth century, but he was not superstitious.) Five hundred ladies attended Lucrezia when she wed, and the couple received gifts of jewels and gold and silver objects.

A fairly scandalous play, the *Menaechmi,* by Plautus was performed to celebrate the wedding. In brief, it's a play about a comedic misunderstanding in which two separated twin brothers show up at the same prostitute's door, and wacky confusion ensues! It probably involved a lot of nudity and whimsy. I hate that kind of show. Spoiler: It ends with one of the brothers auctioning off his wife. He sells his wife. That's the ending. It's perhaps worth noting that the *Menaechmi* was the inspiration for Shakespeare's *Comedy of Error.* I also hate Shakespeare. (I know that this disclosure may change the terms of our imaginary friendship, but I think we can work past it.)

Pope Alexander supposedly found the play very boring and ordered it to be cut short, either because he hated farces, and had impeccable taste like me, or maybe because he liked his nudity to be very, very serious, and the play was failing on that front. According to the humanist and historian Stefano Infessura, Pope Alexander and several other religious leaders spent the rest of the celebration trying to throw candies and marzipans into the tops of women's dresses. Stefano seemingly disapproved, because he ends his description of the proceedings exclaiming, "et hoc ad honorem et laudem omnipotentes Dei et Ecclesie Romane!" (And this in honor of the Almighty God and the Church of Rome!)

The ceremony to consummate the marriage was curiously lacking from the wedding. Alexander asked that Giovanni not actually *sleep* with Lucrezia until November. That's a little surprising. Lucrezia had been living with the pope's mistress, who had been instructing her on womanly arts. Still, at thirteen Lucrezia was a very young bride by the standards of the time. Yes, Romeo and Juliet give the impression that everyone in the fifteenth century was marrying at age twelve, but that's wrong. The average age for non-nobles to marry was around twenty-two. Royal women, like Lucrezia, were married much earlier, so it wasn't entirely shocking, although there was criticism—say, in Dante—of the practice.

Perhaps you are wondering what a fifteenth-century consummation ceremony was like. After their wedding, a newly married couple would be escorted to their bedchamber and undressed. There was frequently much drinking and joking and general high jinks along the way. While the curtains around their bed would be drawn, witnesses would often spend the night in the room to ensure that coupling actually did take place. And while this seems distasteful by modern standards, that ceremony was probably a *really good idea*. If, say, a marriage was uniting two powerful families, you wanted to be certain that it had been properly consummated so that it couldn't be annulled afterward.

Or did you want that? A lot of people say that Alexander's reason for skipping the consummation ceremony wasn't to protect Lucrezia's modesty, so much as it was to make it possible to annul the marriage if the Sforzas ever turned against the Borgias. Or if the political alliance wasn't useful anymore. Which became the case almost immediately. Rumor has it that within months of Lucrezia's wedding, Alexander was already looking for more advantageous partners. The marriage had been agreed upon before Alexander ascended to the papacy, and he now realized that he might have sold his daughter short.

Lucrezia didn't seem fond of Giovanni, who was twice her age and supposedly had a violent temper, and Alexander didn't like that his daughter was going to have to live on her husband's estate in the country rather than remaining in Rome, where she could visit her family regularly. (Maybe this is evidence of the oft-rumored incestuous relationship between Lucrezia and Alexander, or maybe it is just evidence that parents have always been asking their kids why they don't live closer to home.)

Alexander also had suspicions that Giovanni was plotting against the Borgias. There is a lot of paranoia when you look at Borgia political dealings, but in this case it was justified. Giovanni was spying on the Borgias for the Milanese.

So the Borgias did the sensible thing and tried to kill him. In 1497 Cesare planned to poison Giovanni, but first he told his sister his intent, because . . . manners? Giovanni uncovered the plan. Did Lucrezia tell him? It seems possible. For all that history makes Lucrezia out to be a wily murderer, she was also being passed around as a political tool at the whims of her father—like all women from powerful families of the time. Maybe here she tried to do the right thing. Or perhaps Giovanni just found out by himself.

And so they decided not to poison Giovanni after all. Not just because surprise poisonings, like birthdays, are the most fun, but because they knew that the murder would certainly be traced back to them. Going forward, they were nice about their offers to end the marriage (again, after the whole "plotting to poison him" thing). Alexander proposed to let Giovanni keep Lucrezia's dowry, which was a considerable 31,000 ducats. However, the pope also wanted him to say that he was impotent because the grounds for annulment hinged on the bride still being a virgin.

Giovanni, very accurately, pointed out that he had illegitimate children. And his first wife, Maddalena Gonzaga, had died in childbirth. There was absolutely no way that he was impotent. The Borgias were totally open to him lying, but Giovanni did not have their flexible relationship with the truth.

And then the mudslinging started. Giovanni began to tell people that Alexander wanted the annulment so he could sleep with his own daughter. Lucrezia, who was eighteen at the time, came to be referred to as Alexander's "daughter, bride and daughter-in-law" as a result. The Borgias appealed to Giovanni's uncle to *persuade* Giovanni that divorcing Lucrezia would be a good idea. Giovanni countered by saying that Lucrezia was also sleeping with her brothers.

Starting a smear campaign against a pope who tried to have you killed seems extremely, extremely stupid. People ending relationships have, throughout history, said horrible things about their partners. John Ruskin told everyone his wife, Effie, was repulsive and impossible to sleep with. Caroline Lamb told everyone that Lord Byron was a homosexual and involved in incestuous affairs. *But those people did not have families that were extremely powerful and known for murdering people.*

Giovanni was ultimately persuaded when his uncle told him that the family's protection would be withdrawn, and the Borgias would almost certainly kill him if he did not proceed with a divorce.

During this time Lucrezia, who was pretty upset by the slander, had retired to a convent. She was sent letters about the proceedings by one of her father's messengers, a young Spaniard named Perotto. It was rumored that she quickly began sleeping with him. Six months later, when she needed to speak to the fact that she was a virgin, *Lucrezia was pregnant.*

Seriously pregnant. And even though her father was the pope, I don't think anyone believed she was carrying God's child. Except everyone went along with fiction in this weird, happyish story.

In this situation I think most women would say, "I cannot possibly declare that I am a virgin, given that I am noticeably pregnant. Obviously I will have to remain in this marriage. Sorry about the politics, Dad." But not Lucrezia. The Borgia family just decided to proceed as though she wasn't pregnant, and essentially dared anyone to bring it up.

And it totally worked. Lucrezia was inspected and declared "intacta" by judges (admittedly, judges in the Vatican). Giovanni, who had relented somewhat, especially after it was suggested by Pope Alexander that he prove his virility by having sex in front of Borgia and Sforza family members, attested to her virginity.

While she was pregnant.

I love this story. I have given some thought as to why I enjoy it so much, since, obviously, forcing your husband to annul your marriage is not a very nice thing to do. Having affairs is certainly not something people should be commended for. And lying to Vatican judges is, while admittedly not a situation most of us are going to be in, probably bad. History seems to agree with me, as this incident certainly contributes to the Borgias' reputation for decadence and general mayhem, and the enduring rumor that they were all sleeping with one another.

But you know, she did it with style. I'm impressed by her audacity. *She was exceedingly pregnant and had her marriage annulled by telling everyone her husband was impotent and she was a virgin.* And she knew that she was pregnant. She was not a fourteen-year-old girl from rural Kansas on the hit TV show *I Didn't Know I Was Pregnant.* She was a Borgia. She knew about sex. The Borgias seem to have believed that you could Jedi-mind-trick people into just about anything, and, seemingly, they kind of could. Look, maybe we all can. Maybe we all can be bolder and crazier and decide to act as though other people will just follow our lead. A surprising amount of the time they will.

There's nothing noble about this breakup, but it does seem like proof that if you do things with conviction you can get away with just about anything. And honestly, everything worked out all right in the end. Sort of. For some. Giovanni had to return Lucrezia's dowry, and the Spanish messenger Perotto ended up floating in the Tiber, supposedly killed by the Borgia family so he wouldn't reveal he was having relations with Lucrezia. Or they might have killed him just because his job was to deliver messages, not to sleep with Lucrezia. So maybe they killed him because he was bad at his job. Or maybe they just murdered him because they wanted to kill someone that day. As is the case in much of history, murder was not something that had to be reserved for special occasions.

Lucrezia did give birth to the child she was carrying, or we assume she did, because at almost precisely the same time a new child was introduced into the Borgia household. His mother was not named, but he was called Giovanni. Historians refer to him as the "Infans Romulus," referencing the myth regarding the first king of Rome, who, after being fathered by Mars, was abandoned with his twin and raised by wolves. Which seems fitting.

There was some question as to who exactly would be raising the Infans. A papal edict was released in 1501 claiming that the child, who was then three years old, was the son of Lucrezia's brother Cesare, with a woman who would remain unnamed. Then a second papal bull was released, claiming that he was Pope Alexander's son. It explained, "You bear this deficiency not from the said duke, but from us and the said woman, which we for good reasons did not desire to express in the preceding writing." It was thought that the first statement was made to protect the child's inheritance. As pope, Alexander couldn't recognize new children, and he wanted to name the Infans heir to a duchy. Why, having declared the child Cesare's, he then issued the revision claiming the child as his own is confusing, though the reason likely had to do with additional protection regarding the inheritance. The kid definitely belonged to *someone* in the Borgia family.

Instead of assuming, "Oh, the boy is Lucrezia's, her dad and brother are trying to cover for her," everyone seems to have assumed that Lucrezia was having an incestuous affair with her father and possibly her brother. While the people were relatively sure that the child was hers—they remembered the "announcing she was a virgin while pregnant" thing because that announcement was greeted with great laughter—they couldn't remember who fathered him. Everybody knew Lucrezia had been pregnant, and a lot of people had heard Giovanni's accusations that she was sleeping with every male member of her family. Given the historical speculation, I suppose we should address the obvious possibility that, yes, maybe the Borgias were an incestuous family. It is possible that, instead of having an affair with the unlucky Spanish messenger, Lucrezia slept with her father or her brother or both. They did love sex, and they had offbeat tastes. But just because someone loves watching prostitutes pick up chestnuts with their lady parts does not necessarily mean they are incestuous.

That will be a helpful adage to bear in mind in many instances of life.

The main reason to not think they're incestuous is that if they were, they would have been writing love letters to one another. It seems odd that there were never any letters—in this incredibly verbose family—referencing their unnatural attractions for one another. Lucrezia wrote the prettiest love letters in the world, and while there are many affectionate exchanges between her and other family members, there is nothing that suggests they were having sex. They could have been smart enough not to put that in writing, but it seems more telling that none of Giovanni's close associates or even his household staff seemed to actually think that Lucrezia was having incestuous relations. And Lucrezia was good friends with her father's mistress, Giulia, and Cesare's mistress,

Sancia, which would be a little unusual if she were sleeping with both of them (though I suppose in that case the whole situation would be unusual). You know, it is possible that everyone you meet is incestuous. Who knows? Well, they do, but you don't. It still seems more likely in this case that it was a nasty rumor spread by someone she was in the process of divorcing.

And then Lucrezia was engaged to the seventeen-year-old Neapolitan Alfonso of Aragon. Unfortunately, the whole charming "Borgias being ballsy" thing gets a lot less enchanting during this marriage. Alfonso and Lucrezia genuinely liked each other, which may have been because they were both teenagers when they married. The pope gave them a castle in Nepi and, in an unusual move for the time, granted Lucrezia governorship over Spoleto and Foligno, both of which she was said to rule well. The couple had a child named Rodrigo.

And then Cesare and Alexander had Alfonso killed when he ceased to be politically useful.

He was first attacked when crossing St. Peter's Square and was severely wounded in the head, the right arm, and the leg but managed to return home. So Cesare sent one of his guards to finish the job. Burchard writes, "Since Don Alfonso refused to die of his wounds, he was strangled in his bed." Lucrezia was in the room with him. Alexander reportedly saw her fleeing and screaming.

They were terrible times.

In 1502, twenty-one-year-old Lucrezia was married again, this time to Alfonso d'Este, Duke of Ferrara, who remained her husband until her death in 1519. (In that time she also had affairs with her brother-in-law, Francesco, and the poet Pietro Bembo.) Despite her affairs, Alfonso wrote to her father that Lucrezia was a treasure. When Alexander died, they remained married and Alfonso protected her during the fall of the Borgias. Not in a "he walked on the outside of the street so cars would not hit her" kind of way but in a "her family was no longer in power and they had killed a lot of people who might want revenge" kind of way. When she died giving birth to her eighth child in 1519, she was mourned by the people of Ferrara and her husband.

She never quite got over that first marriage, though. The Ferrarese ambassador in Rome sent this note before the wedding to Alfonso explaining that Giovanni should definitely not be near the location because Lucrezia would freak out if she saw him.

> His Holiness the Pope, taking into consideration such matters as might occasion displeasure not only to your Excellency and to the Most Illustrious Don Alfonso, but also to the duchess and even to himself, has charged us to write to your Excellency to urge you so to contrive that the Lord Giovanni of Pesaro, who, as your Excellency is aware, is in Mantua, shall not be in Ferrara at the time of the nuptials. Notwithstanding that his divorce from the said duchess is absolutely legitimate and accomplished in accordance with pure truth, as is publicly known not only from the proceedings of the trial but also from the free confession of the said Don Giovanni, it is possible that he may still be actuated by some lingering ill-will; wherefore, *should he find himself in any place where the said lady might be seen by him, her Excellency might, in consequence, be compelled to withdraw into privacy, to be spared the memory of the past* [emphasis mine]. Wherefore, his Holiness exhorts your Excellency to provide with your habitual prudence against such a contingency.

To summarize, the pope warns that if Lucrezia even sees Giovanni Sforza, she's going to run into another room and hide. Which is, admittedly, something a lot of us have done when we've seen an ex. Lucrezia was able to cope with having her husband murdered in front of her, but man, if she had to see that guy she had the bad divorce from, she just *could not handle it.*

And it wasn't because she was so scared of Sforza. If you are terrified of your ex-husband and you are a Borgia, you do not say you're going to run away in a huff. You tell any member of your immediate family you want him dead, or maybe just suggest it would be kind of funny if he died, and then he dies. So it's doubtful that she was frightened of him, any more than we're afraid, after a messy but not violent breakup, that our ex will attack us upon seeing us at a party. The exes we feel a need to hide from are the ones who make us feel embarrassed about our treatment of them.

If you sign your ex up for a sex addict's meeting (and your ex is not, in fact, a sex addict—an idea I stole from *White Girl Problems* by Babe Walker), or pretend to be a virgin while pregnant during your annulment proceedings, or commit any number of other vengeful acts that will certainly seem amusing at the time and probably entertain your friends or future biographers, you will still be a little embarrassed eventually. (This holds true even if your ex totally had it coming. Sforza certainly did—what with spreading those incest rumors.) If you're a decent person, you will know that you did something scummy, even if it was nicer than what everyone else around you was doing, and you will never be able to face your ex at a party again. You'll know what you did, and you won't like remembering it. You will be ashamed of yourself because you'll know that—*seriously, even if everyone else around you is behaving so much worse*—you usually behave better. It will make parties awkward. It's a trade-off.

But again, future biographers will think you're cool, and actual sex addicts like Byron will be in love with you two hundred years after your death, so I guess it's your call.

4. Henry VIII

Anne Boleyn and Catherine Howard

$\mathcal{E}$very account of the English king Henry VIII's life should start with the same basic question. How hot was Henry VIII?

That is a private joke that is only funny to me. Every biography you read about Henry VIII and his wives begins with a line like "It's essential to begin our account of Henry VIII by questioning the impact of religion upon the average person in sixteenth-century England" or "We must begin our account of the life of Anne Boleyn by asking the question that has plagued scholars for centuries: what impact did Thomas More have on Henry's divorce proceedings?" Beats me! I don't know! I have no idea about the answer to either of these questions except what I read in Hilary Mantel's prizewinning novels. If quizzed, I will answer, "No one can say for sure."

I am, however, able to answer my own question—the first question posed in this chapter—and the answer is: *smoking*.

Smoking hot.

I think anyone who did not watch the TV series *The Tudors* forgets that Henry VIII was really gorgeous. They think he was a jowly, gout-ridden man wearing a large fur hat, which is the impression that everyone gets from one painting and numerous Renaissance fairs. That impression is exceedingly off base.

In 1519 the Venetian ambassador Sebastian Giustinian described Henry: "Nature could not have done more for him. He is much handsomer than any sovereign in Christendom; a great deal handsomer than the King of France, very fair and his whole frame admirably proportioned."

Would Sebastian Giustinian lie to you? Who knows? But let's believe he

No, I swear, Henry VIII was definitely hot.

would not, because everyone else from the Tudor period seems to agree that Henry was pretty much the most gorgeous man anyone had ever seen or was ever going to see. Thomas More claimed that "among a thousand noble companions, the king stands out the tallest, and his strength fits his majestic body. There is fiery power in his eyes, beauty in his face." He stood six foot two, which is still an impressive height now, and his beard was supposed to appear golden.

If brains matter to you even a little bit, he was also one of the most intellectually accomplished princes in Europe. The theologian Erasmus claimed he was brilliant, with "a lively mentality which reached for the stars, and he was able beyond measure to bring to perfection whichever task he undertook." He spoke French, Latin, and Spanish and was a keen musician: he owned five bagpipes, seventy-six recorders, ten trombones, and seventy-eight flutes (which frankly seems excessive). He supposedly (although maybe not) composed the folk songs "Greensleeves" and "Helas Madame." He was an excellent hunter; he particularly enjoyed pursuing deer and wild boar on horseback, and, according to Giustinian, "never [took] his diversion without tiring eight or ten horses." He was also a skilled tennis player and a jouster. He was an accomplished theologian who wrote the "Declaration of the Seven Sacraments against Martin Luther," for which he was called "Defender of the Faith," and he heard three to five masses a day. He aided the constitutional development of England by decreasing the power of nobles. During his reign, the English navy grew from five ships to fifty, which is why he was also called "the Father of the English Navy."

If any of this sounds too intellectual, he was also apparently fun to gamble with.

Frankly, if a crazy person ever came up to you on the street, held a gun to your head, and demanded you answer the question "What was Henry VIII good at?" you could probably just pick anything. You could say he was an accomplished botanist. There are probably some historical documents to indicate that fact that we haven't yet uncovered. He was good at everything.

Now back to how attractive Henry was, because the thing he was best at was being hot. (If you had lived in the sixteenth century, you would have spent days when you were not worrying about the plague having a huge crush on Henry.) Giustinian again: "His majesty is the handsomest potentate I ever set eyes upon: above the usual height, with an extremely fine calf to his leg, his complexion very fair and bright, with auburn hair combed straight and short in the French fashion, and a round face so very beautiful that it would become a pretty woman."

You know who was sadly not considered a pretty woman? Henry's first wife, Catherine of Aragon. Henry married Catherine, the widow of his brother, for political reasons in 1509, when he was eighteen and she was twenty-three. That may seem like a normal age gap; however, the French king remarked that Henry "has an old deformed wife, while he himself is young and handsome."

Who knows how that opinion was formed because every single picture of women from this period looks the same. Seemingly every woman had a tiny mouth, no eyelashes, and a receding hairline. (That hairline wasn't necessarily due to hair loss, because women plucked back their hairlines and eyelashes. Beauty rituals of the sixteenth century are another story for another excellent book.) To visualize the people in this story properly, you could try playing a game where you imagine them as the actors in *The Tudors*, but that's not a good plan because on *The Tudors* even the allegedly deformed people look the way you or I would appear *on the best day of our lives with a team of hair and makeup professionals standing by*. So it's best if you cast everyone in the story of Henry VIII as someone you know. Just make Catherine someone unattractive whom you don't like very much. That is exactly what Catherine of Aragon looked like. You are very good at imagining historical characters.

Catherine also, critically, had not been able to give Henry a son, which was necessary if the Tudor dynasty was going to continue. As early as 1514 rumors were swirling that Henry was going to divorce Catherine because the three sons she bore him died very shortly after being born.

Frankly, the fact that they eventually broke up is not surprising. Pretty much everyone who needs a dynasty breaks up with women who don't bear sons. Napoleon divorced Josephine, with

Five hundred years later, Anne Boleyn still looks like a pretty lady with excellent taste in lipstick.

whom he *was wildly in love*—so in love that their relationship is remembered as one of the greatest love stories of our time—to marry a younger woman who could bear him sons. Since Henry was not, as far as we can tell, deeply or even a little in love with Catherine, it's really only surprising that they didn't break up sooner. When Henry met Anne Boleyn in 1525, it had been seven years since Catherine's last pregnancy. Henry had certainly not been faithful during that period—Anne's sister Mary was one of his mistresses—but given that Catherine was nearing age forty, his mind had likely turned more seriously to the possibility of divorce.

And Anne was spectacular. The year of her birth is disputed, but she is thought to have been in her early twenties, at least ten years younger than Henry when they met. She was known to be very attractive and sophisticated. She had been educated at the French court. This was considered, as it is today, *extremely* sexy. The bishop of Riez, Lancelot de Carle, wrote, "You would have never taken her for an English woman from her manner and behavior, but a native-born French lady."

She was an excellent dancer. And she could also play the lute, which may have appealed to Henry's musical nature. (I do not know how many lutes Henry owned, but I'm going to guess seven.) And judging from everything you read, she was very, very funny.

Or if your idea of funny implies that she made excellent fart jokes, then she was witty. We'll say she had a dry wit. But her greatest appeal might have lain in the fact that Anne Boleyn was, unlike nearly every single other woman from the period, very disinclined to become Henry's mistress. When Henry suggested that she become his *only* mistress, which was the most serious commitment he could make without leaving his wife, Anne replied, "Your wife I cannot be, both in respect of mine own unworthiness, and also because you have a queen already. Your mistress I will not be."

Being a mistress in the sixteenth century didn't technically imply the same "home-wrecking hussy" stuff that it does today. The ideals of courtly love suggested that a man could take a mistress— a woman whom he idolized above all others at court. He would send her poems and small gifts, and she might give him a handkerchief or a hair ribbon to wear at jousts. It sounds really lovely, but Henry was not interested in that chaste arrangement, we assume. Maybe nobody actually thought that was what being a mistress entailed (with the possible exception of Eleanor of Aquitaine and probably not even her?). Maybe that was just a polite system set up to allow for extramarital affairs. And Anne was a bright enough lady to know that Henry was probably not asking for a hair ribbon.

Perhaps Anne was just politely rejecting Henry's advances because she was genuinely uninterested. Some scholars have argued that Anne was really a victim of Henry's sexual harassment, and that she truly wasn't into him. However, if her initial rejection carried with it the demand that Henry could have her only if he married her and made her queen, then, wow, did she ever pick the right time to issue that ultimatum.

So you may wonder: *How did Henry woo Anne Boleyn? Tell me more!* Here is a letter Henry VIII sent to Anne in 1533:

Myne awne Sweetheart, this shall be to advertise you of the great ellingness that I find here since your departing, for I ensure you, me thinketh the Tyme longer since your departing now last than I was wont to do a whole Fortnight; I think your Kindness and my Fervence of Love causeth it, for otherwise I wolde not thought it possible, that for so little a while it should have grieved me, but now that I am comeing toward you, me thinketh my Pains by half released, and also I am right well comforted, insomuch that my Book maketh substantially for my Matter, in writing where of I have spent above IIII Hours this Day, which caused me now to write the shorter Letter to you at this Tyme, because some Payne in my Head, wishing myself (specially an Evening) in my Sweethearts Armes *whose pritty Duckys I trust shortly to kysse* [my emphasis]. Writen with the Hand of him that was, is, and shall be yours by his will,

H. R.

Two points:

1. *Duckys* is sixteenth-century slang for breasts, and it took me forever to figure that out. I spent a solid two hours Googling "kind of birds sixteenth-century women kept as pets? Ducks, maybe? Did people kiss ducks then, was that a thing?" But it's a great term; I use it all the time.
2. Letters from people during this era are just awful to read. I'll say this for ancient Romans: their letters are straightforward and concise and easy to read. Punctuation was seemingly something that the barbarians just took possession of during the Dark Ages, and it doesn't make a fully triumphant return in England until well into the seventeenth century. (Shakespeare is largely credited with finding a treasure trove of commas and semicolons in a cave near Germany in 1602.)

I guess Anne liked these letters more than I, because she and Henry did, after some time, become lovers. But securing a divorce from Catherine proved difficult, especially because Henry had the title "Defender of the Faith." That would be the Catholic faith, a religion that does not believe in divorce. However, he ultimately annulled his marriage to Catherine, claiming that she had previously been wed to his brother, and quoting a passage of the Bible that said that a couple would not have children if a man married his brother's wife.

If you were a Catholic during the period (welcome to the twenty-first century, time traveler! Admire our wealth of semicolons!) or Thomas More in particular, Henry's divorce from Catherine was probably the ultimate bad breakup in this story. Everyone else is going to find what happened next to be worse, though. Despite the pope's strong objections, Anne and Henry married on January 25, 1533, and in September she gave birth to Elizabeth. On the one hand, this was great news! It meant Anne was fertile; she could bear children! And also, the baby grew up to be Queen Elizabeth, one of the greatest monarchs in English history.

On the other hand, the infant was a girl, so everyone was miserable.

The couple hoped more children would follow. They did not. Instead, there were three miscarriages.

This was probably Henry's fault—some scholars speculate that he might have had syphilis, which could have led to his wives' many miscarriages—though at the time miscarrying was always blamed on the woman and possibly taken as a sign that she was a witch.

Following his divorce from Catherine, and the religious and political repercussions that followed, Henry was not in a rush to divorce another wife. However, Anne possessed a very different personality than Catherine. While Catherine's motto had been HUMBLE AND LOYAL, Anne's was THE MOST HAPPY. And she would not stand for unhappiness. While Catherine had looked the other way throughout Henry's liaisons with other women, Anne raged. This was especially inconvenient given that, as early as 1536, rumors were circulating that Henry planned to remarry, this time to Jane Seymour.

You may be thinking, *Great! I hope Anne gets angry! Things work out great when women refuse to tolerate poor treatment by their husbands and get really ballsy and just decide to Take Over the Country! Did Anne, like Eleanor of Aquitaine, decide to do that?* Whoa, hold up there, reader, you are getting ahead of yourself. Eleanor of Aquitaine had approximately seven million times more power and political influence than Anne, and five more sons. Also, Henry II was a better person than Henry VIII, who would, presumably, not have taken such a rebellion so well. Anne did not stage a coup.

So rather than divorcing the increasingly unfriendly Anne, Henry accused her of bewitching him and engaging in adulterous affairs. Now, it's possible that Anne did have lovers. Some believe that she was in a complicated relationship with the poet Thomas Wyatt based on his poem "Whoso List to Hunt," in which Anne Boleyn is compared to a wild deer who has deserted her former master and now belongs to Caesar:

Whoso list to hunt, I know where is an hind,
But as for me, helas! I may no more.
The vain travail hath wearied me so sore,
I am of them that furthest come behind.
Yet may I by no means, my wearied mind
Draw from the deer; but as she fleeth afore
Fainting I follow. I leave off therefore,
Since in a net I seek to hold the wind.
Who list her hunt, I put him out of doubt,
As well as I, may spend his time in vain;
And graven in diamonds in letters plain
There is written, her fair neck round about,
"Noli me tangere, for Caesar's I am,
And wild to hold, though I seem tame."

I do not believe they were lovers based on this poem. If the poet Charles Bukowski proved anything, it is that poems can definitely just be drunken lies and speculation. I do believe they were lovers because before Henry and Anne married, Thomas Wyatt told Henry:

> Sir, I am credibly informed that your grace intendeth to take to your wife the Lady Anne Boleyn, wherein I Beseech your grace to be well advised what you do, for she is not meet to be coupled with your grace. Her conversation [way of life] hath been so loose and base; which thing I know not so much by hearsay as by my own experience as one that have had my carnal pleasure with her.

Wyatt very clearly and in no uncertain terms says he's slept with Anne. However, that does not mean that Anne was unfaithful when she was married to Henry.

It is also probably not true that she was guilty of witchcraft. Witches aren't real (at least not in the non-Wiccan-hippie-Devil-harlot way Henry VIII meant). None of this, however, made any difference when it came time to imprison Anne. She was tried for a host of crimes—including plotting to poison Catherine and praying for the king's death. And she was found guilty, despite supposedly remaining exquisitely calm in the courtroom, and sentenced to death.

At this point Anne went about handling her breakup better than anybody else in history ever has or ever will again. She apparently replied to the verdict with perfect composure. Lancelot de Carle wrote that Anne stepped forward and addressed the court: "I do not say that I have always borne towards the king the humility which I owed him, considering his kindness and the great honor he showed me and the great respect he always paid me; I admit, too, that often I have taken it into my head to be jealous of him . . . But may God be my witness if I have done him any other wrong."

Henry granted her request that she be executed by beheading

with a sword, not an ax. People often remember this as some sort of chivalrous gesture. I remember my mom taking me to the Tower of London when I was ten and telling me that Henry believed Anne Boleyn was too beautiful to be beheaded by an ax. *Wow, he must have still loved her,* I thought at the time. *Even though she was a witch.*

I no longer think that. I now think beheading people is bad regardless of the instrument employed.

Immediately after agreeing that Anne would be beheaded with a sword, Henry declared Elizabeth, their daughter, a bastard. All things considered, I think Anne probably would have traded the sword for not having their daughter declared illegitimate. But if she was furious—and she had every right to be (because Henry was the second worst, next to Norman Mailer)—she never showed it. The morning of her execution she even made little jokes. The constable of the Tower of London met with her, and wrote that

> this morning she sent for me, that I might be with her at such time as she received the good Lord, to the intent I should hear her speak as touching her innocency always to be clear. And in the writing of this she sent for me, and at my coming she said, "Mr. Kingston, I hear I shall not die afore noon, and I am very sorry therefore, for I thought to be dead by this time and past my pain." I told her it should be no pain . . . And then she said, "I heard say the executioner was very good, and I have a little neck."

And then, right before her execution, she stood up and told everyone that Henry was a very nice guy. Her last words were:

> Good Christian people, I am come hither to die, for according to the law, and by the law I am judged to die, and therefore I will speak nothing against it. I am come hither to accuse no man, nor to speak anything of that, whereof I am accused and condemned to die, but I pray God save the king and send

him long to reign over you, for a gentler nor a more merciful prince was there never: and to me he was ever a good, a gentle and sovereign lord. And if any person will meddle of my cause, I require them to judge the best. And thus I take my leave of the world and of you all, and I heartily desire you all to pray for me. O Lord have mercy on me, to God I commend my soul.

My God, think about the way we talk about our exes today. We go on and on about how they were evil, manipulative, sociopathic narcissists because they cheated on us one time. Meanwhile Anne Boleyn was able to speak well about her ex when her head was on the chopping block. What a superhuman amount of poise that must have required.

I'm not saying that composure is necessarily what everyone should strive toward. There's probably something healthy about venting your frustrations with your ex to some friends, especially when you think they did behave badly toward you. Different people have different coping techniques. But I will say that Anne Boleyn is my personal breakup role model. Honestly, I'm such a jerk about breakups. Even when things have gone wrong for completely understandable reasons and it's clear that we're incompatible, after someone breaks up with me, on some level I still want to think that it is because they have fundamental personality defects that make them unlovable or unable to love. Your ex is, as likely as not, not really a narcissist or a sociopath or emotionally disturbed or any of the other accusations that you've come up with to make yourself feel better about the relationship being over. Those are often just things we tell ourselves because feeling angry is more satisfying than feeling sad.

That does not change the fact that you may not immediately feel like speaking in glowing terms about someone who just dumped you. And honestly, if any woman in the sixteenth century was capable of coming up with witty but mean-spirited cracks about her ex, it was almost certainly Anne Boleyn. The seeming sincerity of her speech is more startling given that she'd always been a very forward-thinking, clever, spirited woman. Obviously, most of us have never succeeded in being as polite about exes as Anne was immediately after her breakup, and none of them sentenced us to death for being a witch. (When I wrote that witches aren't real, I was trying to throw you off the scent. I actually am a witch.)

I can't resist interjecting a quote by Rudyard Kipling here. He wrote, "If you can keep your head about you while all others are losing theirs . . . then you'll be a [really good person]." But that is a weird reference when talking about a beheaded person. Though Anne did make a joke right before her execution about how some rulers were remembered as the Great or the Terrible, and she would be remembered as "the Headless." She was the best. She was absolutely the bee's knees. I wish we could go out and have a Scotch with her right now because she would be a great friend for us. (She seems like a Scotch drinker, right? Or do you think she'd order fruity cocktails to make fun of how absurd they are? Discuss in a group.)

It's really not surprising that people are more apt to remember her than Catherine Howard, Henry's fifth wife, and the second to be beheaded. Maybe that's because Catherine erred more on the side of behaving the way most of us do after a breakup.

Following Anne's beheading, Henry did marry Jane Seymour. She died giving birth to his sickly son, Edward VI. Then Henry married Anne of Cleves—a marriage that was later annulled. Anne of Cleves, of all of Henry's wives, may have gotten the best deal. Henry was supposedly unable to consummate the marriage and decreed that she would live on as his sister and be free to remarry.

And in 1540 he met the young Catherine Howard. She was Anne Boleyn's cousin and bore a physical resemblance to her, which she cultivated. She dressed her ladies in the French fashion. However, she adopted the motto NO OTHER WISH BUT HIS. She seemed more docile than her late cousin.

I honestly cannot imagine why she would emulate Anne

Boleyn, because it's not as though Henry was in a state of great mourning for that wife. He was married to Jane less than two weeks after Anne was beheaded. So maybe Henry just liked French dresses, and that was a style that worked well on young women.

It's still a little baffling why Catherine Howard styled her whole look after Anne Boleyn because things did not work *out well for Anne.*

Catherine was unlike Anne in that she did not withhold sex as a strategem. She had grown up in the household of her step-grandmother, the Dowager Duchess of Norfolk, who was known for taking in young, aristocratic charges and then letting them raise themselves. By the time Catherine was thirteen, she was sexually active with her music teacher, Henry Mannox. He claimed of Catherine, "I know her well enough . . . And she loves me and I love her, and she hath said to me that I shall have her maidenhead, though it be painful to her, and not doubting but I will be good to her hereafter."

Whether or not he actually *took* her virginity is still in dispute. A little later, she was very probably raped by Francis Dereham. In 1541 she contended: "Frauncez Derame [*sic*] by many persuasions procured me to his vicious purpose and obteyned first to lye uppon my bedde with his doblett and hose and after within the bedde fynally he lay with me nakyd and used me in suche sort as a many dothe his wife many and sondry tymez but how often I know not." (Sixteenth-century letters are the worst. You read these, and you could swear they were just making up words.) Dereham then began referring to Catherine as his wife, which by the standards of the time might have signified they were precontracted to marry, which meant that though the finer details of their engagement had not been worked out, she could not marry another. Basically it was like having a boyfriend. But, in this case, one who raped you and whom you did not want to date.

But the main point here is that by the time Catherine was a teenager she was already sexually experienced. That was sad for two reasons. First, because *she was raped as a fourteen-year-old*. Second, because it would ultimately cause her to be beheaded.

You see, Henry believed that Catherine was a virgin. The queen of England was supposed to be a virgin to ensure that any sons were indeed Henry's. Anne almost certainly was not a virgin, but Henry had been alerted to that fact before the marriage and just chose to believe that Thomas Wyatt was lying, or decided he really didn't care. Maybe he felt that since Anne resisted him for so long she'd resisted other suitors. Catherine, on the other hand, did not resist him and was supposedly great in bed. And Henry seemingly attributed her sexual skills to the fact that . . . she loved him? They were in love? And that made her know how to do all the sex stuff?

I think you can find a partner who is absolutely untouched, or you can find a partner who has bedroom skills, but you can't have both. You pick. (I would 100 percent choose the sex-stuff option, but I am not a sixteenth-century ruler of England.)

In any case, the marriage started out extremely well. The French ambassador, Charles de Marillac, wrote, "The King is so amorous of her that he cannot treat her well enough and caresses her more than he did the others." He lavished gifts upon her—the number of jewels he gave her must have gone into the hundreds.

And Catherine responded pretty much the way any teenager would act when a much, much older man who was no longer hot and weighed three hundred pounds dotes on them.

She found a younger lover. Sorry! Sorry, old guy readers.

It's not that loving and happy relationships between much younger women and much older men don't exist. They do. It's simply that Catherine sleeping with a man closer in age to her teenage years was not entirely surprising.

She chose a lover whom she'd probably slept with before she met Henry. Thomas Culpeper was a gentleman in Henry's privy chamber, which meant he was a high-ranking man at court, and very close to Henry himself. He was young and attractive, and many women in court doted on him as they might once have doted on Henry. He and Catherine supposedly had a tempestuous relationship before she married Henry, with a lot of speculation about whether or not they might get engaged. If you're interested, Thomas Culpeper was also a rapist (there's a lot of rape in this part). There's a story the religious activist Richard Hilles tells in *Original Letters Relative to the English Reformation* that states:

> Culpeper had violated the wife of a certain park-keeper in a woody thicket, while, horrid to relate! three or four of his most profligate attendants were holding her at his bidding. For this act of wickedness he was, notwithstanding, pardoned by the King, after he had been delivered into custody by the villagers on account of his crime, and likewise a murder which he had committed in his resistance to them, when they first endeavored to apprehend him.

It makes me proud and excited that people in this historical era were able to see that rape was different from consensual sex and that it was "horrid." Civilization is on the march! Being not horrible is becoming a thing, already, even in a world without grammar.

This news either didn't make its way to Catherine or didn't bother her. She and Thomas began exchanging gifts, which, again, was not completely uncommon given that courtly love was thought to be acceptable. As long as she did not actually sleep with them, it was assumed the queen might have admirers. However, she also started writing Thomas letters. Consider this one, which is preserved in her own handwriting:

Master Culpeper, I heartily recommend me unto you, praying you to send me word how that you do. It was showed me that you were sick, the which thing troubled me very much till such time that I hear from you, praying you to send me word how that you do, for I never longed so much for thing as I do to see you and to speak with you, the which I trust shall be shortly now. The which doth comfort me very much when I think of it, and when I think again that you shall depart from me again it makes my heart to die, to think what fortune I have that I cannot be always in your company. Yet my trust is always in you that you will be as you have promised me, and in that hope I trust upon still, praying you then that you will come when my Lady Rochford is here, for then I shall be best at leisure to be at your commandment, thanking you for that you have promised me to be so good unto that poor fellow my man, which is one of the griefs that I do feel to depart from him, for then I do know no one that I dare trust to send to you, and therefore I pray you take him to be with you that I may sometime hear from you. One thing I pray you, to give me a horse for my man, for I have much ado to get one, and therefore I pray send me one by him, and in so doing I am as I said afore; and thus I take my leave of you, trusting to see you shortly again, and I would you was with me now that you might see what pain I take in writing to you,

Yours as long as life endures,

Katheryn*

---

*Every different text seems to spell everyone's name differently. I thought of calling her Kythern.

At this point, I'm just putting up letters from this period so you have to suffer through them with me. Basically, she's sad he is sick, and she wants a horse, and she loves him and wants to be with him forever and always. Catherine has the concerns of a teenager, most likely because she is a teenager. On second thought, that is not a fair comment. Eternal love and a horse are the things everyone wants, in any age, at any age. Most people just hide their desires better in their letters.

Catherine was incapable of hiding any emotion she ever had. Anne of Cleves once noted that "she was too much a child to deny herself any sweet thing she wanted." Which is fine, but *do not put anything in writing.* The fact that she was composing love letters at all, while married to a man who had famously killed her cousin for being an adulterous witch, strikes me as a kind of stupidity akin to women in horror movies walking into abandoned factories all by themselves. Of course he's going to kill you, Catherine! You are definitely going to die! Why did she have no friends to point this out to her?

Unsurprisingly, Catherine's infidelity came to light.

The court tried to let her off the hook by stating that if she had been precontracted to Francis Dereham, her marriage to Henry was not binding and Henry could annul the arrangement. She would likely have been exiled, and her reputation would be ruined, but she would not have been dead. She could have retired to a nunnery or gone overseas.

Anne Boleyn would have taken this deal in about one hot minute. She would have moved to France and made a lot of jokes and been fine. Catherine, whether because of some sort of deeply felt allegiance to honesty or because she stupidly thought she could win Henry back, continued to claim that Francis Dereham had raped her and that they were not precontracted.

I think Catherine was very truthful. I believe she had integrity or at least enough conviction to know that one fact—that she had definitely been raped—was accurate. Those are admirable qualities.

Still, this was one of the dumbest moves in history. Ancient Romans were terrified of exile, and that makes sense because it often meant life in a wildly inhospitable no-man's-land, but things weren't *that* bad by the sixteenth century. Anne Boleyn, before she was executed, supposedly prayed that Henry might let her retire to a nunnery rather than lopping off her head. And considering that she was the cause of the rise of the Church of England, Anne would probably not have done well at a nunnery.

I think Catherine somehow could not conceive of the fact that she might actually die. She would, though. She didn't pull off her execution with Anne Boleyn's aplomb. There was a second where it seemed as if she might. She had the chopping block sent to her cell so she could practice placing her head on it in the most dignified fashion, but I think Catherine just thought this was an elaborate kind of playacting, and that afterward she would walk offstage and resume her life as a pampered, sex-kitteny queen. Unlike Anne, who went boldly to the block, when Catherine approached she was, according to Marillac, "so weak that she could hardly speak." On the scaffolding, she is said to have said that she was justly condemned and "required that people take example [from her] for amendment of their ungodly lives and gladly to obey the king in all things."

People often say that the ending—this likely historically accurate ending—was in keeping with the mores of the period and similar to Anne Boleyn's. I don't think it was. Saying that someone should obey the king is not quite the same as saying that Henry was a good or just king.

My favorite part of Catherine's story is the folklore relating to her beheading. I like to believe this story, though it is very likely apocryphal. It's rumored that her last words were "I die a queen, but I would rather die the wife of Thomas Culpeper!" Yes. Most of us would also rather be the wife of a known rapist/killer than a guy who was actively in the process of beheading us, though neither option sounds great to a twenty-first-century onlooker. But more than that, yes, if it is true, it was probably the first truly modern response to a breakup.

It's always important to point out—as Julian Barnes does in *England, England*—that the past wasn't just a giant costume party. People did not behave the same in the Middle Ages as they do today, no matter how trendy movie directors try to make that life seem. (Sixteenth-century aristocrats swore all the time and listened to the Sex Pistols! No, they did not. They mostly listened to the Ramones and some Blondie.) Concerns were fundamentally different than they are today. No one said their main life goal was "to be happy" or find "work-life balance." Instead, simply surviving was a very real, daily concern for many people. Then there were the questions of how to live honorably and how to get into heaven when you died.

Anne died in a way that was absolutely in keeping with the values of her time. Her concern on the scaffold was *not* sharing her feelings; it was being remembered in an honorable light and preserving the monarchy in the country. And I admire those values. Even today we can understand that avoiding talking terribly about a not-so-great ex is taking a higher road than shouting insults about how you wish you'd never met that person. And when an ex was *obviously* terrible, as everyone knew Henry was, it just makes you look really composed and forgiving and great.

But we may relate more to Catherine. We live in a time that admires being truthful and sharing your feelings. There's a premium placed on emotional honesty—think about all the people you have heard derided for being "fake." The premium we place on being "real" may be a youthful luxury that we indulge in before we start thinking about our legacies. The fact that Catherine possibly went to her death ranting reminds us of her youth. I sympathize with her. Didn't she respond to her breakup the way most of us did when we were teenagers? I mean, hopefully very few of us had breakups that ended in beheadings, but still.

If you want to see the two breakups as a sort of Thunderdome between Anne and Catherine and say, "Who broke up better?" well, that sounds like a fun game and one I would like to play with you at our costume drama movie nights. You know I'd be Team Anne. You know who else was Team Anne Boleyn? Thomas Wyatt, who once advised Henry not to marry her. He wrote about Anne's death in his poem "Innocentia Veritas Viat Fides Circumdederunt Me Inimici Mei":

These bloody days have broken my heart.
My lust, my youth did them depart,
And blind desire of estate.
Who hastes to climb seeks to revert.
Of truth, circa Regna tonat.

Anne had the good fortune to have slept with a really talented poet in her younger years. That, coupled with her quick-witted and supposedly seductive ways, and, of course, the dramatic nature of her death, means that Anne is remembered fondly. She has been depicted by actresses from Merle Oberon to Geneviève Bujold to Charlotte Rampling to Natalie Portman to Natalie Dormer. (There seems to be a contractual obligation for the most beautiful actresses of the day to appear in at least one adaptation of the life of Anne Boleyn.) You'll find plenty of people who will take Anne Boleyn's side.

I imagine the Catherine Howard camp is smaller, although she was portrayed by the actresses Emily Blunt—who depicts her screaming as she is about to be executed—and Binnie Barnes, and, bizarrely, comes up in one episode of *The Simpsons*.

But whether you think that you should repress your feelings and maybe just drink martinis quietly, or whether you think people should hear the truth about what's going on with you, whether you respond to being dumped by taking the high road or taking a slightly lower path, there are going to be people who understand.

And you know whose side no one ever, ever takes? Henry's.

All of this wife killing did not work out well for him. According to Eustace Chapuys, the imperial ambassador to England, Henry mourned Catherine's passing more than that of any of his other wives. Though Chapuys didn't necessarily think that was because he loved Catherine more. He wrote:

> I should say that this King's case resembles very much that of the woman who cried more bitterly at the loss of her tenth husband than she had cried on the deaths of the other nine put together, though all of them had been equally worthy people and good husbands to her. The reason [is] that she had never buried one of them without being sure of the next. But after the tenth husband, she had no other one in view: hence her sorrow and her lamentation.

In the years between Anne and Catherine, Henry had gone from being a good-looking, middle-aged man to the bloated, drumstick-gnawing monster you remember from royal portraits. And he still could have been a superstar if he'd just not started killing his wives. The breakups killed his reputation.

Normally the takeaway from these stories is "Your breakup will not define your life. In the story of you, this will not be the central narrative." However, Henry VIII beheaded not one but two wives. So maybe the takeaway should be "Your breakup will not define your life. In the story of you, this will not be the central narrative *unless you murder not one but two spouses, in which case it totally will; then it will be the central narrative for sure.*"

I can't help feeling pleased that while Anne and Catherine might have lost their heads, they're both remembered well. They're played by lovely, America's Sweetheart–type actresses, whereas

Henry VIII is played by Jonathan Rhys Meyers with an increasingly crazy glint in his eyes. If people today are asked about Henry VIII, the one thing they will say is "the guy who killed his wives?" Henry is the only one in this story who we have decided isn't getting into heaven, regardless of what Anne Boleyn might have said. Which is sad, because, you know, he was probably a really good botanist.

5. Anna Ivanovna

I suspect if you ask people what the worst possible outcome of a breakup could be, most would say, "I will never love again." And that would be terrible! It's unlikely that would happen, but it would certainly be very sad.

However, that is not the worst outcome. You could become a crazed supervillain who goes about systematically destroying other people's relationships, trying to make sure everyone's experiences of the pitfalls of love mirror your own. You running amok and locking people in torture chambers—that would be the worst.

This will also probably not happen. Partly because your life isn't a novel written by the Marquis de Sade. And because very few people have the power to seriously and maliciously influence others' romantic circumstances. I suppose you could try to break up happy couples by seducing one party or both of them, but not only is that wrong, it is difficult and time-consuming. If you are not interested in a serious relationship with either of the parties you are devoting your energy to seducing, that project is going to get really old really fast.

But you know who had a ridiculous amount of time on her hands, almost limitless power, and an unhappy romantic history? The eighteenth-century Russian empress Anna Ivanovna.

Born in 1693, Anna was the daughter of Czar Ivan V, who is often referred to as "Ivan the Ignorant." This descriptor makes him sound more competent than he was. Ivan was apparently mentally deficient to such an extent that he would remain in a nearly vegetative state for hours on end. He could walk only with the support of courtiers and was capable only of performing ceremonial functions as czar, while Peter the Great, Anna's uncle and co-czar, performed most of the real court duties. There's a story about peasants storming the castle when both Ivan and Peter were young. Peter ended the conflict by rebuffing the peasants authoritatively; Ivan allegedly cowered and wet himself. It was decided that they should both rule and sit on twin thrones. By the time he was twenty-seven, Ivan was mostly blind and considered mad.

Ivan had five children. If you ever need proof that it's good to be czar, look no further than the fact that women in the late seventeenth century competed to marry Ivan.

So Anna had something of an odd childhood. Her mother wasn't a happy woman and sternly believed in maintaining the old Russian ways. That meant little education for girls; Anna was barely literate. And she wasn't pretty. The author Thomas Carlyle once cruelly described her cheeks as "Westphalian ham." She is said to have had terrible manners and a grim demeanor. She was a nice dancer, though, and later founded a ballet school! That's seriously one of the only nice things we can say about Anna Ivanovna for this entire chapter, so treasure that tidbit.

Her notable lack of pleasing attributes did not keep her from being married off, because if we've learned anything from Ivan the Ignorant, it is that if you are a Russian noble nothing will stop you from being wed. In 1710 she married Frederick William, the Duke of Courland (part of today's Latvia).

And Anna was so excited about this! Before their wedding she wrote a letter to him, which declared:

> I learned with the greatest pleasure of our marriage, which is to take place thanks to the will of the Almighty God and their Imperial Highnesses, my dear relatives. At the same time I cannot but assure Your Highness that nothing could delight me more than to hear of your declaration of love for me. For my part, I assure Your Highness that I share your feelings. At our next happy meeting, to which I look forward eagerly, I shall, God willing, avail myself of the opportunity of expressing them to you personally.

The wedding was beautiful. Anna wore a cape embroidered with gold and a bejeweled tiara, and the ceremony ended with a display of fireworks.

Two days after the couple's marriage, Anna's uncle, Czar Peter the Great, staged a wedding of two dwarfs as a companion celebration to Anna's. It was an incredibly elaborate affair. According to Lindsey Hughes in *Peter the Great: A Biography*:

> Peter had planned both weddings simultaneously, evidently seeing the second as a sequel to the first. In August 1710, a day after he ordered a pair of diamond earrings for his niece, he had instructed Prince-Caesar Romodanovsky to round up all the dwarfs in Moscow and send them to St. Petersburg. Their owners were told to provide smart outfits for the dwarfs in the latest Western fashion, with plenty of gold braid and periwigs ... On the day about seventy dwarfs formed the retinue for the wedding ceremony, which was accompanied by the stifled giggles of the full-sized congregation ... a spectacle made all the funnier by the fact that most of the dwarfs were of peasant extraction with coarse

manners. At the feast . . . the dwarfs sat at miniature tables in the centre of the room, while full-sized guests watched them from tables at the sides. They roared with laughter as dwarfs, especially the older, uglier ones whose hunchbacks, huge bellies and short crooked legs made it difficult for them to dance, fell down drunk or engaged in brawls.

I assume the dwarf wedding was intended as a cruel parody of Anna's—a horrible commentary on how ugly and ill-mannered Anna was. And that's kind of true. But according to Hughes, it was a bigger, more elaborate joke, where Peter was expressing his contempt not only for Anna but for the entire Russian court. "Like all Peter's mock spectacles," Hughes writes, "the dwarf wedding also operated on a more symbolic level. Its juxtaposition with the wedding of Anna and the duke and its imitation of certain elements suggested that the full-sized guests were watching caricatures of themselves, miniature 'lords and ladies' clad, like them, in unfamiliar Western dress. Peter's courtiers . . . still had a long way to go before they were fully fledged, 'grown-up' Europeans."

It is also interesting that Peter the Great was trying to breed a race of little people. For real. He wanted to breed a race of dwarfs in his spare time.

He attempted to breed a race of giants, too. In addition to the dwarf wedding, he married a seven-foot-six-inch man to an equally tall woman, with the intention of producing giant children. Peter kept the man on salary and brought him out to parties dressed up as a baby.

I know I've said this before, but it is such a good thing we have television. Anyone who complains about people spending too much time watching reality shows and playing video games does not know what people with spare time got up to in a world without mindless amusements to keep them occupied. They made giants dress up as babies for their entertainment, that's what they did.

People often talk about Russian president Vladimir Putin's

eccentric behavior today, but I think we forget that Russian rulers throughout history, even the good ones, have had a taste for unconventional pageantry.

Between his marriage to Anna and attending the weird dwarf wedding, Frederick William, the Duke of Courland, drank a *lot*. He even engaged in a drinking contest with Peter the Great, which—just based on what you have recently learned about the czar in this chapter—you already know was a terrible idea. In his book *Vodka Politics: Alcohol, Autocracy, and the Secret History of the Russian States*, Mark Schrad notes that, according to Russian lore, "even in his early teens, Peter drank a pint of vodka and a bottle of sherry over breakfast, followed by about eight more bottles before going outside to play." Trying to keep up, Frederick drank so much that he fell ill immediately after the marriage and died two months later.

Anna was a widow. And desperate to remarry. She wrote her family more than three hundred letters, most of them expressing her fervent desire for a husband. Peter the Great rejected every suitor until Anna seemed to sour on the concept altogether.

Now, you could say that this story doesn't "technically" qualify as a breakup because Frederick William died. You are right. If we were saying that "one member of the couple dies" is a breakup, then everyone would break up. *The Notebook* (2004) would be a story about a couple who seem to work through their differences and then break up.

If you want to move immediately on to the next chapter, I will understand.

But I think Anna's reaction to her uncomfortable wedding, and not being allowed to remarry, is *astonishing*. Bitterness—a very understandable sentiment—overtook her. She wanted to punish people who were happy in love and make a mockery of the concept of weddings.

Think of the times following a breakup when you audibly groaned when you saw a couple making out on a street corner. No? You are more reserved? Well, I like to groan and fake retch and throw garbage at them because I'm a garbage queen, so I guess Miss

Havisham and I can have our own party. Sometimes there's nothing more irritating than seeing other people embracing something that caused you pain. That's why you can probably think of a recently divorced man who wants to warn his buddies off marriage altogether (often with terrible jokes) or a spurned wife who will tell you at length about how all men cheat. (She is not joking; she is simply incorrect.) On some level when we do this, we are trying to fight back against an institution we feel has betrayed us. If marriage did not work out for us, by God, we'll bring down marriage altogether.

No one epitomizes this mind-set more than Anna Ivanovna. In fact, her bizarre reaction to her romantic disappointment is *without question* what she is most remembered for.

With Frederick William's death, Anna became ruler of Courland. And then, most surprising, in 1730 she became empress and autocrat of *all* the Russias.

She was never supposed to become empress. It happened because fourteen-year-old Czar Peter II died of smallpox the night before (or the day of, depending on your source) his wedding. This wasn't a great loss politically as Peter II was mostly known for loving drinking and amusements. His major political accomplishment had been forbidding serfs from joining the military because it gave them a chance to earn their freedom. At the time officials claimed, "All of Russia is in terrible disorder . . . money is not paid to anyone. God knows what will happen with finances. Everyone steals, as much as he can." Weddings seemed really cursed for Russian rulers during this particular period. No one had a happy wedding. Except maybe the dwarfs.

When the Supreme Privy Council appointed Anna as empress, they thought she would be malleable but not necessarily a good ruler. Shortly after she took the throne a Russian nobleman remarked, "Although we are confident of her wisdom, high morals, and ability to rule justly, she is still a female, and thus ill adapted to so great a number of duties."

Cheeks like Westphalian ham.

No one thought of Catherine the Great as "ill adapted" when she became empress thirty years later. So this statement may have less to do with general feelings about women being the weaker sex than with concerns about Anna specifically. Compared to male rulers who were alcoholics at thirteen and those with mental issues so severe they could not walk, it was hard to do worse just because you were a woman. This statement may instead have had something to do with Anna being a strange, bitter, unpleasant woman, with absolutely enormous cheeks.

Upon ascending to the throne, Anna was given the following set of conditions by the Privy Council:

We hereby give a most binding promise that my main concern and effort shall be not only to maintain but to spread, as far as possible and in every way, our Orthodox faith of the Greek Confession. Moreover, after accepting the Russian crown, I will not enter into wedlock so long as I live; nor will I designate a successor, either in my lifetime or after. We also promise that, since the safety and welfare of every state depends upon good counsel, we will always maintain the Supreme Privy Council as it is at present established with its membership of eight persons. Without the consent of this Supreme Privy Council:

1. We will not start a war with anybody.
2. We will not conclude peace.
3. We will not burden our faithful subjects with new taxes.
4. We will not promote anybody to high rank—above the rank of colonel—either in the civil or military service, be it on land or sea, nor will we assign any important affair to anybody; the guards and other important regiments are to remain under the control of the Supreme Privy Council.
5. We will not deprive members of the nobility [*shliakhetstvo*] of life, possessions, or honor without a court of law.
6. We will not grant any patrimonies [*votchiny*] or villages.
7. We will not promote anyone, whether Russian or foreign, to an office at court without the advice of the Supreme Privy Council.
8. We will not spend any revenues of state.

And [we also promise] to maintain an unalterably favorable disposition toward all our faithful subjects. Should I not carry out or fail to live up to any part of this promise, I shall be deprived of the Russian crown.

Those conditions don't seem unreasonable to me, although they did imply that Anna would be something of a puppet of the Privy Council. Some other people might think, *What's the point of being an eighteenth-century ruler if you can't even start a war?* Because if you've ever played any video game in the *Civilization* series, you know that going to war is the most fun part of the game.

Anna quickly restored the security police to terrorize any officials who opposed her, so never let it be said that a woman can't be a strong ruler. The twenty thousand high-ranking officials whom she exiled to Siberia certainly would not say that. And under Anna's rule, Russia did go to war with Turkey, so I'm guessing she felt the same as a lot of people about the whole "we will not start a war" idea.

Being a strong ruler is very different from being a good ruler, though. With the exception of founding the Cadet Corps school for military training and the first professional ballet school, Anna didn't have many positive domestic transformations to show for her reign. Those two accomplishments are really all anyone can come up with when trying to think of "good things Anna Ivanovna did for Russia."

Anna may not have had Peter the Great's leadership qualities, but she did have his tendency toward bizarre behavior. In her case, though, that behavior crossed the line from "whimsical" to "sadistic" in a very bold leap. The fact that she meticulously recorded all the small animals she killed is often mentioned. She was also envious of how many friends her mother seemed to have, so she brought all the living ones to court so that they could be *her* friends. For those who had died, she found similar-looking replacements to impersonate them. That's not necessarily bad; it's just very weird. There's more sadistic stuff like having a Jew who attempted to convert a sailor to Judaism burned alive in the town square, and ringing the fire bell so that people fled their houses in panic. The fire bell stunt really upset people, though unlike Nero she did not actually set the city on fire. It is now up to you to decide whether any of that is stranger than trying to breed a race of giants.

The most famous instance of her cruelty, however, related to Prince Mikhail Alekseyevich Galitzine. While Anna had lovers— Peter Bestuzhev-Ryumin and Ernst Johann von Biron most notably—I don't think she ever recovered from the grotesque dwarf spectacle of her own wedding or the fact that she was never allowed to marry again. And she certainly had no reason to think well of the institution, considering that her parents' marriage seemed to be made solely for political reasons, and Peter II's was tied in popular memory to his death. So when Prince Mikhail, from one of the most noble houses in Russia, married a Catholic Italian woman, it was as if he was making out on a street corner in front of her forever. Anna may have hated love and marriage in general, but she despised Catholics. And they were *really happy*, Prince Mikhail and his Catholic bride. Anna went apeshit.

Prince Mikhail's wife died shortly after their marriage, to his great sorrow, so you would think that would be the end of it. However, Anna didn't seem to believe that this was sufficient punishment for falling in love in the first place. She turned Mikhail into a court jester. And not just any court jester. He had to pretend to be a chicken. He had to sit on a nest of eggs in Anna's reception room and pretend to lay them when visitors came to see her.

It's mystifying to imagine how that conversation took place. If you are in a position of power over anyone, I'd like you to say, "Your job is to be a chicken now" and just see how people respond. Maybe they'll agree? I bet employees at chain restaurants would try it for a limited period. The people at the Cheesecake Factory really just seem to want you to be happy. But it was a horrible thing to do to a grieving widower. Also, eighteenth-century Russians must have had low expectations for their court jesters telling jokes and making merriment. There was a lot of drinking going on back then.

You would think that *this* would be the end of the story, but Anna wanted to punish Mikhail further. Seemingly, she intended to show him—and everyone—the folly of love and marriage— especially to Catholics—and wanted a "total victory over all infi-

This seems like fun—because elephants are party animals—except for the part where a couple is supposed to be going to their death inside an ice palace.

dels." So in 1739 she ordered the construction of a massive ice palace eighty feet long and thirty-three feet high, where all the blocks were "glued" together with water. Inside was a furnished bridal suite. Made of ice! The bed, the pillows, even the clocks! Outside there were ice trees in which ice birds nested. There was even an ice statue of an elephant that spouted water from its trunk. The elephant could also bellow in a realistic manner because a man sat inside it blowing a horn. (The number of terrible jobs in old Russia are absolutely endless, and the revolution was completely understandable.)

It sounds like a staggering waste of resources building this palace. Not that creating for the sake of beauty alone is bad. Obviously the French monarchy did a great job of that. Every historical example of beautiful decadence leads to revolution, but lots of us love the decadent remnants. (We'll never stop taking photographs at Versailles.) The giant ice palace might have been a fun—if useless and temporary—national point of pride. It might be remembered for its whimsy if Anna hadn't attempted to use it to stage a deadly wedding.

Because it wasn't just an ice palace. It was also intended to serve as a torture chamber.

Bitter Anna decided to marry Prince Mikhail to one of her maids, a Kalmyk woman called Avdotya Ivanovna. The maid was apparently very old and ugly, so this union was clearly not intended as a reward for the prince or, as we'll shortly see, a prize for the maid. On the day of their wedding the couple were dressed as clowns and made to ride an elephant to be presented to a laughing crowd. They were tailed by a group of people deemed ethnically undesirable, and the physically handicapped.

In many ways, the farcical (*by the standards of the time, good God, it would not be considered funny now, I hope*) nature of the wedding was similar to what Anna must have seen and felt when Peter the Great staged the mock dwarf wedding after her marriage. This time there were real nobles, not little people dressed up like them, though.

That wasn't the torture part. That was just run-of-the-mill, garden-variety sadism on Anna's part. The cruel part was that immediately after the wedding the couple was forced to spend their wedding night inside the ice palace. Naked. During one of the coldest winters in Russian history. The expectation was that they would freeze to death, horribly.

But they did not! They emerged the next morning. Because their love was a glorious fire that burned not just in their hearts but physically in the ice palace. Their love actually turned into real fire because love turns all of us into Johnny "The Human Torch" Storm from the Fantastic Four.

No. Not really. I embellished. Supposedly they survived because the bride, Avdotya Ivanovna, traded her pearls for a coat from one of the guards. So if the heat of passion can't keep you alive, bribes quite often work. They also spent the night running around wildly and apparently breaking anything they could find. So exercise is also helpful.

The popular legend is that the couple went on to enjoy a happy marriage and have twins, conceived that terrible night on the ice mattress. Historians now say that's unlikely, and records point to the fact that the woman, already in weak health, died a few days after the ice palace experience. She likely contracted pneumonia. It wouldn't take much to kill a frail, elderly woman in a country without great medical care, especially if she'd had to spend a night surrounded by ice.

I choose to believe that sometimes historians make up sad lies for no reason, because just as Anna hated marriage, historians hate happy stories that tie everything together with a fun ending. You can, accordingly, believe whichever version of the tale suits you. A lot of people like the ending with the twins.

As for Anna Ivanovna, she died the following October of kidney troubles. Her lover, Biron, was banished to icy Siberia. She left no heirs, and she's mostly remembered for the ice palace event.

She does not emerge as the heroine in this story. Because no one who comes down against love can ever be the heroine in any story. People who are bitter, and who try to make everyone else as miserable in love as they were, only emerge from stories like these as, well, as quite literal ice queens. No one speaks lovingly of Anna Ivanovna, and no one wants to date that guy who keeps making jokes about how his ex-wife screwed him. A quote often attributed to Buddha says, "Holding on to anger is like drinking poison and expecting the other person to die." And they *will not die*. Not even if you imprison them in an ice palace torture chamber. They will just keep on living and maybe have twins, mostly to spite you.

To this day, people often describe Anna as the worst ruler in Russian history. She wasn't, really. Even if we look only at people mentioned in this chapter, her father was worse by far. She certainly wasn't the only sadist in Russian history, and the ballet was a lovely cultural accomplishment. I don't even believe she was as opposed to love and marriage as the ice palace makes her out to be. On her deathbed, her last words dictated that her lover Biron be appointed regent. In the end, love thaws even the weirdest and iciest of hearts.

Love and marriage and the institutions that celebrate love—those are all great and good. Seriously. I mean that. They ultimately tie society together. Love doesn't work out for everyone, and it's natural to be upset when a relationship doesn't work out for us, but that doesn't change the fact that love gets a lot of people out of bed in the morning.

So when you have just suffered through a rocky breakup, and you want to tell those lovers on the street corner that they're in for a terrible surprise, wait awhile. Those icy feelings have a way of thawing. Wait, because deep down, you know that you will want to love again, and no number of servants pretending to be chickens will fill the void in your heart. And because when the stories are told, the people like Anna Ivanovna who align themselves against love always come out looking *terrible*.

6. Timothy Dexter

*H*ave you ever been the victim of a phenomenon known as *ghosting*? It's a rather unpleasant way to end a relationship where, after dating for some time, your partner simply stops returning your calls or e-mails or texts. There is no official breakup; your partner just . . . disappears into the ether. As though either you or your partner simply no longer exists. It is as if your partner has chosen to live on a completely different plane of being.

It's awful.

Ghosting is an understandable if tasteless way to break up. There will be no tears or shouting or otherwise awkward breakup behavior. But it is also inconsiderate. People who are ghosted don't have any closure and are always left wondering why that person never responded to them again. Let alone thinking that individual might have died or been kidnapped into slavery.

But you know what is infinitely more maddening than that? *Your husband telling everyone you are literally a ghost.*

Thank goodness you're not married to Timothy Dexter.

Dexter was an eighteenth-century businessman known for being hilariously eccentric, even by the standards of the day. He may also have been the luckiest idiot who ever lived. According to his autobiography, "I was born when great powers ruled, on January 22, 1747. On this day, in the morning, a great snow storm; the signs in the seventh house; whilst Mars came forward Jupiter stood by to hold the candle. I was to be one great man." This is steps away from North Korea's Kim Jong Il declaring that a double rainbow appeared on the day of his birth.

The signs were not wrong, however. Timothy Dexter did become a very wealthy man. With no formal education, Dexter apprenticed in his teens as a leather dresser, tanning and preparing skins before they were sold. And at age twenty-two he married a wealthy widow, Elizabeth (Lord) Frothingham, of Newburyport, Massachusetts, and moved into her home. She was ten years his senior. Seemingly, the marriage started out well. They liked each other, and she probably appreciated being married to an ambitious younger man. Timothy plied his trade—he advertised his sheep, deer, and moose skins in the *Essex Journal*—and Elizabeth ran a small shop from the basement of their home selling fruits and vegetables. They had two children, a son born in 1771 and a daughter in 1776.

For most people, that would have been enough. Timothy had already advanced up the social ladder by marrying into comparative wealth, and the couple could have had a comfortable life. However, Timothy Dexter had greater aspirations; he was determined to be accepted into high society. So he began petitioning the governing council of Newburyport for a role in public office. Unfortunately, since he was barely literate, most of his petitions were nigh on incomprehensible. Finally, seemingly exhausted with trying to decipher his appeals, the councilmen awarded him the title "Informer of Deer," a job that entailed enforcing the killing of deer. Though he was rarely called upon to actually enforce any deer killing (how would one do this?), he was reelected yearly for twelve years until 1788.

Despite the fact that Dexter was definitely keeping those deer in line, many of his (mean guy) contemporaries thought he was an absolute idiot, and attempted to trick him into making bad investments. And this is where we have to decide if Timothy Dexter was a supremely savvy businessman or the luckiest man alive. Because he turned that bad business advice into gold.

Timothy was encouraged to buy up Continental currency during the end of the Revolutionary War. It was of no value—"not worth a Continental" had even become a common phrase to describe something worthless. However, remarkably, after the war, the U.S. government decided that Continental currency could be traded for new Treasury bonds at 1 percent of face value. Nothing had become something, and since Timothy had been collecting tons of Continentals for almost nothing, he was suddenly a very wealthy man.

He used his new wealth to acquire two merchant ships, leaving the obvious question of what cargo he was going to ship. He realized that many British products were being shipped to the West Indies by way of the United States. To come out ahead, he had to think hard about items that weren't yet being exported. He realized that no one had been shipping warming pans.

Of course they hadn't. Warming pans were used to heat bed covers on frigid evenings, and the West Indies were not known for their cold climate. The clever commander of the ship, realizing that this was not really workable cargo, and assuming there had been some sort of miscommunication, attached handles to the pans and sold them as devices to ladle the local molasses. They sold like hotcakes. Timothy was now much, much richer.

After hearing about this, people jokingly suggested he should next send woolen caps and gloves south. Dexter thought that was a great idea—there were no woolen caps and gloves in Guinea! After he sent them to that tropical climate, they were by bizarre luck purchased (at his great profit) by a group of Asian merchants who were on their way to Siberia.

His good fortune continued in ways no one could ever have

predicted. He heard whales were dying, and bought all the carcasses that could be found—from which he made a fortune, as whalebone was needed for corsets.

By this point people were baffled and also outraged by Dexter's insane, completely illogical windfalls. The next suggested endeavor was "shipping coal to Newcastle." Newcastle was where people produced coal. That's really all they did in Newcastle. For that reason, "selling coal to Newcastle" is an idiom used to describe doing something pointless. Timothy Dexter clearly wasn't familiar with that turn of phrase, so he shipped a ton of coal to Newcastle. His shipment happened to land during a miner's strike. After that I think he just determined, "You know how you make money? Shipping anything. Literally anything. Just take an object and put it on a ship to somewhere that is not here, and you make boatloads of cash." So he shipped stray cats off to the Caribbean . . . where they were welcomed as a solution to a recent rat infestation.

Timothy Dexter became one of the wealthiest men of the period. He had such good luck that merchants did not want to sell their goods to him because they assumed that if Timothy Dexter was buying something, its value was bound to skyrocket.

The message from this success is either: (1) You should always listen to advice given by strangers, even malicious strangers trying to trick you or have fun at your expense, and follow it to the letter. Or: (2) A pact with the devil is the key, and you should sell your soul as soon as possible. (Here it may be worth pointing out that before Timothy made any business decision, he met with the local fortune teller, Madam Hooper of Newburyport. Pacts with the devil have been made many times. There is no other way to explain the popularity of the book *Fifty Shades of Grey*.)

Throughout, Dexter remained close to his community and took his "Informer of Deer" duties very seriously. He also provided funds for a bell for the local church and gave generously to the poor. His reputation might have improved if not for his infamous "Deer Island" speech in 1793, which onlookers jokingly described as "truly Ciceronian." Though the speech's intended content is lost to us, he recorded the following:

> Mr. MyCall, Messrs. Blunt and Robinson took notice in their last Herald that I delivered on the fourth instant on Deer Island a speech in French. This speech I now send you in English, and should you think it worth of a place in your useful paper, you may insert. I did not deliver all that I intended on account of the ill-breeding of a blue puppy, who impertinently endeavored to upset my pulpit, or rather the table on which I stood. The public, considering the small chance I have had to learn French, are a little surprised to hear of my having endeavored to speak it; but, if Gentlemen and Ladies will give themselves the liberty to reflect that Frenchmen express themselves very much by gestures, and that Englishmen have made such a proficiency in the art that a whole play can now be acted without speaking a word, they will cease to wonder.

He attempted to give a speech in French to an English-speaking audience *without knowing how to speak French himself.* He seemed to think that the entire French language was maybe just a series of primitive hand gestures. It's like the episode of the television show *30 Rock* in which really good-looking people get away with outrageous behavior, like ordering off-menu at restaurants with no problem and receiving exemplary customer service wherever they go. Alec Baldwin's character notes that until he was in his midthirties he was so handsome that people allowed him to think that he spoke fluent French.

Timothy Dexter was rich, but he was not that handsome. Someone ended his insane pretend-French speech by knocking over the table he had jumped on. No one thought of Timothy Dexter, *Oh, it's so sad I can't understand him; my ear for accent must be terrible.*

You do have to wonder what his wife, Elizabeth, made of all this. (He had not yet ghosted her.) She certainly couldn't fault him for failing to support the family, although initially it might have been a worry that he would live off her income. However, as he seemed to earn more and more money, he also seemed to behave in more and more erratic ways. Elizabeth had been a woman of some refinement when she met Timothy. That is to say, she probably knew that French was not just a language of hand gestures. She must have been mortified, although they had come a very long way from the bourgeois household where they started their marriage.

Timothy acquired a giant house in Chester, and then an even larger one in Newburyport. The latter was as eccentric as his Deer Island speech. It had minarets and a golden eagle flying from the cupola. In the garden were forty statues of men whom he considered "great," including John Adams, George Washington, a traveling preacher, George III, an Indian chief, and . . . himself. Twice. (You cannot possibly be surprised by that.) All of them were gaudily painted and didn't necessarily look like the figures they were originally intended to be; General Morgan, for instance, was turned into Napoleon Bonaparte.

He began calling himself "Lord" around that time, seemingly under the misconception that anyone who is very rich is a lord. That's not true.

The *Essex Antiquarian* claims, "He styled himself 'King of Chester' and undertook to exercise kingly prerogatives over his neighbors; but they put an end to his audacity and impudence by the aid of the horsewhip." He was, however, sometimes jokingly called the Marquis of Newburyport. That seemed appropriate, as he issued an open invitation for any members of Louis XVI's family who had survived the French Revolution to come and stay with him.

The estate was described in a poem by Jonathan Plummer, who claimed he was "poet lauriet [sic] to Lord Timothy Dexter," as follows:

His house is fill'd with sweet perfumes,
Rich furniture doth fill his rooms;

Inside and out it is adorn'd,
And on the top an eagle's form'd.

His house is white and trimm'd with green,
For many miles it may be seen;
It shines as bright as any star,
The fame of it has spread afar.

The images around him stand,
For they were made by his command,
Looking to see Lord Dexter come,
With fixed eyes they see him home.

Four lions stand to guard the door,
With mouths wide open to devour
All enemies who dare oppose
Lord Dexter or his shady groves.

So it was the most ostentatious, over-the-top house ever. Lions! Massive statues! It sounds (a) supergreat and (b) supertacky, especially by early American standards where everyone else was living in a tasteful Colonial. There was apparently some conflict when Dexter asked that the statue representing Jefferson be shown holding a scroll that read CONSTITUTION. The carver/painter refused to do so because he knew that Dexter meant the Declaration of Independence. Another time, when a stranger was looking at the estate, Timothy ordered his son to shoot the visitor. When his son refused, Timothy said he would shoot the boy instead. Thus threatened, his son then shot at the stranger—fortunately missing.

If any of this seems like tall tales told by envious business associates or snobs who didn't like gaudy, new-money upstarts (or minarets!), you have not yet read Timothy Dexter's autobiography, *A Pickle for the Knowing Ones*, which he wrote in 1802.

I just love that there are two statues of Timothy Dexter adorning this house.

No one knows why he chose that name for a book, but it was commonly referred to as *Pickle*. One explanation might be that the title derived from the original meaning of *pickle* as it presents in John Heywood's 1562 poem:

Time is tickell
Chaunce is fickell
Man is brickell
Freilties pickell

In which *pickell* means a "difficult situation." But honestly, no one really knows, not even "the knowing ones." Maybe he just liked pickles. Maybe if we spoke French like he did, we'd understand. The book is written by "Lord Timothy Dexter, First in the East, First in the West, and the Greatest Philosopher in the Western World." If you ever write a memoir, please make up a fun little egotistical description of yourself for your title page. Be bold about it.

The book details Timothy's life in his own somewhat incoherent way. It was written entirely without punctuation. When it was pointed out that the greatest philosopher in the Western world would probably use at least *some* punctuation (since it was, thank God, no longer the sixteenth century), in the second edition (there were ultimately eight printings) Dexter added a page of punctuation at the end, so readers could insert the marks wherever they liked or, as he claimed, "I put in A Nuf here and they may pepper and salt it as they plese."

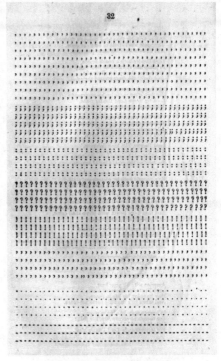

If I was really committed to following Dexter's teaching, I'd have written this chapter without punctuation and just presented you with this page.

In addition to telling readers that his massive home possessed a fine library (he wasn't making much use of it), we learn in *Pickle* that Lord Timothy Dexter, Informer of Deer, was not happy in his personal life. Things weren't going well with Elizabeth. Timothy rants about a lot in his little book, which was approximately twenty pages long, but significant passages are devoted to the evils of his nagging ghost of a wife. Yes, his ghost wife.

By that point, Timothy and Elizabeth had been married for thirty-two years, and they were not one of those couples going hand in hand into their twilight years. Timothy just decided to behave as though the twilight had already come for Elizabeth and, indeed, the dark. He explains that his wife has become a ghost. At first you think: *Oh, Elizabeth died? Well, early America: lots of superstitions—"The Legend of Sleepy Hollow" and all that; sure, lots of grieving widowers probably saw their wives as ghosts. Especially those with the early onset of dementia that was probably not fully understood at the time! That's sad. That makes sense.*

But Timothy wrote (punctuation added):

> **To save his Life from the Attacks of the Ghost,**
> **offers to sell House, Lands, and Equipage.**
>
> NOW TO ALL ONNEST MEN, to pittey me that I have bin in hell 35 years, in this world, with the gost—A woman I maried, and have two Children, Now Liveing; Abram bishup maried my Dafter—sence, the troubel is such that words Cant be Expressed; Nine years disordered for a tun of silver for three months; I could Not have the gost in my palles; sleep Not to be had; now to save my Life I will sell—if Not, I will let the house; it is as Noted as any hous in the oile shouls, and fourder, in the world, or sence Noers Arke & sence the floud; taking in my self, finly, such a plas No whare in the world; all goes with it—hoses, carages, all but plate and gouels, and Reserve the holey bybel and one bouck more. My old head has wore out three boddeys; it would take a jourey of Doctors one our to find and Count the scars on my head, given by the gost & others. A men.

Preceding that paragraph was the following: "Forbid by the Ghost of his Wife to become a Mason; Makes a contract with the Ghost to quit his estate."

So he would part with all his worldly goods to be rid of this ghost and would happily give up even his Xanadu-esque estate. It would indeed be troublesome to free yourself from a ghost haunting your estate; the movie *Beetlejuice* proved this at length. The thing is, Elizabeth was alive and well. Timothy's wife was definitely not dead. Apparently she just threw things at him and made his life miserable and didn't like his gaudy minaret-studded house. While these are things ghosts are known to do, they are not necessarily proof that your wife is a ghost. As far as I know, most ghosts have no feelings about whether or not you should become a Mason, but that could have just been Dexter's eccentricity talking.

Now, you might wonder whether divorce was a foreign concept at the time. I did, because I associate early America with Puritans, George Washington maybe having wooden teeth, and "Rip Van Winkle," and divorce does not come up in any of those stories. But no, divorce wasn't uncommon. In fact, Timothy's own daughter had been divorced in 1797 after being married for three years. Timothy didn't disown her or anything—though it is said that he wasn't particularly interested in either of his children—so there's no reason to think that he clung steadfastly to the "till death do us part" aspect of the marriage vows. If he was unhappy, it seems it would have been easier to divorce than to pretend your wife does not exist, especially when she was still living in your home and throwing things at you.

I'd be inclined to write all of this off as a bit of quirky insanity. Dexter might have legitimately believed that his wife was dead. He was, after all, maybe a very lucky idiot, and he could have easily believed some things that were clearly not true if someone told him a convincing story. Basically, if he was trusting enough to believe that selling coal to Newcastle was a good idea, he might believe anyone who told him that his wife had become a ghost.

But we actually know that isn't true. We know that Timothy understood how death worked because he *staged his own death.*

He had been telling everyone his wife had been dead for some time by then. When guests showed up at his estate and, you know, noticed his wife, who was living there as an alive person, he just told them to ignore the "crabby" presence. He had become obsessed with death in general and, rather than sharing a bed with his wife, had begun sleeping in a coffin. It was apparently a very beautiful coffin, made of mahogany and silver and intricately lined, and he took great pleasure in displaying it to visitors to his house.

And then he chose to fake his own death. Honestly, who hasn't thought about how great it would be to attend their own funeral? Everybody, right? It's a party where everybody just says nice things about you. Timothy Dexter had extra-special reason to be excited, as Plummer's poem had claimed that:

When Dexter dies all things shall droop,
Lord East, Lord West, Lord North shall stoop,
And then Lord South with pomp shall come,
And bear his body to the tomb.

They wouldn't have to bear him far—Dexter had already set up a tomb in his garden.

Everyone *did* show up for Timothy's funeral. His wife and children went along with it because he bought them all mourning attire beforehand. He was, certainly, the most famous figure in town. So while the lords of all the points of the compass did not arrive, because they're not real, it was well attended. Three thousand people came, and Timothy, while lying in state, seemed gratified, by all accounts. That is until he noticed that his wife did not seem to be grieving sufficiently.

Maybe because he had been telling everyone that she was a non-entity.

In any event, in front of all assembled, Dexter leaped up, very much alive, and began caning Elizabeth for not weeping satisfactorily. He then supposedly began throwing money out of the windows of his mansion. His son cried buckets because he was very, very drunk and maybe also because he was the progeny of a lunatic.

The preface to *Pickle* notes that Timothy Dexter "was addicted to drunkenness, and with his son and other companions, kept up his revels in the best apartments of his house, by which in a very short time, all his costly furniture was ruined, or very much injured." Alcoholism would probably account for a lot of erratic behavior, though consistently telling people that your spouse is a ghost still qualifies as one of the weirdest ways to try to sever ties with a romantic partner.

Timothy died for real in 1806, and his long-suffering non-ghost, totally human wife lived for three more years.

It is somewhat baffling how he went from running a vegetable shop with her out of their basement—like some sort of charming Brooklyn couple—to caning her in public and declaring her a ghost. And yet—and this is something many of us feel during breakups—even though Timothy had told everyone that Elizabeth had literally ceased to exist, he still wanted her love and approval when she was at his fake funeral. Even though she knew it was fake! He wanted her to be in tears at even the *thought* of him being dead. No matter what, he expected her to go on loving him. Or at least loving him enough to outweep anyone else at that fake funeral.

We may decide to pretend that the person we were once close to doesn't even exist. The way we ghost now can take many forms, whether it means we ignore our ex at a party (either with a polite nod or by whirling around like an icy wind has touched our backs and fleeing for the other side of the room) or just refuse to respond to any of our ex's messages. As always, there's no great way to break up. If a relationship was happy, there would be no need for a breakup at all. During that period of completely ignoring our ex, maybe we feel cool and in control. But wait, just wait, until there is some evidence that this person does not care about you anymore. Whether your ex takes to Facebook to show off all those great times with a new girl or friend or refuses to mourn adequately at your fake funeral—you will want to go *insane*. Maybe that's because ghosting means that nothing is ever resolved. The person you've decided is a ghost doesn't feel a sense of closure, but neither do you, so you sort of assume that resuming the relationship is always an option. Then one day it becomes clear that it's not possible, and that's when people leap out of coffins and start caning their spouses and throwing their money out the windows.

Unless you are King Henry VIII, there may not be a way to get a real sense of "closure" about a relationship. You may never feel good about its end, but at some point it's probably important to say something to the effect of "we are parting ways now" rather than just deciding the other party is a phantom. You'll have to figure out how to be polite if you meet in passing. Because if trying to pretend your ex is a ghost didn't work for Timothy Dexter, the Informer of Deer, and the luckiest man who ever lived, then it won't work for anyone else.

7. Caroline Lamb

Lord Byron

I'm convinced that anyone who has never written stupid post-breakup letters to an ex-lover either is not fully human or has never actually experienced a bad breakup. We have all written or texted or e-mailed our former lovers something we regret.

Sometimes correspondence revolves around an exchange of items. If your ex left her iPhone behind as she fled, for instance, it would be polite to pack it up, maybe with a note that reads, "Here's your iPhone, you bloodsucking succubus." Obviously, you should not write exactly that. If your ex is male, you should substitute *incubus* for *succubus*.

Instead of communicating only when you need to, you suddenly see four of your ex's blue Bic pens lying on your coffee table, or a leaf that fell off his coat after a beautiful day you spent together in the park, and you decide you should reunite him with those objects immediately. So you write a note saying, "I know how attached you are to your writing utensils, so I'm sending these to you. I'm

This portrait of Caroline Lamb's head does not demonstrate her vigorously hacking off her pubic hair, which is a pity.

also enclosing a leaf." When you are sending off Bic pens and foliage—or demanding them back in an indignant fashion—the real reason you do so is that you want to maintain contact. On a sentimental level, keepsakes of a relationship might remind your ex that something once happened between you two. Maybe we're optimistic that our former beloved is going to open that letter or delicately wrapped package and say, "Lisa sent me four Bic pens *and a leaf?* What was I thinking? I have loved her all along, more than I have ever loved anyone."

And it's not that it could never work. Perhaps you could make someone take you back in exchange for a dinosaur or something retrieved from space. I'm pretty sure, however, that one item that will never convince someone to take you back is a bloody lump of pubic hair. But that didn't deter Lord Byron's lover, Caroline Lamb.

After their breakup, she sent him a letter suggesting they exchange items. Unlike most sane people's writing, her letter read, "I asked you not to send blood but yet do—because if it means love, I like to have it. I cut the hair too close & bled much more than you need—do not do the same & pray put not scissors points near where quei capelli grow. Sooner take it from the arm or wrist—pray be careful." And she signed it "from your wild antelope," although "your shorn antelope" might have been more appropriate, considering the circumstances.

Have you ever sent your ex-lover a bloodstained hunk of pubic hair and demanded in return a moderate amount of blood? No, you have not. You are good at handling your emotions and keeping private bodily parts private.

Are you thinking, *Did it work?* Oh, God, no. It did not.

So what kind of woman sends pubic hair? Caroline was born in 1785 the Honorable Caroline Ponsonby, the only daughter of the 3rd Earl of Bessborough and Henrietta, Countess of Bessborough. Her aunt Georgiana claimed that, at seven, Caroline was "very naughty and [said] anything that [came] into her head" and had "too much anxiety about what she love[d]." She apparently asked a lot of bizarre questions, had a tendency to leap over furniture, and when she did not like people, would, well into her middle childhood, scream until she was blue in the face. She justified the latter by maintaining, "It is a common practice to condemn children to the society of those with whom parents cannot endure even for a moment to associate."

She had strong opinions about people. By the time she was a teenager she was variously nicknamed Ariel, Sprite, and the Young Savage, and was taking laudanum in an attempt to soothe her nerves.

In 1805, when she was nineteen, Caroline met William Lamb, the heir to the 1st Viscount Melbourne. She immediately affected a childlike lisp and spoke baby talk around him. When you think about it, this is still a thing being done by slim blondes today, and it seems to work out. Caroline and William were, at least at first, very happy. Caroline wanted to follow him around constantly and sit in his lap, which might be a red flag today but was, I suppose, considered charming then.

William Lamb was, by most accounts, an extremely decent guy. He went on to become the prime minister in 1834, six years after

William Lamb was in fact heavily into S & M, which you would not guess from this kindly-looking picture.

Caroline's death, and was a great mentor to Queen Victoria. He was described as "kind, honest, and not self-seeking." Alas, those are rarely qualities that women go wild for.

Their marriage produced two children. Sadly, their son, born in 1807, had a mental disability now thought to be autism, while their daughter died almost immediately after her birth in 1809. And the sex was not good. In 1810 Caroline wrote, "He called me prudish, said I was strait-laced, amused himself with instructing me in things I need never have heard or known—and the disgust that I at first felt for the world's wickedness I till then had never even heard of—in a very short time this gave way to a general laxity of principles which little by little unperceived of you all has been undermining the few virtues I ever possessed."

Reading this, you might assume that maybe William just wanted a blow job or to have sex with the lights on, and Caroline thought it was unspeakably gross. Not the case! A lady willing to chop off her pubic hair and send it to someone isn't likely to be that prudish. I think she would have been comfortable letting William have sex without the candles snuffed, which was probably the standard for nonprudish behavior in 1810 based on more than a few costume dramas I have seen.

However, costume dramas are not real life. Later scandals suggested that William not only fetishized spanking (which may have been the reason Caroline wanted to appear more childlike around him) but also enjoyed whipping women. Neither partner seemed satisfied.

Two years later, in 1812, Caroline met Lord Byron. He had published Cantos I and II of *Childe Harold's Pilgrimage* and was as close to being a rock star as you could be in the 1800s. Caroline was a *huge* fan. Her friends told her that he was ugly, had a club foot, and was a compulsive nail biter (ladies apparently really hated nail biters then), but Caroline just replied, "[Even] if he's as ugly as Aesop, I must know him." However, when she was presented with the opportunity at the home of their mutual friend Lady Westmorland, she fled Byron and his surrounding throng of admirers. Perhaps regretful that she missed the opportunity, perhaps preemptively jealous, she wrote that she thought Byron was "mad, bad, and dangerous to know," which is basically the polar opposite of

"kind, honest, and not self-seeking." But, much sexier (unless you are into S & M, in which case, seriously, William sounds great).

Byron, on the other hand, had noticed her at Lady Westmorland's. That was probably because she hadn't flocked to him as other women did. So this sounds like the plot of a high school movie directed by John Waters, until you find that when Byron actually did meet Caroline,

Lord Byron: nail biter.

he dismissed her almost immediately. He wasn't attracted to her and told his friend Thomas Medwin that he thought she was "too thin to be good." She was so slim, in fact, that John Hobhouse later called her a "mad skeleton." Byron liked them busty. The nonrelationship should have vanished except that after the same meeting, Caroline was in love, writing, "That beautiful pale face is my fate."

They did have interests in common. Caroline, provided you saw through her baby-talk voice, was intelligent. She spoke Latin and Greek (which was unusual for a woman of the era) and had a tremendous knowledge of poetry (which was, obviously, what drew her to Byron in the first place). They had terrific banter, too. Byron fondly recalled one dinner party where she told her brother-in-law that the seventh commandment was "thou shall not bother." She was also intelligent enough to flatter Byron with her appreciation of his talents. And wow, did she ever value him. She wrote fan letters about how no one else in the world deserved to be happier than he did. Sometimes people fall in love with others just because they seem to like them very much, and that may well have been the case here. Soon after Caroline decided Byron was her fate, they began an affair. He wrote, "I have always thought you the cleverest, most agreeable, absurd, amiable, perplexing, dangerous, fascinating little being that lives now or ought to have lived 2000 years ago."

No, you didn't, you thought she was too thin, but that's a good line. So their affair began, and it was wonderful for about two days. Byron claimed that he'd never met a woman with "greater or more pleasing talents . . . something of everything." After that (very brief) honeymoon period, they began having colossal public fights. Byron described her as having a heart like a "little volcano that pours lava through your veins" and "a total want of common conduct." Caroline was excessively jealous and convinced that Byron was pursuing other women, which, as it happened, he was. He often made a point of comparing William to a saint and himself to a devil. This isn't entirely surprising. Remember, Byron *in*

Not pictured in this view of Venice are any women because Byron was busy having sex with all of them.

one year slept with 250 women in the city of Venice alone. It seems unlikely that he was really as "ugly as Aesop." Yet Byron was also jealous, flying into rages when Caroline refused to say she didn't love her husband.

All of this played havoc with Caroline's emotions. Once, she saw him talking to another woman at a party, and she bit down on her glass so hard that it shattered. When they went to parties, she insisted that they go together, rather than just "unexpectedly" meeting as propriety would demand, given that Caroline was *married to someone else.* If Byron was attending a party that Caroline was not invited to, she would just stand outside, waiting for it to be over. In the rain.

Byron really wasn't a French New Wave type of guy. He was a man who desperately wanted to be accepted by aristocratic society and accordingly seemed simultaneously fascinated and repulsed by these scenes with Caroline. If Byron ran off with a married lady, it would be scandalous, but I expect it also temporarily excited him to see someone who felt sufficiently secure in her position to flout convention. So he demanded that Caroline elope with him. She declined, probably on account of her husband and autistic son. Byron wrote a letter back swearing to "wring that obstinate little heart!" Well, that was all the persuasion she needed, so she agreed. And then he realized that he didn't want to marry her after all. Most likely he just wanted to prove that she would give up everything for him. But Caroline took that call to run away with him very seriously. She showed up at his house disguised as a page. Lord Byron's friend John Hobhouse was with him at the time and wrote:

> I did think that to leave my friend in such a situation, when . . . every soul in the house servants & all knew of the person in disguise, and not to endeavor to prevent the catastrophe of an elopement which seemed inevitable, would be unjustifiable. Accordingly I stayed in the sitting room whilst the Lady was in the bed room pulling off her disguise—under which she had a page's dress . . . at last she was prevailed upon to put on a habit, bonnet & shoes—belonging to a servant of the house and, after much entreaty did come out into the sitting room.

A lot of historians talk about Caroline's eccentric tendency for disguises. Who doesn't dress up as a page boy sometimes, when the situation calls for it? I think we've all done that. I'm wearing a page boy costume right now, just because it's fun.

Hobhouse attempted to prevent the couple from eloping, at which point Caroline grabbed a knife and tried to stab herself, exclaiming, "There will be blood spilt . . . it shall be mine!" There is also much discussion of the many instances in which Caroline tried to stab herself, but this is the first recorded one. Byron and the noble Hobhouse sent her back home to William.

And then, soon afterward, probably still somewhat unhinged, Caroline sent Byron her pubic hair. Coincidentally, surely, it was around this time that Byron's interest began to seriously wane.

Caroline was appealing when she seemed to exist primarily to adore him but was considerably less alluring when engaged in suicide attempts and demands for body-part trades. To be fair, almost all of us are less interested in that, unless we're part of a very small minority of a certain kind of rock star. Byron told Hobhouse that if he went away with her he would "blow his brains out."

Lady Jane was the original mean girl.

Caroline continued to write to him. But Byron had moved on to Lady Jane, Countess of Oxford. He and Lady Jane, like the nineteenth-century nightmare version of high school movie villains, read Caroline's letters together and made fun of them. Lady Jane convinced Byron to write a letter back, which read:

> I am no longer your lover; and since you oblige me to confess it, by this truly unfeminine persecution,—learn, that I am attached to another; whose name it would of course be dishonourable to mention. I shall ever remember with gratitude the many instances I have received of the predilection you have shewn in my favour. I shall ever continue your friend, if your Ladyship will permit me so to style myself; and, as a first proof of my regard, I offer you this advice, correct your vanity, which is ridiculous; exert your absurd caprices upon others; and leave me in peace.

Byron and Lady Jane—and this fact is often glossed over in history books—were monster-people. Lady Jane's heart was made of live cobra, and she later went on to serve as inspiration for the fictional supervillain the Joker and all the unsympathetic characters in the film *Mean Girls* (2004). (There's nothing to back this claim, but it feels right in my heart, which is made of love.)

When Caroline returned to London from Ireland, where she'd been staying, Lord Byron had to see her socially, so he couldn't be such an unmitigated asshole in person. Does this description of Byron seem too harsh? He was, after all, in a difficult situation himself. But, you know, his treatment of Caroline continued to suck going forward, so let's just go with that feeling. Let's give ourselves the freedom to hate him.

When Caroline again requested a lock of his hair—presumably the normal kind, not the pubic kind—he sent her a lock of Lady Oxford's. He joked, "It was a lucky coincidence of colour & shape for my purpose . . . surely it is a very innocent revenge for some very scurvy behaviour."

This part of the story is particularly upsetting because Byron is a good writer and I'd love to be on his side, but I can't. Oscar Wilde writes in *The Picture* of *Dorian Gray* that "the tears of those we no longer love always seem faintly ridiculous," and maybe they do. But if painful breakups are good for anything, it is because they remind us to try to be decent and *extremely* sensitive when we're on the other side of things. You really shouldn't kick people when they're down, and you definitely shouldn't kick them when they are down, prostrate, and sobbing at your feet.

Byron, who once quipped, "Think you, if Laura had been Petrarch's wife / He would have written sonnets all his life?" wasn't a man who was rebuffed often. I'm not saying that people who've never had their hearts broken tend to be shittier people on the whole, but I'm implying it, strongly. Byron in particular seemed to lack empathy for Caroline's great sadness. He wrote one poem about the loss of a loved one, which runs:

Near this Spot
are deposited the Remains of one
who possessed Beauty without Vanity,
Strength without Insolence,
Courage without Ferosity,
and all the virtues of Man without his Vices.

This praise, which would be unmeaning Flattery
if inscribed over human Ashes,
is but a just tribute to the Memory of
BOATSWAIN, a DOG.

Right. He only ever really loved his dog.

Caroline altered all the buttons on her servants' clothing to read NE CREDE BYRON, which means "Don't Trust Byron." This would just be good advice, considering the circumstances, but it was particularly fitting given that Byron's family motto was CREDE BYRON, and, indeed, Byron had sent her a locket with the motto inscribed on it when she requested pubic hair.

BYRON + BOATSWAIN = TRUE LOVE 4EVER

Some time before that, she had decided to dispose of all the gifts he ever gave her, including, presumably, that locket. This reaction seems normal. A lot of today's lady magazines advise you to dispose of trinkets left behind from prior relationships. There's even a "Breakup Museum" in Zagreb, Croatia, where you can donate objects from past relationships. But Caroline didn't want to simply take Byron's trinkets and toss them in a box to go out with the trash. She would host a massive party. At the party she'd throw all the gifts on a giant bonfire and have local village girls dressed in white dance around the flames, the way club-footed Byron never could.

It's worth pointing out that she was still married throughout all of this mess. To poor, long-suffering William.

She went through with her plan, by the way. If you thought there was some dramatic about-face when she realized that this party was a little melodramatic, you thought wrong, buddy!

She erected her giant bonfire and tossed all of Byron's writing and all of his gifts on it. Then, in a final stroke of genius or mania, she burned him in effigy. She recited her own poetry to the assortment of dancing locals, which contained lines like "Ah, look not thus on me, so grave, so sad / Shake not your heads, nor say the lady's mad / Judge not of others, for there is but one / To whom the heart and feelings can be known" and "Burn, fire, burn, while wondering boys exclaim / And gold and trinkets glitter in the flame."

I get the feeling the wondering boys were *very* judgmentally exclaiming, "Why are we here, at this oddly angry, extremely self-indulgent party?" but you probably just didn't question free festivities back then. And all this happened on Christmas Day. William Lamb must have been very tolerant because that's not how most people like to spend the holidays with their families.

Sadly, this party did not end Caroline's obsession. The letters she threw onto the bonfire weren't even Byron's original letters. They were only copies. In 1813 she broke into his home to inscribe a book on his desk, REMEMBER ME! Byron wrote a poem in response:

Remember thee! remember thee!
Till Lethe quench life's burning stream
Remorse and shame shall cling to thee,
And haunt thee like a feverish dream!

Remember thee! Aye, doubt it not.
Thy husband too shall think of thee:
By neither shalt thou be forgot,
Thou false to him, thou fiend to me!

And then he wrote her a letter, essentially saying that enough was enough. He was pretty cool and self-effacing about it: "You say you will '*ruin me*'—I thank you—but I have done that for myself already—you say you will 'destroy me,' perhaps you will only save me the trouble.—It is useless to reason with you— to repeat what you already know—that I have in reality saved you from utter & impending destruction."

Byron's half sister Augusta came to visit that summer, which may have made Byron feel less ruined. There's speculation about whether Byron and his half sister were having an affair. The answer is "Maybe." Or "Probably. Byron slept with everybody." Byron certainly let Caroline think so, though his motivation might have been to make her think he was an unsuitable partner. Byron and Augusta were affectionate with each

Augusta may have the most amazing hair of anyone in any of these stories.

other at parties and had cutesy nicknames for each other and Byron doted on her. But when Caroline started telling people Byron was having an affair with his half sister, he wrote that she should stop spreading outrageous lies about him. Caroline replied, "I know not from what quarter the report originates. You accused me, and falsely; but if you could hear all that is said at this moment, you would hear one who . . . though your enemy, though forever alienated from you, though resolved never more, whilst she lives, to see or speak or forgive, you would perhaps die to save you."

I will be on Byron's side here. Byron did not believe her protestation of innocence. Nobody believed it. Nor should they have. There's evidence that suggests that Caroline said Byron was having an affair not only with Augusta but also with "three schoolfellows whom he had thus perverted." Accusing your ex-boyfriend of being an incestuous, homosexual pedophile would be a big deal today and was a considerably more serious accusation in the nineteenth century.

Their last public fight happened at a ball at Lady Heathcoate's slightly less than a year after they'd thought of eloping. Caroline approached Byron and—remember he hated dancing because of his club foot—said, "I conclude I may waltz, *now*." Byron replied, "With everybody in turn—you always did it better than anyone." Later he sneered, "I was admiring your dexterity." Sometimes it's hard to parse how people are insulting each other in the nineteenth century because it's all sort of under the surface, but I'm fairly certain that he is calling her a tramp. In response Caroline brandished a knife. There seem to have been knives everywhere in 1813. Byron replied, "Do, my dear. If you mean to act a Roman's part, mind which way you strike with your knife—be it at your own heart, not mine—you have struck there already." And then, depending upon the account, either she ran away shouting "Byron," or she was carried away. The spectacle was written about in all the gossip columns, and the *Satirist* ran a picture of the events with a caption that read, "With horn-handled knife / to kill a tender lamb as dead as mutton."

Remember that there was probably no one more famous at the time than Byron. If this stuff happened with any celebrities today, it would dominate tabloids for a while, and then what would happen? Well, one of them, probably the less famous one, would almost certainly write a thinly veiled tell-all. The writer Henry Miller would claim, one hundred years after these events, that "the best way to get over a woman is to turn her into literature." Which is exactly what Caroline Lamb did with Byron.

She wrote a book called *Glenarvon*. As you can probably guess, Byron's fictional stand-in wasn't portrayed all that positively. That's somewhat to be expected given that she'd gone from addressing him as "Childe Harolde" in her letters to addressing him as "Mefistocles [*sic*], Luke Makey, De La Touche, Richard the 3rd, Valmont, Machiavelli, Prevost, the wicked Duke of Orleans." Her book's rakish main character, Lord Ruthven, is a habitual seducer of women. *Glenarvon* ends with Ruthven literally pursued by the devil, and then he commits suicide, haunted by the women he wronged.

The book sold like hotcakes. People were fascinated by the depiction of Byron—though less thrilled to find satiric depictions of their own households throughout the novel. Caroline was promptly shunned from polite society, which seemed to bother her only vaguely. Her husband—her extremely tolerant husband—encouraged her to go ahead and publish a second edition, which she did.

Lord Byron had his own feelings. He claimed the novel was not so much a kiss-and-tell as it was a "— and publish." In 1817 he composed a poem in response to *Glenarvon*:

> *I read the "Christabel;"*
> *Very well:*
> *I read the "Missionary;"*

Pretty—very:
I tried at "Ilderim;"
Ahem!
I read a sheet of "Marg'ret of Anjou;"
Can you?;
I turned a page of Webster's "Waterloo;"
Pooh! Pooh!
I looked at Wordsworth's milk-white "Rylstone Doe;"
Hillo!
I read "Glenarvon," too, by Caro Lamb;
God damn!

Caroline published two more novels. Today, she is largely remembered for *Glenarvon*, and periodically you might see women dress up as page boys at certain costume parties. She never really stopped obsessing over Byron, and when he published *Don Juan* in 1819, she dressed up as that character for a masked ball. She had some reason to; there is a line in the poem that reads, "Some play the devil—and then write a novel." The line was the cause of much commentary in the papers. Caroline wrote her own snarky response to Byron's *Don Juan*. Her poem, *A New Canto*, imitated his style, containing stanzas like:

What joke?—My verses—mine, and all beside,
    Wild, foolish tales of Italy and Spain,
The gushing shrieks, the bubbling squeaks, the bride
    Of nature, blue-eyed, black-eyed, and her swain,
Kissing in grottoes, near the moon-lit tide,
Though to all men of common sense 'tis plain,
Except for rampant and amphibious brute,
Such damp and drizzly places would not suit.

It's true. No one wants to have sex in grottoes unless they are at the Playboy mansion, and that is different. The *Monthly Review* claimed, "The writer of this lively nonsense has evidently intended it as an imitation of Lord Byron. It is a rhapsody from beginning to end, describing the sudden arrival of dooms-day; and to those who are fond of extravagance, and doggerel versification, it may seem to possess merit."

When Byron died in 1824, fighting for Greek independence, Caroline claimed, "I am very sorry I ever said one unkind word against him." That kind of statement holds more weight if one hasn't already written an entire book full of unkind words.

You may come away from this chapter believing that Caroline Lamb had an extremely exciting life, and she certainly did. Byron did, too. They did some, as Byron might say, "scurvy things," but they were certainly not bored. Indeed, some historians admire Caroline for feeling all her feelings. But while there can be a sort of drama in the frenzy of heartbreak, there can also be drama to good relationships. (For instance, instead of dressing up as a page boy and trying to stab yourself, someone may ask you to marry them, and then you do, and that's exciting.) Drama isn't really as pleasurable as having someone who will sit and support you and love you—which William seemed perfectly willing to do. It seems a shame that Caroline missed out on that.

While Caroline may not have been the writer Byron was, she does have one great line in her book. In the death speech of her character in *Glenarvon,* one can't help but feel tenderly toward her. The character's last words are: "Peace to the broken hearts." That is the hope for anyone experiencing the despair of heartbreak. It's only a shame that Caroline never seemed to find any of that peace herself.

8. John Ruskin

Effie Gray

When I was younger, I used to read an advice column in some sexy grown-up ladies' magazine (almost certainly *Cosmopolitan*). In one column, addressing the subject of being on top while having sex, a woman was concerned that her boyfriend would see her belly fat in that position and be repulsed. The columnist replied, "Anyone who is close enough to you that you are having sex with them should be close enough to you that they would not care." This struck me as good advice, way better than the response I'd composed in my head, which was "Turn off the lights, maybe?" That is why fifteen-year-olds should not be advice columnists.

But yes, in real life, it's very unlikely that someone you care about is going to see you naked and suddenly run for the hills because of anything about your body. Unless you are married to John Ruskin, in which case, I am so sorry.

Not that, at first glance, Ruskin seemed in any way a bad person to marry. He was a brilliant art critic—surely the best of his age. He was also a prolific writer, painter, and philanthropist—he used his family fortune to build model apartments! He was even an amateur botanist and geologist who wrote a mineralogical dictionary at age twelve. He was interested in environmentalism long before it was fashionable to be interested in that subject, and the Pre-Raphaelite Brotherhood artistic movement was influenced by many of his ideas. He even founded

John Ruskin: Handsome!
But awful!

the Guild of St. George, which denounced industrial capitalism and pollution, and which still exists today! He was also very nice-looking. Gabriel Byrne could play him in a movie, that is, a younger Gabriel Byrne.

Ruskin seemed like a really cool husband candidate all around. This claim should be explored because in a *New York Times* book review of Suzanne Fagence Cooper's biography *Effie: The Passionate Lives of Effie Gray, John Ruskin and John Everett Millais*, Charles McGrath says:

> Though Ms. Fagence Cooper is somewhat sympathetic to him, you would not immediately gather from her book that Ruskin was not just an undersexed, self-absorbed workaholic but also one of the towering figures of his age—a brilliant and

indefatigable writer, critic and social reformer who changed the way Victorians looked at the world—or that his end was tragic and pitiable.

Oh, Charles McGrath, you are going to hate this chapter. Because, indeed, Ruskin was all of those praiseworthy things. Unfortunately, those positive attributes made him no less of a creepy dude and a terrible husband, and his creepy terribleness overshadows his merits.

Even Ruskin knew this about himself. He wrote, "If I had been a woman, I never should have loved the kind of person that I am." That's mostly because he was shy, and hesitant around the opposite sex, as well as some things considerably less savory.

Euphemia Gray (thank goodness she shortened her name to Effie, which we shall choose to use; I already misspelled *Euphemia* twice in typing it here) was the daughter of Ruskin family friends. She didn't seem to think John was unlovable when she met him when she was twelve. Nor should she have. He wrote the Victorian classic *The King of the Golden River or The Black Brothers: A Legend of Stiria* for her. The fairy tale sums up a lot of his philosophical arguments, namely, that nature is great, it's good to help the needy, and capitalism is corrupt.

And as Effie grew older, seemingly no one thought *she* was unlovable. Seriously, no one. She was lively and flirtatious, and it was said that she was "amused as well as flattered by the rapturous admiration she created." Ruskin, though engaged when he met Effie, quickly fell captive to her charms, writing her letters saying, "You saucy—wicked—witching—malicious—merciless mischief-loving—torturing—martyrising . . . mountain nymph that you are." He introduced her to literary and artistic London society, which she loved, and proposed when she was nineteen and he was twenty-nine. Effie later said of the time, "It almost made me weep with joy to think myself so beloved."

Ruskin seemed excited by their impending wedding and wrote

her shortly before the day in 1848, "That little undress bit! Ah—my sweet Lady—What naughty thoughts had I," and that he would welcome her into his home with "such a long-long kiss."

However, Ruskin's naughty thoughts came to an abrupt halt on their wedding night when he reportedly drew back from his wife, repulsed. It's commonly believed that this was because he did not know that women had pubic hair. This seems ridiculous today—and some historians speculate that Effie's menstruation was the cause of Ruskin's horror—but it is not completely illogical. It was the Victorian era, so a nightmare time when respectable people were taught very little about sex. Ruskin was an art critic. He saw a lot of naked women but in the form of marble statues and Renaissance oil paintings, where there is always, say, a bundle of grapes covering the woman's lady parts. He may have expected women in real life to look like art. Or maybe he knew that *some* women might have pubic hair but expected a wife to be more statuesque.

So Ruskin was maybe a very smart, handsome guy who just did not know that women had pubic hair. Effie later wrote a letter to her father explaining that Ruskin had refused to consummate the marriage:

> I had never been told the duties of married persons to each other and knew little or nothing about their relations in the closest union on earth. For days John talked about this relation to me, but avowed no intention of making me his Wife. He alleged various reasons, hatred to children, religious motives, a desire to preserve my beauty, and, finally, this last year, told me his true reason (and this to me is as villainous as all the rest) that he had imagined women were quite different to what he saw I was, and that the reason he did not make me his Wife

Effie had, sadly, lost her freshness.

was because he was disgusted with my person the first evening.

Poor Effie.

I'd like to say that Effie ended the marriage on that first night and stormed out of the room saying that she deserved to be with a man who both loved and desired her. But she didn't. I would like to say that is how women *today* would respond if a man claimed he was unattracted to them, and made them feel as if something was wrong or ugly about their body. I don't know if that would actually happen, though. Today's women are exposed to many harmful messages telling them what is potentially wrong with their appearance: *Lose five pounds fast! Have a bikini body! Discount breast implants! Best teeth-bleaching values! The new celebrity eyebrow waxer! NO ONE WILL EVER LOVE YOU IF YOUR BELLY BUTTON KEEPS LOOKING WEIRD LIKE THAT; STITCH IT UP.* (The last one I made up.) And so a woman tends to think that if a man doesn't like the look of her, she is culpable. But she isn't.

If you marry someone, you have every right to expect that person to treat you as though you are desirable, especially on your wedding night. Indeed, one of the most remarkable things about truly happy couples is that despite the physical changes that happen over time, they still seem to desire each other. One of the loveliest compliments I ever heard was when a man in his eighties said that his wife was just as beautiful to him as she had been when he married her nearly sixty years previously. The prospect of that alone—that there will be someone who will always think of you as you were when you were young—actually seems like one of the most wonderful perks of being married and one reason it would be nice to be with someone for a lifetime.

The fact that Effie should have responded to Ruskin's initial rejection by throwing up her arms and shouting, "Effie out!" is not often addressed (though she did claim that she initially thought it might have been because they were married during Lent, and

Ruskin might have been piously abstaining from sex). More frequently, there's some dispute about whether Ruskin rejected Effie because he had no idea what the naked female form looked like, or whether there was something actually unusual about her body—maybe it was made entirely of stitched-together doll parts. (I apologize to my stitched-together-doll-part readers and am glad that Tim Burton found work for each and every one of you.) Ruskin certainly seemed to believe there was something disgusting about Effie's body. During the annulment proceedings, years later, Ruskin stated publicly, "It may be thought strange that I could abstain from a woman who to most people was so attractive. But though her face was beautiful, her person was not formed to excite passion. On the contrary, there were certain circumstances in her person which completely checked it."

This is a terrible thing to say. Anne Boleyn would *never* have spoken about her ex that way. What that statement essentially boils down to is "Yes, she looks pretty from the outside, but underneath her dress she is disgusting." That is a scummy thing to say about your ex in a public forum; I don't care if underneath her clothing she is part lizard.

Yet Ruskin did not initially seem to think that there was anything about her physically that would impede their eventual union. She was not, say, as some Ruskin apologists strangely suggested, born without a vagina. Ruskin promised her that they would become man and wife in six years, when Effie was twenty-five. Indeed, he claimed that on her second bridal night he would "again draw [her] dress from [her] snowy shoulders." Dude, six years is a really long time to wait.

Some historians speculate that Ruskin's reluctance was because Ruskin wanted to make sure that Effie loved him for *himself* and not just his family's money. Maybe that's a valid point, though in an age where women were expected to marry men of good families since they had absolutely no way to support themselves, it seems unrealistic that Ruskin would have been scandalized that his financial situation might have played a role in Effie's acceptance of a marriage proposal. It is easier to imagine that he knew nothing about the female form, coming from a strict household and having immersed himself in his studies, than that he knew nothing of economics or social dictates. He certainly knew that Effie's family had financial difficulties when he married her.

That's not to say that Effie entered into the marriage with bad intent. If Effie thought about Ruskin's money when she married, it indicates simply that she probably considered the prospect in the way that every single woman of her age would have *had* to consider the prospect. Women in Victorian England could not hold property of any kind, so they had better pick a husband who had the means to support them and their eventual children.

Despite the fact that he tried to push off the consummation of the marriage, few historians seem to speculate that Ruskin thought that age nineteen was uncomfortably young for a woman to be a wife, and, certainly by the standards of the time, it wouldn't be seen as that young. However, there are indications that maybe Ruskin strongly preferred that his women be very young. Considerably younger than nineteen. In Effie's case he mentioned that she had lost some of the marvelous good looks she had when she was twelve. That is a bizarre thing to say.

During the next six years, despite her dissatisfaction with the marriage, and the fact that her husband clearly found her repulsive, Effie remained spirited and lively. Once, in Verona, two men fought a duel to see who would dance with her. She wrote that "these young men think as little of dueling as they do of smoking a cigar." Ruskin never really discouraged her, perhaps because when she was out it left him more time for his writing.

Ruskin liked to sit alone and write. That was his thing, solitude and thinking and writing unbothered by any kind of adult women's bodies.

In a letter, Ruskin recalled:

Looking back upon myself—I find no change in myself from a boy—from a child except the natural changes wrought by age. I am exactly the same creature—in temper—in likings—in weaknesses: much wiser—knowing more and thinking more: but in character precisely the same—so is Effie. When we married I expected to change *her*, she expected to change *me*.

Some historians read this letter and wonder, *Was Ruskin a homosexual, with all those unchangeable likes?* During this particular period in England, Ruskin would not have wanted to reveal that tidbit of information if he was. But that theory doesn't seem likely because if he was a homosexual, those naughty thoughts about Effie's little undressed bits are then very confusing.

Either way, their sex life did not change. Effie cried herself to sleep most nights—which prompted Ruskin to write a letter to her father asking if Effie perhaps suffered from a "disease affecting the brain."

And if you're still thinking, *Maybe Effie was born without a vagina, and Ruskin was just telling her they'd have sex later as a kind of polite lie*, well, it turns out that was simply not true, and we know that for certain.

In 1853, five years into her marriage, Effie was reintroduced to Ruskin's protégé, John Everett Millais (whom she had first met as a teenager), one of the foremost Pre-Raphaelite Brotherhood painters of the period, when Ruskin invited

John Everett Millais is great, just great. Try to imagine a younger version of him as a movie star you find attractive.

The Order of Release *(John Everett Millais), featuring Effie being cool and heroic, just like in real life.*

him to join the couple in Scotland. Millais quickly asked Effie to pose for him. The result was the excellent and aptly named painting *The Order of Release*, which depicts her as the Scottish wife of a prisoner being released from captivity.

Millais found Effie extremely attractive, which must have been appreciated given that Ruskin had been telling her she was physically repellent. Millais was also staying in the bedroom next to the couple's, and the rooms were tiny, so he could probably hear that she wasn't intimate with her husband.

Effie began to confide in Millais about her marital problems.

After she did so, he—almost immediately—came to hate his old mentor. He became so upset that he wrote a letter to Effie's mother, claiming:

> The worst of all is the wretchedness of her position. Whenever they go to visit she will be left all by herself in the company of any stranger present, for Ruskin appears to delight in selfish solitude. Why he ever had the audacity of marrying with no better intentions is a mystery to me. I must confess that it appears to me that he cares for nothing beyond his Mother and Father, which makes the insolence of his finding fault with his wife (to whom from the beginning he has acted most disgustingly) more apparent . . . If I have meddled more than my place would justify it was from the flagrant nature of the affair—I am only anxious to do the best for your daughter . . . I cannot conceal from you the truth that she has more to put up with than any living woman . . . She has all the right on her side and believe me the Father would see that also if he knew all.

Millais wasn't going to reveal all to Effie's mother, but it seems that he did know all. However, the innocuousness of this letter seems amazing when read today. Would a mother now read that and think, *Her husband forces her to talk to strangers? She should divorce him immediately!* Either Victorian social mores were very different, or people were very good at reading between the lines.

Happily Millais's encouragement gave Effie the nerve to finally end her miserable, unconsummated marriage, which was an incredibly difficult thing to do at the time. Divorce was costly in the 1850s, and only four divorces during Queen Victoria's reign were granted to women who attempted to initiate them. In two of those cases the women's husbands were proven to have committed incest. Moreover, as mentioned, women weren't entitled to property of any kind, so there were very few options, except to go back to their families. According to Cooper, in her last letter to her mother-in-law, Effie wrote that Ruskin had said he would "break her spirit" and cause her to return to her childhood home.

He did not.

Effie wrote to her father, asking for his help in ending her marriage. "[I do not] think I am John Ruskin's wife at all," she confided, "and I entreat you to assist me to get released from the unnatural position in which I stand to him." She also revealed to her father that when she continued trying to initiate some kind of physical intimacy, in the hopes of producing children, Ruskin told her that if she was not "very wicked," she was "at least insane."

Her family immediately began helping her arrange an annulment; her father was surprisingly cool and progressive about it. As he was a lawyer, he even reassured Effie that he had hopes for a good outcome because he had seen cases where wives had been released from similarly unhappy marriages. Annulling a marriage after six years, though, wasn't easy. It was generally expected that Victorian wives would defer to their husbands' desires, and that those desires would include sex. Annulling her union required Effie to submit to a medical exam to prove that she was still a virgin. Poor Effie—having your first intimate physical experience be with a doctor must have been humiliating, especially for someone who had been led to believe sexual relations were disgusting. When she had the exam, the results confirmed her case—though they just as easily might not have. She could have been an avid horseback rider; not like Ruskin, who was, as you may have heard, a terrible, repellent, cruddy horseback rider. (I hate Ruskin.)

Effie claimed she wanted an annulment on the grounds of Ruskin's "incurable impotency." Ruskin disputed the charge, claiming, "I can prove my virility at once!" and telling people that he masturbated, which is an interesting fact for everyone to know. Weird how much things had changed since Lucrezia Borgia's annulment. He decided to counter-file, maintaining that he could not have sex with Effie because of her "mental imbalance," which a child risked inheriting.

He lost.

Effie married Millais a year after her annulment from Ruskin was finalized. And wow, did they ever consummate that marriage. They kept consummating until they had eight children and Effie was compelled to write letters exclaiming, "No more!" None of their children seemed to have any "mental imbalances," and their grandson was so adorable that Millais' painting of him was used to advertise Pears soap. So it seems she was capable of arousing passion, even with her doll-part body or pubic hair or menstruation or whatever it was that Ruskin found so disgusting.

The marriage wasn't perfect. Millais was possibly briefly infatuated with Effie's beautiful younger sister Sophy, who modeled for him, enough so that Effie asked her to stop staying at their house, but it seems nothing much came of it. Effie and Sophy remained close and visited regularly; Sophy was invited back to stay with Effie and Millais in 1861.

Sadly, Effie's annulment meant she was not allowed to attend events at which Queen Victoria was present. This restriction limited her social life to some extent, but she remained a lively hostess, and the couple was well liked. Between Millais's artistic talent and Effie's charm, their house was generally full of celebrated individuals.

Millais continued to paint Effie—perhaps most

It turned out that Effie had lots of children, and it was basically like this, except for the wounded soldier. Peace Concluded *(John Everett Millais).*

memorably as a symbol of eternal love and fertility in *Peace Concluded,* which depicts her as the wife of a wounded officer, cradling him in her arms, while their children play at their feet. Even Ruskin claimed it "among the world's best masterpieces." As Millais grew older and his family became larger, he shifted into doing more society portraits, the quality of which remained superlative. In 1885 Millais was given the hereditary title of baronet.

Effie and Millais lived happily ever after, and today they dance together in the part of heaven where painters and socialites live. It's a fairly big section, at least the size of New York.

Ruskin remained bitter about the annulment/divorce, claiming that he was glad to have been freed of his "commonplace Scotch wife" and writing, "I never knew what it was to possess a father and mother—till I knew what it was to be neglected and forsaken of a wife." Ugh, dude, you told her she was crazy and deformed, and refused to sleep with her; *you are not the victim here.*

But Effie wasn't the only woman he would ever love. When Ruskin was thirty-nine years old, he was asked to tutor a ten-year-old girl named Rose La Touche. He recalled:

In the eventful year of 1858, a lady wrote to me from—somewhere near Green Street, W.,—saying, as people sometimes did, in those days, that she saw I was the only sound teacher in Art . . . that she wanted her children—two boys and a girl—taught the beginnings of Art rightly; especially the younger girl, in whom she thought I might find some power worth developing.

Ruskin promptly fell in love with Rose. He claimed, "I don't know what to make of her . . . She wears her round hat in the sauciest way possible—and is a firm—fiery little thing."

She was *ten.*

She seemed to feel some affection for him in return. She referred to him as "St. Crumpet," and he kept the letters she wrote him wrapped in gold leaf. A letter she wrote to him on vacation at age thirteen read:

> I wish so very much that you were happy—God can make you so—We will try not to forget all you taught us—It was so nice of you. Thank you so much from both of us.—Mama is very glad you went to Dr. Ferguson[.] She says you must not give him up. How very kind of you to see & talk to our old man[.] Certainly the name is not beautiful[.] We have all read your letter & we all care for it[.] That was indeed a "dear Irish labourer." Will you give them our love please & take for yourself as much as ever you please. It will be a great deal if you deign to take all we send you. I like Nice, but I don't much like being transplanted except going home. I am ever your rose.

That sounds like a letter a thirteen-year-old would write—especially when you consider she signed it "Rosie Posie." Ruskin really hated the idea of his Rosie Posie getting older and, shortly after this letter, wrote, "I shan't see her for ever so long . . . and then she'll be somebody else. Children are as bad as clouds at sunrise—golden change—but change, always!"

It's probable that the mere fact that Effie at age nineteen had the body of a fully grown woman might have been what Ruskin found undesirable. He may well have been expecting her to look the way he imagined her as a twelve-year-old—reminiscent of that nice guy who still sees his eighty-year-old wife looking the way she did at twenty-five. Except, in Ruskin's case, different and upsetting and not at all sweet. That theory seems plausible. Adding to its credibility is the fact that Ruskin began to write letters to the students of a local girls' school, one of which expresses his predicament with Rose:

My dearest Birds,

I am so much obliged to you for finding the letter for me and copying the end of it, though after all I can't show it to Rosie—for her father—staunch evangelical of the old school—does not believe in Greek, and might not like some expressions in this letter speaking mercifully of Error. Rosie, believing at once in him, & her mother and me, is growing up quite a little Cerberus, only her mother and I make two heads bark one way; but the third barks loudest—Indeed I should not say she believed in me—but would like to do so if I did not every now and then say much out of the way things—she pets me as she would a panther that kept its claws in—always looking under the claws to see that the velvet is all right & orthodox. She petted me yesterday, up, or down—(I don't know which)—to such a point that when I began drawing in the evening I found I didn't like the Venetians—but could only look at Angelico—But I can't write you a Sunday's letter to-day; it is all dark and rainy and I can't think now, unless in the sunshine.

I kept this letter to try and put some more in it—being reduced to a state of frantic despair by Rosie's going away to Italy next week.

I am not saying that anyone who doesn't find you sexually attractive must necessarily be a pedophile. Maybe I am saying that Ruskin was, based on the fact that he seems to have been very attracted to young girls. But there are some who think this fascination was normal, including Ruskin's biographer, Robert Hewison, who wrote: "Like other men of his class and culture . . . Ruskin enjoyed the company of young girls . . . It was their purity that attracted him; any sexual feelings were sublimated in the playful relationship of master and pupil that characterized his letters to several female correspondents."

Really? Huh. People always want to bring up Lewis Carroll and

Alice Liddell, but their relationship was also extremely discomfiting. There are certainly people who can have close relationships with children without developing sexual feelings for them, but that does not mean that pedophilia did not exist in the nineteenth century.

Ruskin waited until Rose was eighteen years old to propose marriage. Rose didn't reject him but did ask him to wait three years. Then the La Touche family—who already had religious differences with Ruskin—reached out to Effie Gray and John Millais, asking for information about why the marriage between Ruskin and Effie had ended. Millais responded to Rose's mother, informing her that Ruskin's conduct toward his wife had been atrocious. He further implored her not to write again, claiming that any mention of her prior marriage upset Effie terribly. However, she did write again because, well, that wasn't really much of an answer and mothers can be persistent. Effie wrote back saying that Ruskin's "conduct to me was impure in the highest degree" and that he had told her they could not consummate the marriage because she had an "internal disease."

As soon as Rose's family saw the letters, Rose stopped considering an engagement to Ruskin.

The running theme throughout this book is that "it's generally a bad idea to trash your ex publicly. You probably will because emotions run high and it's something a lot of us have done, but, seriously, try not to." However, the information Effie gave the La Touche family seemed reasonable to share.

Alas, her narrow escape did not lead to a happy ending for Rose. She died in 1875 when she was twenty-seven years old. Some said it was due to a broken heart, but it was more likely anorexia. It is terrible that she probably died from a disease that led her to believe her body was repellent. There's certainly a parallel there—Rose believed her body was unacceptable, and Effie was made to believe that hers was, too. Either way, the women in Ruskin's life really did not feel great about their womanly bodies.

Ruskin went mad after Rose's death. He became obsessed with spiritualists and with attempting to contact her from beyond the grave. That's not necessarily insane—there are different ways to grieve; people like horoscopes; my toilet flushes by itself sometimes, and I am fairly sure it is because my apartment is haunted—but he also began to hallucinate, and his letters became increasingly disjointed.

He also became overly harsh in his reviews. At one point he criticized James Whistler's painting *Nocturne in Black and Gold— The Falling Rocket* by saying, "I have seen and heard much of Cockney impudence before now; but never expected to hear a coxcomb ask two hundred guineas for throwing a pot of paint in the public's face." That is maybe the quippiest statement Ruskin ever made, and Whistler promptly sued him for libel. At the trial in 1878, Whistler was awarded one farthing in damages. (There used to be four farthings in a penny.)

But the case wasn't all that lighthearted. With some reluctance, Ruskin gave up his chair as art professor at Oxford in early 1879. "Although my health has lately been much broken," he explained, "I hesitated in giving in my resignation of my Art Professorship in the hope that I might still in some imperfect way have been useful at Oxford." That is sad.

If you do not dislike Ruskin as much as I do, you'll take comfort in knowing that in 1883 he seemed to have recovered somewhat and was reelected to a professorship. This was a good thing because he wasn't that great to have around the house. His cousin Joan Severn, who was tending to him, wrote the following while being "down in the depths after a good cry":

It is so difficult *not to mind* when he speaks in such a calm and deliberate voice, accusing me of the most dreadful things—saying he knows that I am the cause of all this—and that *through me* he has been poisoned, or that he is lying dead in his coffin, as he holds my hand, and that I only *think* he is living, and that I have set everybody against him, and that I have killed him to get his house and property—it breaks my heart!

People always attribute his madness to grief over Rose's death, but it seems possible, even likely, that he suffered from a neurodegenerative disorder, most likely CADASIL syndrome, which leads to dementia. He finally died of influenza in 1900 at age seventy-nine.

The British prime minister William Ewart Gladstone was once asked about Ruskin and said, "Should you ever hear anyone blame Millais, or his wife, or Mr. Ruskin remember there was no fault. There was misfortune, even tragedy: all three were perfectly blameless."

That's a nice sentiment that I don't think anyone reading this chapter will agree with. Now, readers, go tell your significant others that you find their physical presence attractive. Or tell your friends that they look great. And remember, anyone who has ever made you believe that your body is repulsive is probably, like Ruskin, a sad, lonely person who is going to go crazy later in life and *die alone,* while you will go off with a sexy artist who loves you and cannot keep his hands off you. That, in addition to healthy self-esteem, is an excellent way to feel better about your body.

9. Oscar Wilde

💔

Lord Alfred Douglas

The tale that follows is the saddest story in this book. It does not feature insane behavior or murder. Stories about wild and crazy people aren't that heartrending. There is a voyeuristic satisfaction in learning what two awful people will do to each other after a breakup.

Look at the very dramatic Caroline Lamb and Lord Byron. It's fun to read about them just going at each other, and you can't help but think that this is what they were made for—that their strong personalities were not suited for love but for war. I always think that Caroline Lamb and Lord Byron, if they went to heaven, embraced each other's skills and enjoyed fighting for all eternity. There is also something moving about stories with a clear victim. We come away from the tale of Nero and Sporus fairly certain that a popular miniseries will be made about them. It is a decadent horror story. That's why Ryan Murphy is going to direct! (When the miniseries is adapted as a dark Broadway musical, the big bucks will start rolling in. I expect residuals from anyone who even thinks about this project.)

But then there are stories that are about frailty and ordinary stupidity and unfair societal pressures. They are stories about wonderful, smart, delightful people meeting with bad ends. They are so sad because they are so banal. They are terrible reminders that life is not a fairy tale, and often not even a fair tale, and sometimes bad people triumph. Not even interestingly and obviously villainous bad people, but just petty and unkind and intolerant

Oscar Wilde appears to have a Katy Perry–esque firework of a flower growing out of his lapel.

people. Sometimes stupid triumphs over clever and kind and sparkling.

I take no pleasure in writing the story of Oscar Wilde and Lord Alfred Douglas.

Oscar Wilde was the wittiest playwright of his age—perhaps best known for *The Importance of Being Earnest* and *Lady Windermere's Fan*. If you have not seen those plays, go to the repertory theater in any small town in Kansas. You can see them there right now. And, as Dorothy Parker first quipped, numerous audience members will be remarking upon the language, as though they are the first to realize that this Oscar fellow had quite a way with words.

I could rattle off fifty Oscar Wilde phrases that show how witty he was. However, since we've already hauled her into this, Dorothy Parker probably said it best when she wrote: "If, with the literate, I am / Impelled to try an epigram / I never seek to take the credit / We all assume that Oscar said it."

That established, here is my favorite Oscar Wilde quote: "If you want to tell people the truth, make them laugh, otherwise they'll kill you." This quote is, unfortunately, particularly relevant in the life of Wilde, who was a homosexual. One could say that Victorian England was a bad time to be a homosexual, but all of history has been a tough time to be a homosexual. In England in 1533, King Henry VIII made it an offense punishable by death, and it remained a capital offense until 1861. By the late nineteenth century it was punishable only by imprisonment, which is slightly better, but still did not bode well for Wilde and his young lover, Lord Alfred Douglas.

I wish I could say that all of the difficulties that arose for Oscar were worth it because Lord Alfred was delightful. I would be able to slant this as a "world well lost for love" story, and it would not be in this book at all! Still, while I'd like to describe Lord Alfred Douglas's numerous good qualities, I am having trouble with that, because he had so few.

Alfred Douglas will always look like a beagle to me.

He was considered handsome at the time, but I'm not even on board with that. He had one of those droopy, bored faces that make Englishmen look as if they're having a stroke or are a member of the monarchy. Apparently, Oscar

Wilde was one of those people who found that look attractive. People make their own choices.

He met Lord Alfred Douglas in 1891, when he was thirty-six. Lord Alfred Douglas (nicknamed Bosie), the rather pampered son of John Douglas, 9th Marquess of Queensberry, was twenty-one.

In a weird bit of minutiae suitable for your next appearance on a big-time trivia show, the 3rd Marquess of Queensbury (who lived around 1700) was a cannibal. When he was ten years old he was found eating a servant whom he'd been roasting on a spit. Again, that is *when he was ten*. So we can't even say that Bosie came from a nice family.

Bosie was, or at least is often viewed as such in the aftermath of his relationship with Oscar Wilde, a whiny little brat with wild pretensions about his own literary ability. He never, ever stopped talking about what a talented writer he was, although there was nothing to indicate that this was the case.

But I can at least see why Lord Alfred Douglas might have been appealing initially. As an undergraduate at Oxford, he edited a magazine called *The Spirit Lamp,* which began its run with an editor's letter saying that the magazine would attempt to appeal "exclusively to the enlightened." According to the biographer Richard Ellmann, it was also Bosie's "attempt to win acquiescence at Oxford for homosexuality." That seems like a bold move. This is one moment when Bosie is going to seem like a cool, forward-thinking person. Treasure this moment.

You might ask how a magazine went about winning acquiescence at Oxford for homosexuality. The answer is that in its fourteen-month existence it published four original works by Oscar Wilde and three other articles discussing the greatness of Oscar Wilde. The magazine was probably not intended so much to win acquiescence at Oxford for homosexuality as it was to win Oscar Wilde's personal acquiescence for Lord Alfred Douglas.

And it worked. Oscar Wilde hired Bosie to translate his play *Salome* from French into English. This was a big deal. Wilde wrote

Salome while he was residing in Paris in 1891. Supposedly while writing it Wilde wandered into the Grand Café and asked the gypsy orchestra to play the kind of music that would appeal to someone who has just slain their lover and danced in his blood.

What they played was Katy Perry's "Firework."

No. We don't know what they played. But the fact that "dead lover blood dance" was the sound track to its creation illustrates that *Salome* was a fairly wild and provocative work. Censors seemed to agree. The work was banned in England before it could ever be presented onstage. And the task of translating this outrageous and controversial work fell to a twenty-one-year-old man who did not speak French very well. Bosie thought he spoke French, probably because he was handsome by the standards of the time, and he was not contradicted nearly enough.

Oscar and Bosie fought over what is generally agreed to be Bosie's absolutely terrible translation of *Salome*. To make peace, Oscar gave up correcting the translation and dedicated *Salome* "To my friend Lord Alfred Bruce Douglas, the translator of this play."

Much later, when he was in prison (we'll get to that), Oscar wrote letters to Bosie still lamenting that the translation was *terrible*. Wilde claimed, "I took you and the translation back."

But this failure did not deter Bosie. He was absolutely convinced he was a literary genius. He later claimed in *Without Apology*, "I suspected I was a great poet when I was twenty-three, and as the years went by my suspicion became a conviction." This statement might have been amusing if a blustering literary genius had said it. We'd all probably chuckle with Hemingway because it would be arrogant yet true. Like the Teenage Mutant Ninja Turtle Raphael, Hemingway would come off as cool but rude. But if you're going to make that kind of statement, you'd better make sure most people agree that it's true.

Anyway, they seemed to be happy together—Oscar Wilde, literary luminary, and that pretentious kid with the droopy face.

By 1893 their affair was in full swing. Oscar was writing Lord Alfred love notes, such as: "It is a marvel that those red-roseleaf lips of yours should be made no less for the madness of music and song than for the madness of kissing. Your slim gilt soul walks between passion and poetry."

Bosie proceeded to leave one of Oscar's beautiful letters in the pocket of a suit he gave to a young male prostitute named Alfred Wood, who then attempted, unsuccessfully, to blackmail Oscar. Wilde's defense was that all the letters he wrote were intended to be published as sonnets.

Around this time Oscar Wilde went from being fairly discreet about his homosexuality—he had a wife and children—to embracing it more openly. He did not proclaim it, but he did, on Lord Alfred's introduction, begin seeing a series of young male prostitutes. Wilde later noted that being with them "was like feasting with panthers; the danger was half the excitement."

And in 1894 Lord Alfred wrote:

> *"What is thy name?" He said, "My name is Love."*
> *Then straight the first did turn himself to me*
> *And cried, "He lieth, for his name is Shame,*
> *But I am Love, and I was wont to be*
> *Alone in this fair garden, till he came*
> *Unasked by night; I am true Love, I fill*
> *The hearts of boy and girl with mutual flame."*
> *Then sighing, said the other, "Have thy will,*
> *I am the love that dare not speak its name."*

"The love that dare not speak its name" became a synonym for homosexuality until, well, until right now. Until this minute, unless you are reading this book in the enlightened future, where absolutely no one hides their sexual preferences. (If you are, write back, please. Time travelers should *always* write back!)

Lord Alfred Douglas's father, the Marquess of Queensberry, had heard about Oscar Wilde's involvement with his son, and he was not pleased. In keeping with our "Bosie came from a weird family" angle, it feels worth mentioning that the Marquess of Queenberry was an absolutely hilarious human being. He was an atheist who was prone to going to church services to shout at the ministers. He wrote some demanding, extremely instructional poems, one of which read:

> When I am dead cremate me
> Please let my ashes lie
> In mother Earth's dear bosom
> I have no fear to die

I like all of my poems to actually be dictates about things I want done.

Another fun tidbit (no pun intended): his second wife demanded an annulment after finding "malformation of the parts of generation, frigidity and impotence." The biggest mystery is what is meant when people say their significant historical other was genitally malformed. Do you think he had a microphallus? I do. But we'll never know. It's going to be a mystery forever. In the future, if you accuse anyone of being malformed in their genitals, please take pictures *for historians.*

In any case, the marquess presumably couldn't have much sex, regularly, despite fathering Alfred, he really didn't like anyone else doing it either, and he was not afraid to die. By 1893 he was writing Lord Alfred Douglas, threatening to disown him if he didn't stop having contact with Oscar Wilde.

Some of the marquess's erratic behavior might have been due to the fact that he was a boxer, and he could have been punch-drunk most of the time. He invented the modern rules of boxing; they're called the Queensberry rules. Accordingly, when he approached Oscar Wilde and told him, "If I catch you and my son again in any public restaurant, I will thrash you," Wilde responded, "I don't know what the Queensberry rules are, but the Oscar Wilde rule is to shoot on sight."

Then the marquess started showing up at Wilde's plays clutching bundles of vegetables, presumably to hurl at the stage. He wasn't allowed in. Wilde claimed he "prowled about for three hours, then left chattering like a monstrous ape." Stop and think for a moment how weird this is. Remember this is an extremely influential man of notable standing. Imagine if a U.S. senator started showing up on Broadway intending to hurl vegetables at the performers and had to be barred at the door. Wouldn't that be kind of great?

Nothing cool ever happens these days.

It's no wonder Oscar Wilde didn't take him all that seriously. Nobody did. Even Lord Alfred Douglas once replied to one of his father's tirades by saying, "What a funny little man you are," and that feels about right. He also told his father, "If O.W. was to prosecute you in the criminal courts for libel, you would get seven years' penal servitude for your outrageous libels."

The Marquess of Queensberry, despite being a funny little man, may have realized that a trial for libel would actually prove to the world that Oscar Wilde was having an affair with his son. In 1895 the marquess left a card for Wilde at his club that read, "For Oscar Wilde, posing somdomite."

Somdomite? That is not a word.

Upon receiving it, Oscar Wilde later wrote, "I felt I stood between Caliban and Sporus." Presumably that references the Marquess of Queensberry and Alfred Douglas, though if Bosie had resembled Sporus *too* closely, Oscar might have been less interested in him.

So Oscar Wilde, at Bosie's behest, sued the marquess for libel. Bosie was so adamant he do this that he promised that one of his brothers and his mother would cover Oscar's legal expenses.

Moreover, Wilde was in an extremely socially secure place as he sued. *The Importance of Being Earnest* had just run, with a review from the *New York Times* stating, "Wilde may be said to have at last, and by a single stroke, put his enemies under his feet."

Alas, that would not be the case here.

The Marquess of Queensberry agreed to go to court enthusiastically, claiming that he had indeed called Oscar Wilde a "posing somdomite" and that he had done so for the good of the public.

Friends were not enthusiastic about Wilde participating in this trial because, again, homosexuality was illegal. Wilde perhaps wasn't as worried as you and I might be, though. He was used to being a controversial figure. People often speculated about his homosexuality, especially after the publication of *Dorian Gray*, which had homosexual undertones. He'd even been accused of plagiarism by James Whistler, an episode from which we get the wonderful exchange:

OSCAR WILDE: My God, James, I wish I'd said that!

JAMES WHISTLER: You will, Oscar, you will.

And Wilde had emerged from those episodes unscathed, with people finding him even more vibrant and interesting than before. So he might have thought himself equally invulnerable in this new libel suit. Just for the record, never sue for libel if you have actually done the things you're accused of. As any good attorney or historical essayist will tell you: truth is an absolute defense to a claim of libel. When Oscar went to trial, he adamantly assured his barrister that all twelve instances of sodomy that the marquess claimed he committed were false. This was a pretty absurd strategy considering that he not only talked about his romances but talked about them *at length*. After he told Aubrey Beardsley about his seduction of various messenger boys ("they were all dirty, and appealed to me for that reason"), Beardsley remarked, "I don't mind his morals, but his lamentable repetitions bore me to death." So it's not a huge surprise that his friends were begging Oscar to leave the country and go to America—or France. (An aside: France is always the right answer. So many people in this book could have led happy lives if only they'd fled to France.)

Oscar Wilde's first trial is reminiscent of the trial of Socrates.

The philosopher was put on trial for supposedly corrupting the morals of the young men of Athens. Socrates treated the entire proceeding in a very dismissive way, probably because the charges were absurd, and when asked to defend himself, he began by claiming: "I do not know what effect my accusers have had upon you, gentlemen, but for my own part I was carried away by them; their arguments were so convincing. On the other hand, scarcely a word of what they said was true." Midway through the trial he was asked to propose a punishment for himself, and he suggested that the government provide him with free dinners forever for his service to the city. Socrates was witty and charming and the smartest person in the room, and he made people laugh as he told them the truth. He was sentenced to death by hemlock.

I guess no one told Oscar Wilde about Socrates.

When, during the trial, the opposing counsel recounted Queensbury's accusations, Wilde quippily countered:

[Lord Queensbury] said, "You were both kicked out of the Savoy Hotel at a moment's notice for your disgusting conduct." I said, "That is a lie." He said, "You have taken furnished rooms for him in Piccadilly." I said, "Somebody has been telling you an absurd set of lies about your son and me. I have not done anything of the kind." He said, "I hear you were thoroughly well blackmailed for a disgusting letter you wrote to my son." I said, "The letter was a beautiful letter, and I never write except for publication."

Then I asked: "Lord Queensberry, do you seriously accuse your son and me of improper conduct?" He said, "I do not say that you are it, but you look it."

I prefer his statement that he only writes for publication, but it was apparently the line about not being a homosexual but looking like one that made the court laugh. However, this was a pretty brilliant move on the marquess's part. By claiming that he'd only called Wilde a *posing* sodomite, he only had to prove that Oscar Wilde gave the *appearance* of a homosexual.

However, Wilde did continue to charm the court for some time, as with this exchange:

CROSS EXAMINER: Have you ever adored a young man madly?

WILDE: No, not madly. I prefer love—that is a higher form.

C: Never mind about that. Let us keep down to the level we are at now.

W: I have never given adoration to anybody except myself. (Loud laughter)

The judge, unfortunately, did not take to Oscar's humor. If you are ever on trial, it is not the time to be witty.

And then this exchange sealed Wilde's fate:

CROSS EXAMINER: Do you know Walter Grainger?

WILDE: Yes.

C: How old is he?

W: He was about sixteen when I knew him. He was a servant at a certain house in High Street, Oxford, where Lord Alfred Douglas had rooms. I have stayed there several times. Grainger waited at table. I never dined with him. If it is one's duty to serve, it is one's duty to serve; and if it is one's pleasure to dine, it is one's pleasure to dine.

C: Did you ever kiss him?

W: Oh, dear no. He was a peculiarly plain boy. He was, unfortunately, extremely ugly.

Despite Oscar's repeated insistences that he was making a joke, the cross examiner continued to contend that Oscar Wilde *would* have kissed the boy if he'd been handsome. Because that was true, probably! *Oscar—why did you get into this trial?*

Wilde once wrote, "You can produce a tragic effect by introducing comedy. A laugh in an audience does not destroy terror but, by relieving it, aids it. Never be afraid that by raising a laugh you destroy tragedy. On the contrary, you intensify it."

That may be true because it makes you like the characters more and thus dread unfortunate circumstances befalling them. Or it may be because you should not make any jokes at a trial.

The court found in the marquess's favor on the charge of libel and forced Wilde to pay the court costs. Those expenses bankrupted him.

There was, however, some hope that the marquess would take no further action. Wrong. The marquess sent all of the notes from the libel trial as well as the information his private detective had found about Wilde's male prostitutes to Scotland Yard, evidence upon which Wilde was charged with gross indecency. A date for a second trial was set, this time to decide whether Wilde should be imprisoned for being a homosexual. The jury at this trial was hung.

At a third trial he was found guilty of every count of sodomy except one.

The judge ruled:

The crime of which you have been convicted is so bad that one has to put stern restraint upon one's self to prevent one's self from describing, in language which I would rather not use, the sentiments which must rise to the breast of every man of honor who has heard the details of these two terrible trials . . . I shall, under such circumstances, be expected to pass the severest sentence that the law allows. In my judgment it is totally inadequate for such a case as this. The sentence of the Court is that you be imprisoned and kept to hard labor for two years.

Let us now rail against Victorian society as a whole, but especially those people in the courtroom who *loved* this verdict and responded to it by hissing "Shame!" at Wilde. The sentence seems not only unjust but wasteful. Wilde could have spent those two years producing some good plays. But then, in any era, the persecution of homosexuals is nonsensical. Anyone who reads the Great Commandment and the story of the Good Samaritan in the Bible and comes away saying "Gays will burn in hell" has missed an essential message. Those people make no more sense than, as humorist Mallory Ortberg quipped, the people who read the Bible and say, "The first thing I've got to do is get a bunch of snakes and start handling them." They might also be the same people who read this chapter and say, "The way to become a great writer is to listen to angry gypsy music."

Obviously, we were not there to give impassioned defenses at Oscar Wilde's trial. And so he was sentenced to two years of hard labor, which was terrible. Not just because he was an aesthete but because hard labor is bad for anyone. He suffered from severe hunger, and while at Wandsworth Prison he burst an eardrum; the resulting infection was later thought to have contributed to the meningitis that killed him. He was initially allowed no books or pen or paper, and visitors were permitted for only twenty minutes every three months.

His friends campaigned for his eventual transfer to Reading Prison. The warden there, a Major Nelson, who was seemingly a very nice man, offered Wilde a book from his personal library, claiming, "The home office has allowed you some books. Perhaps you would like this one. I have just been reading it myself." The gesture brought Wilde to tears, and he claimed that they were "the first kind words that have been spoken to me since I have been in [Reading] gaol." Wilde later gave Nelson a copy of *The Importance of Being Earnest* inscribed, A TRIVIAL RECOGNITION OF A GREAT AND NOBLE KINDNESS. In 1897 he was allowed to write—but was supposed to turn in whatever he had written to Major Nelson at the end of the day, so he could not see the manuscript's flow. Despite the fact that it was against the rules, Nelson supposedly let him consult some of the prior pages and returned the entire manuscript to Wilde when he was set free.

In "The Ballad of Reading Gaol," his poem about his prison years, Wilde wrote:

The vilest deeds like poison weeds
*   Bloom well in prison-air:*
It is only what is good in Man
*   That wastes and withers there:*
Pale Anguish keeps the heavy gate,
*   And the Warder is Despair.*

For they starve the little frightened child
*   Till it weeps both night and day:*
And they scourge the weak, and flog the fool,
*   And gibe the old and grey,*
And some grow mad, and all grow bad,
*   And none a word may say.*

Each narrow cell in which we dwell
*   Is a foul and dark latrine,*
And the fetid breath of living Death
*   Chokes up each grated screen,*
And all, but Lust, is turned to dust
*   In Humanity's machine.*

Despite this despair and the increasing rarity of Lord Alfred's visits, and his upset upon hearing that Lord Alfred planned to publish some of his letters from prison, nothing changed his feelings toward Bosie.

Immediately after his release from prison they reunited in Naples, and Wilde wrote his new publisher, Leonard Smithers, in 1897:

How can you keep on asking is Lord Alfred Douglas in Naples? You know quite well he is—we are together. He understands me and my art, and loves both. I hope never to be separated from him. He is a most delicate and exquisite poet, besides— far the finest of all the young poets in England. You have got to publish his next volume; it is full of lovely lyrics, flute-music and moon-music, and sonnets in ivory and gold. He is witty, graceful, lovely to look at, lovable to be with. He has also ruined my life, so I can't help loving him—it is the only thing to do.

It is amazing that Oscar Wilde is able to treat his years in prison—and truly, the ruination of his life—as a sort of amusing footnote in a romance. Because from an outsider perspective, his involvement with Bosie did completely ruin Oscar's life.

Really. Unambiguously. It *ruined* his life.

And he just forgave him. He wasn't able to treat Bosie in the same indulgent way that he had before prison because Wilde emerged if not broken, then certainly broke. He was a persona non grata in England. Bosie came into his inheritance around that time, and while he did not give Oscar a substantial portion, as friends of Oscar's suggested he should, he did provide him with an allowance. But he eventually separated from Oscar when his family threatened to cut off funds. Bosie wrote, admittedly fairly practically, to the editor More Adey, "If Oscar and I are to be starved to death for living with each other, it does make a reason for not doing so." Bosie also once said of Wilde, "When you are not on your pedestal you are not interesting" and wrote to his mother toward the end of his relationship with Wilde that he was "glad to go."

Oscar was never able to write again. Or rather he claimed, "I can write, but have lost the joy of writing." He spent his last years, before his death from meningitis in 1900, drinking steadily. His last words are often recorded as being "either that wallpaper goes or I do." Though I think he'd prefer to be remembered for that phrase, Father Dunne, who administered Wilde's last rites, claimed, "When

I repeated close to his ear the Holy Names, the Acts of Contrition, Faith, Hope and Charity, with acts of humble resignation to the Will of God, he tried all through to say the words after me."

Bosie was shooting in Scotland at the time.

De Profundis, Wilde's fifty-thousand-word letter to Douglas from prison, was published in its entirety. This is probably the basis for our anti-Bosie bias because many examples of Bosie not being very nice (from Oscar's perspective) are presented in that work.

We could probably say that Oscar had selective memory about events if not for *Oscar Wilde and Myself,* Bosie's memoir published in 1914. By that time Bosie had married and found religion, so perhaps it's not surprising that the book is not sympathetic to Wilde. In it he claims:

> [Oscar Wilde had] a shallow and comparatively feeble mind, incapable of grappling unaided with even moderately profound things, and disposed to fribble and antic with old thoughts for lack of power to evolve new ones. It was a mind which was continually discovering with a glow that two and two make four, or pretending to discover with a much warmer glow that two and two make five. In every scrap that he wrote, leaving out, of course, the poems, you will find this feeble, medio-cre, but, withal, vain-glorious instrument hard at work on the fearful business of saying nothing in such a way that foolish people will shout about it.

That's simply incorrect. That is not factual in the least. Let's take a moment and say, "No, he was a literary genius. You are confused." Let's say that collectively. We all did that? Good! We put that matter to rest.

Bosie didn't hear you.

Oscar Wilde and Myself, which was partly ghostwritten by his former assistant editor Thomas William Hodgson Crosland— because Bosie could not write a whole book himself despite constantly claiming to be a literary genius—goes on and on about what a great luminary he is compared to old, feebleminded Oscar Wilde. The guy helping him ghostwrite a book went along with it. Bosie continued making statements like this until the end of his life and tried to disown anything other than peripheral friendship with Wilde, stating in his second autobiography, *Oscar Wilde: A Summing Up,* published in 1940, "I have, as I hope is well known, nothing but abhorrence for homosexuality," though that work is, mercifully, somewhat kinder to his former partner. But still. Bosie was definitely a homosexual who introduced Oscar Wilde to male prostitutes, evidence of which was proven in a court of law. It seems a little late in the game to start protesting, "What, no, I don't like dudes!"

I suppose it is a possibility that everyone in the world except Lord Alfred Douglas was lying and he was straight as a girder, but I am not a conspiracy theorist. It seems more likely he just didn't want to have to endure the same punishments that Oscar Wilde did, and which he'd witnessed firsthand. Disowning any love or intimacy with Wilde was certainly one way to do that. Obviously, the fact that Alfred Douglas lived in an age when he had to label his sexual preferences abhorrent is very sad. That is a shame. Alfred Douglas isn't a real villain; he just kind of sucks. He's not a monster; he just remained a whiny brat until the day he died.

Oscar Wilde, on the other hand, not only was a genuine literary genius but had the added distinction of not being a whiny brat. He was a brave champion against humorlessness, bullies, ugliness, and bad wallpaper. All the important stuff.

But then, Wilde had a remarkable ability to see the world as he wanted it to be, filled with beautiful, imaginative, funny, loving people. I think that is the way everyone reading this book would like to see the world. And I am sorry that he was disappointed.

There is another Wilde quote that is perhaps not as funny as the others but strikes me as a fitting end to this story. It runs: "To be good, according to the vulgar standard of goodness, is obviously quite easy. It merely requires a certain amount of sordid terror, a certain lack of imaginative thought, and a certain low passion for middle-class respectability."

The ultimate triumph in life seems to be retaining a sense of bravery and imagination and an inner sense of decency. If those things don't make us "good" in the eyes of our contemporaries, well, perhaps we should strive to be more than just good. At the very least, you look better in the history books. Which is why a barrier was placed in front of Wilde's gravestone in Paris. So many people had kissed it that the stone was beginning to wear away.

And if you are still dedicated to finding a little bit of virtue in Lord Alfred Douglas, as I'm sure Wilde would have wanted us to, then I'll let him sign off with what is regarded as one of the better poems he wrote, which is, unsurprisingly, about Oscar Wilde, "The Dead Poet."

I dreamed of him last night, I saw his face
All radiant and unshadowed of distress,
And as of old, in music measureless,
I heard his golden voice and marked him trace
Under the common thing the hidden grace,
And conjure wonder out of emptiness,
Till mean things put on beauty like a dress
And all the world was an enchanted place.

And then methought outside a fast locked gate
I mourned the loss of unrecorded words,
Forgotten tales and mysteries half said,
Wonders that might have been articulate,
And voiceless thoughts like murdered singing birds.
And so I woke and knew that he was dead.

10. Edith Wharton

Morton Fullerton

$\mathcal{S}$ometimes, we are fond of writers because they appear normal, just like you and me. For instance, Dave Barry seems like a regular guy. He would tell funny jokes at a pool party, but not all of them would land. He'd have perhaps a 75 percent heartfelt laughter rate, which would be enough to make you glad he was at the party, but not enough to make you feel you were suddenly, strangely, attending a comedy show. And he would let other people get a word in edgewise. If you formed a neighborhood rock band, Stephen King would probably want to play in it, and he would not even be the coolest guy in the group. I am pretty sure that Jennifer Weiner is friends with both of our moms, which is a good reason to remember to ask your mother about what is going on in *her* life the next time she calls.

And then there is Edith Wharton, a writer whose life in no way resembled that of anyone you probably know or are ever going to know. It is safe to say she is not friends with your mom, even if your mom had been alive in the early 1900s. There are people who wonder whether Edith Wharton can ever be seen as a sympathetic figure, if only because she was so outrageously, absurdly wealthy. So well-off that F. Scott Fitzgerald's quote about the rich being very different from you and me is periodically tossed back into the past at her. But she wrote so well about her era's superrich that we love her anyway.

Do you know my absolute favorite story about the author of *The Age of Innocence*? It's that she did all of her writing, longhand, after breakfasting in bed and that, when finishing a page, she would just toss it on the floor. Her secretary would then be left to assemble all of the pages in the correct order. It is a testament to the quality of her staff that her work does not seem more disjointed.

The fact that Edith was going to be the kind of woman who could spend a lot of time lounging in bed was determined from the day of her birth. She was born in New York in 1862 to George Frederic Jones and Lucretia Stevens Rhinelander. That saying "Keeping up with the Joneses"? That referred to Wharton's family. As she grew up, Edith's hobbies included yachting and, later in life, visiting harems. Somehow on a trip to Morocco she managed to enter the sultan's harem, where she claimed the women reclined "in clothes such as [the costume designer] Bakst never dreamed of."

Edith Wharton in a sparkly ball gown looked like a babe, so I don't know why so many people want to talk about how unattractive she was.

Yet great wealth and privilege, as the TV series *Downton Abbey* has taught us, do not necessarily lead to happy relationships. In a *New Yorker* essay titled "A Rooting Interest: Edith Wharton and the Problem of Sympathy," Jonathan Franzen writes: "Edith Newbold Jones did have one potentially redeeming disadvantage: she wasn't pretty. The man she would have most liked to marry, her friend Walter Berry, a noted connoisseur of female beauty, wasn't the marrying type. After two failed youthful courtships, she settled for an affable dud of modest means, Teddy Wharton."

That description may be a cruel overstatement. While Edith Wharton may not have been beautiful, she was smart enough to know how to work her looks and style to her benefit. She was also good with men. As a child she preferred to spend her time with boys—a preference that continued well into her later life, when her best friends were men, foremost among them Henry James. In *No Gift from Chance: A Biography of Edith Wharton*, the historian Shari Benstock writes:

> Although a tomboy, Edith was already familiar with the feminine arts, and she displayed her gifts to best advantage. Playing ball or skipping rope with the Harrys, Willies and Georgies, she shook out her long red hair "so that it caught the sun!" A few years later she amused herself by stealing the handsome German fiancé of a daughter of the Livingston family. He was attracted to her "sense of fun" and she enjoyed "keeping his poor fiancée on the rack for a few weeks."

Usually when you encounter women who boldly declare "all my friends are men," they are often implying, "I do not like relationships with people I cannot seduce." Edith Wharton was not that kind of woman. Even in the situation with the fiancé, who did eventually return to his intended, she felt terrible about it for weeks afterward. What's perpetually surprising to me is that a lively, emotionally complex woman who stole someone's fiancé for fun, hung out in harems seemingly unperturbed, and wrote *The Age of Innocence*—one of the most heartbreaking romances of all time (read it right now if you haven't!)—would have *only one orgasm in her life with a man who left her immediately afterward.*

That man was not her husband, Teddy Wharton.

The blame for this inexperience and inhibition lies, once again, at the feet of Victorian repression. Edith certainly faulted society and specifically her mother, who, when teenage Edith remarked that she felt pleasant tremors while riding her pony or dancing with the boys next door, supposedly replied, "It's not nice to ask about such things." It was the age of innocence, and by God people were determined to keep it that way.

Her mother just did not *understand.* Edith, at age eleven, showed her mother a novel she was working on that contained the dialogue: "Oh, how do you do, Mrs. Brown?" said Mrs. Tomkins. "If only I had known you were going to call I should have tidied up the drawing room." To which her mother said, seemingly bewildered, "But drawing rooms are always tidy."

Edith was from a world where the furnishings were always impeccable, but understanding of female sexuality and attraction between partners was considerably flawed.

So when Edith married Teddy Wharton, it was a *marriage blanc.* That is a polite way of saying they never had sex. Or maybe they had sex once or twice. Having no information whatsoever about intercourse probably wasn't helpful. Edith claimed that immediately before her marriage to Teddy in 1885, she asked her mother how sex worked, and the interaction went as follows:

> A few days before my marriage, I was seized with such a dread of the whole dark mystery, that I summoned up courage to appeal to my mother, & begged her, with a heart beating to suffocation, to tell me "what being married was like." Her handsome face at once took on the look of icy disapproval which I most dreaded. "I never heard such a ridiculous question!" she said impatiently; & I felt at once how vulgar she thought me.

But in the extremity of my need I persisted. "I'm afraid Mamma—I want to know what will happen to me!"

The coldness of her expression deepened to disgust [and the question went unanswered] . . . I record this brief conversation, because the training of which it was the beautiful and logical conclusion did more than anything else to falsify & misdirect my whole life.

It falsified and misdirected her entire life.

This chapter is for everyone who is sitting around thinking, *God, dating must have been so much better in the days when you married after a long courtship in your early twenties and then you had one sexual partner for your whole life.* I see you. I see you reading those Jane Austen fan-fiction books with oil painting covers and titles like *Lydia Kills Mr. Wickham* and thinking that the Victorian dating scene would be wonderful. It was, in fact, not great. It might have been different, and different can be easier in some ways, but on the whole it just meant that you probably didn't have an orgasm until you were forty and the heartbreak you endured would be the worst because you would only kind of, sort of, understand what was even happening.

It's hard to convey how stultifying the sexual environment was for everyone in Victorian times—in England and in the United States. Between this chapter and the two preceding ones (on Oscar Wilde and poor Effie Gray), this book could be subtitled, "Victorian Times: The Worst or The WORST?" Edith Wharton's story shows how dating only one person ever in a superromantic way actually works out.

No part of this unfortunate situation stems from Teddy being a terrible choice for a husband. He gets a bad rap, and it's not quite fair. He was thirty-five years old when Edith, at age twenty-three, married him. He had a great love for travel, just as Edith did, he came from a very well-to-do family, he liked pets, and he once saved his cousins when they fell through the ice on a pond they were skating on. Nothing in the historical record makes him seem like an awful human being (at least, except for the time he embezzled money from Edith's trust fund, but he did later make restitution). However, there was supposedly a history of what we would now better understand as clinical manic depression in his family. His father "just wouldn't get out of bed" and committed himself to psychiatric care. Teddy was also an alcoholic, which may have been a result of or contributed to his intense unhappiness. At the time, he was thought to suffer from melancholia

It is impossible not to like poor Teddy Wharton a little when he loved small dogs so much.

(depression). Edith and her family might not have noticed that at first because during the Victorian era if you weren't somewhat melancholy, you were just a moron. Sorry.

However, his reticence to have sex with Edith might also have stemmed from the fact that she did not seem to know what it was. Edith was really, really upset with her mom, pretty much forever, for refusing to tell her about sex. Given that the understanding at the time was that "nice" women would not know anything about sex, Teddy may just not have wanted to educate her and be thought a brute. He did tell her about the "process of generation," but not until several weeks after their wedding. This was the closest she had come to the topic since age ten, when she asked her mother if babies came from flowers, and her mother declined to answer. Being met with such a . . . it seems unfair to say naive, so let's just say a bride who was a product of the times, it's probably understandable that Teddy, who was not a robust lothario, was reluctant to enlighten her. Supposedly, on their wedding night, she expected him to perform some manner of concert for her, which may be the only known example where this phrase is not a euphemism.

Their marriage remained either, depending on the source, entirely or virtually celibate until their divorce in 1913. Maybe they made out or got to second base—we really don't know. But Edith Wharton was not sexless for her entire life or even for the duration of her marriage. She began what was believed to be her first and only love affair with the journalist Morton Fullerton in 1907 when she was forty-five. By that time, she was already a famous novelist; she had published *The House of Mirth* in 1905. She'd also been celibate for—if those earlier, concert-performing reports are to believed—her entire life, which may explain why, as the writer Nicole Cliffe pointed out, "*The House of Mirth* reads like a poorly played game of choose your own adventure," particularly when it comes to any situ-

Look at the mustache on Fullerton—just look at it. Are you weak at the knees yet?

ations that could be sexual in nature. (Just flee and lie about even having been there. That'll work out great!) Edith Wharton couldn't write about sex because she'd never had any.

Until Morton Fullerton.

He was, admittedly, a pretty cool person with whom to have an affair. A scoundrel and a possible sociopath, but cool nonetheless. After graduating from Harvard, Morton had moved to Paris, where he lived with an older stage actress named Madame Mirecourt, despite being engaged to his half cousin and adopted sister, Katherine. The engagement did not work out. Edith and Morton were introduced by their mutual friend Henry James. Fullerton was a Paris correspondent for the *Times of London*, and Edith Wharton considered him "an ideal intellectual partner." He was also a man who was certainly not celibate. Again, he had a romance with his adopted sister, which is an uncomfortable thing to think about unless you have *just* seen the film *The Royal Tenenbaums* (2001), which notes that such situations are merely "frowned upon." Jennie Fields, who wrote *The Age of Desire* based on Wharton's life, claimed on NPR: "[Morton Fullerton] had had affairs with other successful people, both men and women. He was something of a sociopath because he would have these affairs and he would just disappear; [that] was his MO."

Meanwhile, in *Henry James: A Life,* Leon Edel claims that Fullerton was a "libertine," "an elegant seducer," and a "middle-aged mustached Lothario." Edel also asserts that he was totally irresistible; people were really attracted to the "dashing well-tailored man with large Victorian moustache and languid eyes, a bright flower in his button-hole, and the style of a 'masher.'" This would explain how he ended up being friends with Oscar Wilde, the theater designer Percy Anderson, and the novelist George Meredith, as well as Henry James. Fullerton was bisexual; he even had an affair with Lord Ronald Sutherland Gower, who was supposedly the inspiration for the character of Lord Henry in *Dorian Gray*. He probably did not have an affair with Wilde, though the latter did once ask him for a loan at the end of his life, and Morton turned him down.

I am kind of attracted to Morton Fullerton right now. He just seems like someone who super-did-not-give-a-damn about the restrictive mores of the time. Henry James even wrote a letter to him, which reads in part:

How, my dear Fullerton, does a man write in the teeth of so straight a blast from—I scarce know what to call the quarter:

the spice-scented tropic isles of Eden—isles of gold—isles of superlative goodness? I have told you before that the imposition of hands in a certain tender way "finishes" me, simply—and behold me accordingly more finished than the most parachevé of my own productions . . . You do with me what you will . . . You're at any rate the highest luxury I can conceive, and . . . I should wonder how the devil I can afford you. However, I shall persist in you. I know but this life. I want in fact more of you . . . You are dazzling, my dear Fullerton; you are beautiful; you are more than tactful, you are tenderly, magically tactile.

I don't know what that is if it is not a love letter.

So we have established that Morton Fullerton was irresistible to men and women. And Edith Wharton was a woman who was not used to the attentions of sexually liberated men, so she fell for Morton quickly, and they began a sexual relationship. She was psyched, probably because *she'd never really had sex and/or never had satisfying sex before.*

In *The Love Diary* Wharton wrote:

I felt for the first time that indescribable current of communication flowing between myself & someone else—felt it, I mean uninterruptedly, securely, so that it penetrated every sense & every thought . . . & said to myself: "This must be what happy women feel."

I have drunk of the wine of life at last, I have known the thing best worth knowing, I have been warmed through and through, never to grow quite cold again till the end.

Of course, that could just mean the experience of being in love, but it seems telling that the following excerpt, which Wharton labeled an "unpublishable fragment," came after her affair:

As his hand stole higher, she felt the secret bud of her body swelling, yearning, quivering hotly to burst into bloom. Ah, here was his subtle forefinger pressing it, forcing its tight petals softly apart, and laying on their sensitive edges a circular touch so soft and yet so fiery that already lightnings of heat shot from that palpitating center all over her surrendered body, to the tips of her fingers and the ends of her loosened hair.

So, yeah, that was not just the experience of being in love; that was an orgasm. An orgasm she experienced with Morton, not with poor, alcoholic, sad Teddy.

You know, it's probably fair to feel bad for Teddy. Some biographers dismiss him as a pathetic layabout, but depression is terribly hard, and he just wasn't bold enough to make her secret bud burst hotly into bloom. Morton had a mustache and was turning on famous writers left and right, so he was different.

And this entire affair, all of this might have been a fine thing. We can all feel happy that fiery lightning shot all over Edith Wharton's body. Today we have whimsical romantic comedies starring Steve Carell with this very premise, where a lovable middle-aged virgin finally has sex. All could have ended well if she had gone off with Morton Fullerton or learned about her sexuality and then gone on to have many other happy relationships or initiated things with Teddy or just felt great about the whole affair.

But that is not the way it ended. Morton left her. There's some debate over how quickly he vanished. Historians used to think that their affair must have lasted for some years because of the sheer volume of letters Edith wrote him afterward. However, it's now thought that it might have lasted only a matter of weeks. By Edith's estimation, though, it lasted a few months.

In 1908, a year after their affair, she wrote him this fairly painful letter begging—*begging*—him to write back to her. Skip to the end if you can't bear the heartbreak.

Dear, won't you tell me the meaning of this silence? . . .

I re-read your letters the other day, & I will not believe that the man who wrote them did not feel them, & did not know enough of the woman to whom they were written to trust to her love & courage, rather than leave her to this aching uncertainty.

What has brought about such a change? Oh, no matter what it is—only tell me!

I could take my life up again courageously if I only understood; for whatever those months were to you, to me they were a great gift, a wonderful enrichment; & still I rejoice & give thanks for them! You woke me from a long lethargy, a dull acquiescence in conventional restrictions, a needless self-effacement. If I was awkward & inarticulate it was because, literally, all one side of me was asleep.

I remember, that night we went to the "Figlia di Iorio," that in the scene in the cave, where the Figlia sends him back to his mother (I forget all their names), & as he goes he turns & kisses her, & then she can't let him go—I remember you turned to me & said laughing: "That's something you don't know anything about."

Well! I did know, soon afterward; & if I still remained inexpressive, unwilling, "always drawing away," as you said, it was because I discovered in myself such possibilities of feeling on that side that I feared, if I let you love me too much, I might lose courage when the time came to go away!—Surely you saw this, & understood how I dreaded to be to you, even for an instant, the "donna non più giovane" who clings & encumbers—how, situated as I was, I thought I could best show my love by refraining—& abstaining? You saw it was all because I loved you?

And when you spoke of your uncertain future, your longing to break away & do the work you really like, didn't you see how my heart broke with the thought that, if I had been younger & prettier, everything might have been different—that we might have had together, at least for a short time, a life of exquisite collaborations—a life in which your gifts would have had full scope, & you would have been able to do the distinguished & beautiful things that you ought to do?—Now, I hope, your future has after all arranged itself happily, just as you despaired—but remember that those were my thoughts when you were calling me "conventional" . . .

Yes, dear, I loved you then, & I love you now, as you then wished me to; only I have learned that one must put all the happiness one can into each moment, & I will never again love you "sadly," since that displeases you.

You see I am once more assuming that you do care what I feel, in spite of this mystery! How can it be that the sympathy between two people like ourselves, so many-sided, so steeped in imagination, should end from one day to another like a mere "passade"—end by my passing, within a few weeks, utterly out of your memory? By all that I know you are, by all I am myself conscious of being, I declare that I am unable to believe it!

You told me once I should write better for this experience of loving. I felt it to be so, & I came home so fired by the desire that my work should please you! But this incomprehensible silence, the sense of your utter indifference to everything that concerns me, has stunned me. It has come so suddenly . . .

This is the last time I shall write you, dear, unless the strange spell is broken. And my last word is one of tenderness for the friend I love—for the lover I worshipped.

Goodbye, dear.

Oh, I don't want my letters back, dearest! I said that in my other letter only to make it easier for you if you were seeking a transition—

Do you suppose I care what becomes of them if you don't care?

Is it really to my dear friend—to Henry's friend—to "dearest Morton"—that I have written this?

If that letter is a bit too long, we can summarize it by saying:

- Why won't you write me?
- How could you say you loved me and never, never write me?
- We were happy.
- I love you.
- Oh my God, I love you.
- I'm never, ever going to talk to you again, you bastard.
- Sorry about how I angrily told you to return all my letters.
- *NOT THAT YOU CARE ANYWAY, SHITHEAD.*

Some people are inclined to see the tone that Edith Wharton took with Morton Fullerton as unnecessarily hyperbolic, considering what must have been the short duration of their relationship. This can be attributed to the impression of Wharton as an extremely dramatic woman, with her breakup letters being another of her eccentricities, like throwing the pages of her manuscripts on the floor as she wrote. And Wharton herself seemed baffled by her behavior, writing in *The Love Diary*: "I, who dominated life, stood aside from it so, how I am humbled, absorbed, without a shred of will or identity left! . . . How the personality I had moulded into such strong firm lines has crumbled to a pinch of ashes in this flame!"

I don't think her behavior is strange, though. Fullerton received a lot of letters from people complaining about how he'd abandoned them. (The author Charles Hamilton Aidé wrote to him saying, "I am now so accustomed to your silence that it was almost a shock to see your handwriting.") What Wharton in particular was going through, though, seems *extremely* painful. It hurts if someone you believe you love, whom you've slept with, won't have contact with you afterward. It does; I don't care what era we're in.

What's more, she had absolutely no one she could talk to, given that the belief that good women didn't discuss such matters was completely ingrained in her. It's likely the only person she felt she could talk about sex with was the person with whom she'd had sex, who was not returning her letters. I cannot imagine a much more frustrating situation, especially for someone who, as she said, usually had a very strong personality. Considering the circumstances, Wharton wasn't being melodramatic at all.

And the fact that it was short doesn't make it a less meaningful affair for her. It always seems unfair that the emotional impact of a relationship is judged by how long it lasted. Well-wishers always want to suggest that the amount of time you'll need to get over a relationship is exactly half of the time you were in that affair—or the entirety of the time or double or really just anything quantitative, as though in exactly eight months and three days you're going to feel great. A couple breaking up after years together might have found that the passion has faded and will be able to part amicably as friends; but if one of them were to tell someone their relationship had ended after many years, they would receive a great deal of sympathy. And you know, they could be just fine. And maybe someone who broke up after a matter of weeks or months could be devastated in ways and for reasons we can't understand. Like Edith Wharton.

In Sloane Crosley's *How Did You Get This Number*, she describes her reaction to being asked how long she had been with the man who broke her heart:

Your very happiness, you see, depends on how long. How long? How long? Say it fast enough and it sounds like the name of a dead emperor. Ho-lung of the Sad Sap dynasty. *My whole life, okay?* You have been silent for months and more than anything this is what you want to say: *We were dating my whole life. And I don't mean symbolically, as in I keep going for the same type of guy and this is a pattern that needs exploring. Like paisley. I mean, I was born, and he was born, and we*

*fell in love. And now I just have a memory that won't quit and
some choice words for Carly Simon.* Instead you just round up
by a month and leave it at that.

The length of time two people are together isn't the way to gauge
the pain of the ending. Feelings don't work that way.

After a few times when it seemed as if they might, maybe, get
back together (Morton finally replied to one of her letters, and they
met up a year later), Edith moved on in the way many of us do,
writing him:

> What you wish, apparently, is to take of my life the inmost &
> uttermost that a woman—a woman like me—can give, for
> an hour, now and then, when it suits you; & when the hour
> is over, to leave me out of your mind & out of your life as a
> man leaves the companion who has afforded him a transient
> distraction. I think I am worth more than that, or worth,
> perhaps I had better say, something quite different.

Yes, Edith. You *did* deserve more. Yes to all of this.

As for Morton, well, Edith didn't end up hating him. Her letters to him eventually took on a tone of camaraderie, even though
he never returned the letters she wrote him, as she asked him to.
And life didn't work out perfectly for him, either. Later, around
the time of Oscar Wilde's trial, he, seemingly worried that his homosexual tendencies might be discovered, distanced himself from
his old friends. During World War I he joined army intelligence
and later protested the Treaty of Versailles. He died in 1952. Maybe
he broke more hearts—or maybe not. He is largely remembered
today for his friendship with Henry James and his affair with
Edith Wharton.

Unlike the rest of the world, Edith never forgot him. During
the affair Morton had told her the relationship would influence her
writing. He was correct. Falling in love made her view the world

in a new way. Long before her affair, in 1893, she had written a short story called "The Fulness of Life," which reads:

> "You were married," said the Spirit, "yet you did not find the fulness of life in your marriage?"
>
> "Oh, dear, no," she replied, with an indulgent scorn, "my marriage was a very incomplete affair."
>
> "And yet you were fond of your husband?"
>
> "You have hit upon the exact word; I was fond of him, yes, just as I was fond of my grandmother, and the house that I was born in, and my old nurse. Oh, I was fond of him, and we were counted a very happy couple. But I have sometimes thought that a woman's nature is like a great house full of rooms: there is the hall, through which everyone passes in going in and out; the drawing room, where one receives formal visits; the sitting-room, where the members of the family come and go as they list; but beyond that, far beyond, are other rooms, the handles of whose doors perhaps are never turned; no one knows the way to them, no one knows whither they lead; and in the innermost room, the holy of holies, the soul sits alone and waits for a footstep that never comes."

The footstep came for Edith. It comes for most of us. And then it left again, and maybe that is worse than it never coming at all. Surely she must have wondered.

Edith divorced Teddy by 1913. She lived around Paris and on the Côte d'Azur until her death in 1937. She was ferociously productive, writing a novel nearly every year. In 1920 she published *The Age of Innocence*. Many consider it her finest novel, and some consider it maybe the finest novel *ever*. The book is about two people who love each other but can't be together because of the societal restrictions of their times. The central conflict is that the couple can't bring themselves to be impolite and offend other people who might be upset if they were together. At its core, *The Age of*

Innocence is about longing and desires that are never satisfyingly fulfilled. It's about sorrow and pain, but also the gratitude that can come from having had a very small taste of passionate happiness. It may be frustratingly insufficient, that bit of happiness, but if it cannot last, hopefully we can at least appreciate it while it is there. Maybe, too, as it did for Edith Wharton, the pain of loss can be turned into something beautiful.

In the end, it's probably only the inevitability of loss and the way we reconcile ourselves to it that unite everyone. So even if the average person can't sympathize with Edith Wharton's rarefied world, her novels endure because she was able to sympathize with us.

11. Oskar Kokoschka

Alma Mahler

One of my mother's favorite movies is *Lars and the Real Girl* (2007). It's about a man who falls in love with a life-size doll. People seem to go for this kind of plot, judging from the success of other movies like *Her* (2013), in which a man falls in love with an extremely intelligent computer operating system that has Scarlett Johansson's voice. I guess some people like these stories. Not me, though. I find them terrifying, in the same way that I find people who say they prefer animals to human beings terrifying. I always wonder what atrocities they experienced at the hands of people that seemingly caused them to want to give up interacting with actual humans.

I mean, it seems like that situation must have been terrible. Or maybe not. Maybe Alma Mahler just broke up with them, and they took it really, really badly.

The writer Brooke Donatone recently claimed that millennials are unable to process breakups properly and that, "a generation ago, my college peers and I would buy a pint of ice cream and down a shot of peach schnapps (or two) to process a breakup." Well,

Alma Mahler was hot to trot. Look at her. She is seducing you without even looking directly at you.

her generation clearly did not live in Vienna in 1915. Turn-of-the century Viennese were *the* most dramatic generation. Oskar Kokoschka, bad boy artist, definitely required more than two shots of peach schnapps to get over his breakup.

Kokoschka was a celebrated artist of the time. His early drawings were of children in terrifying, corpselike positions, which makes his art sound fairly disturbing. It wasn't all awkward, possibly deceased children, though. He painted a lot of Viennese notables, not all of whom looked grotesque. His *Bride of the Wind*, done in 1914, is particularly beautiful and pensive. It shows him lying next to Alma Mahler, his lover. He is awake, while her eyes are closed, and she is most likely not depicted as a corpse. Or . . . maybe she is. It might depend on how tumultuous their two-year relationship was at the time.

Long before meeting Kokoschka, Alma had a stormy and passionate disposition. She was married to the composer Gustav Mahler in 1902, when she was twenty-two; he was forty-one and the director of the Vienna Court Opera at the time. Alma probably married him in part because she had a great love of music and wanted to compose. Gustav wasn't into that. "How do you imagine both wife and husband as composers?" he wrote to her. "Do you have any idea how ridiculous and subsequently how much such

Oskar and Alma snuggling! Scandalous unmarried snuggling.
Bride of the Wind *(Oskar Kokoschka).*

an idiosyncratic rivalry must end up dragging us both down? How will it be if you happen to be just 'in the mood' but have to look after the house for me, or get me something I happen to need, if you are to look after the trivialities of life for me?"

Basically, Gustav thought it was entirely possible that one day he was going to want her to make him a sandwich, and she would be unable to do so. Because of her art. This all seems absurd by modern standards, but it was 1902. There weren't a lot of power couples. Alma, frustrated, wrote in her diary: "He thinks nothing at all of my art—and thinks a great deal of his own—and I think nothing of his art and a great deal of my own. That's how it is!"

Still, Alma gave up her own pursuits, married Mahler, and became a renowned society hostess. He told her no one would really be interested in her artistic talents if she weren't beautiful.

You can tell Gustav Mahler was smart because he had smart-person wire-frame glasses.

Unsurprisingly, she came to resent her husband's work, even more so after the death of one of their two young daughters, which she claimed he brought about by composing *Kindertotenlieder (Songs on the Death of Children)* in their home. She reported: "I sit down at the piano, dying to play, but musical notation no longer means anything to me. My eyes have forgotten how to read it. I have been firmly taken by the arm and led away from myself. And I long to return to where I was."

When Mahler went to a composing retreat, she began having an affair with Walter Gropius, the architect who founded the Bauhaus School. I do not really like the Bauhaus School. But if you started dating the founder of an architectural movement, I'd support you and think your choice was great, and I'd pretend to like his architectural movement when we were all hanging out because I'm a good friend. So Alma was an adulteress and creatively unfulfilled—but she was just killing it with her choice of men.

When Gustav found out about the affair, he decided maybe Alma should focus on her musical career after all. Hell, maybe he should help her with it. "If you want more freedom and respect from your spouse, definitely have an affair with someone awesome" isn't advice you'll find in *The Rules*—I believe the 1995 advice book mostly just advises against being fun—but it seems to have worked for Alma.

In 1910 she published five of her own songs, with the same company that handled her husband's work. And three movements of Gustav Mahler's incomplete Tenth Symphony are thought to have been inspired by his feelings about Alma's affair and the joy at their reconcilia-tion. So they were actually doing pretty well as a couple, and Alma

Walter Gropius, Alma's sad-eyed second husband.

would never be in this book at all if Gustav hadn't ruined every-thing by dying less than a year later.

Alone, Alma did not, as many people (especially Gropius) expected her to, return to the architect. She seemingly thought, *Well, I've already slept with the most famous musician of the period and the most famous architect, so now I'm going to go find the most famous artist. I will do this because I have a love potion that I will utilize to great effect.*

Not really. As far as I know, witchcraft plays no role in this story. It's not fair to say she was a sorceress just because every successful man in Vienna was in love with her, though love spells would obvi-ously go a long way toward explaining it. Either way, she had an absolutely spectacular track record in terms of dating the most famous men of the time. Her ability in this regard was almost, but not quite, to be matched by model, songwriter, and former first lady of France Carla Bruni. (I am not saying Carla Bruni is a witch. She is lovely and talented.)

So Alma starts dating Oskar Kokoschka. At this point, one might ask, "What kind of a man was Oskar Kokoschka? Was he a relatively normal man, aside from the drawings of dead children?"

Well, he was a fairly normal artist *as* a young man. OK, he hated his father. That antagonistic relationship is sometimes brought up as a factor in what was to come, but theirs was a fairly common story. Oskar's father didn't want Oskar to become an artist, but *Oskar had to paint.* He applied to and was accepted by Vienna's Kunstgewerbeschule in 1904. One hundred fifty-three people applied, and only three were accepted. That's a 2 percent acceptance rate. (Harvard University has a 6 percent acceptance rate, just for comparison.) So he got into that hard-to-get-into school and promptly began creating corpselike drawings of children. In 1907 he also attempted to write a children's book called *The Dreaming Youths* that went horribly awry in that it contained poems like:

> *Little red fish,*
> *little fish red*
> *with a triple-edged knife I'll cut you dead,*
> *then with my fingers I'll tear you in two,*
> *put an end to the silent circling you do.*

That freaked out mothers and fathers everywhere, though not everyone. The painter Gustav Klimt was a fan. (If you are not familiar with Gustav Klimt's work, let me direct you to any college dormitory in the world.)

By the time he graduated in 1909, Oskar had begun to develop a following, at least among the intelligentsia; the press claimed he was "the wildest beast of all" in his set. He took a job teaching nude painting classes at the School for Applied Arts, which, for a wild beast, seems responsible and reasonable. That's what he was doing when he met Alma.

Incidentally, Alma also had a brief dalliance with Klimt. Actually, just name any famous man from the period, and you can assume that Alma Mahler had an affair with him. If there was a man in Vienna at the time with whom Alma did not canoodle, he was not worth knowing. Given that, let's just say she and Oskar had friends in common.

They met at a dinner party given by Alma's stepfather, Carl Moll, in 1912. Alma asked Oskar to paint her portrait, which is the kind of request you make of portrait painters when you sit next to them at dinner. People aren't actually expected to follow up. Except this time, Oskar did, perhaps because he had asked to marry her approximately three hours after meeting her.

Kokoschka decided to paint Alma as the new Mona Lisa, with an elusive, mysterious, sensual smile. She doesn't look like that in Oskar's picture. She also doesn't look like herself either. She was definitely a dark brunette, and the woman in the painting is a strawberry blonde. Alma Mahler pointed out, not incorrectly, that in this painting she looks like Lucrezia Borgia.

But if that one painting seemed not to resemble her, no worries; Oskar would paint dozens more. He spent the next year painting her and sleeping with her and sometimes painting her while she was sleeping (see *Bride of the Wind*).

Recall that John Singer Sargent's painting of Madame X in 1884 caused a scandal because her gown's strap seemed to be slipping off her shoulder. Thirty years later an unmarried couple could be shown curled up in bed together clearly naked, and people

A painting of Alma Mahler that obviously looks nothing like her.

thought it was . . . well, much nicer than Kokoschka's other works. Also note that you couldn't show a similar scene in American movies until the 1960s. Vienna at the turn of the century was a liberated and bohemian place. Vienna then was what people from Iowa think Brooklyn is like today. (Brooklyn's not nearly that cool.)

So the problems in their relationship were not due to society's pressures. The relationship frayed largely due to Oskar's obsessive jealousy. At one point he wrote to Alma, "You may not slip away from me even for a moment; whether you are with me or not, your eyes must always be directed at me, wherever you might be." This seems like a hilarious thing to say to anyone—that they should just know where in general your body would be at any given time, and just keep staring in that direction until you returned.

Alma began to wonder if maybe she'd made a mistake. When she became pregnant with Oskar's child, she had an abortion. Alma was pragmatic about it (it bears repeating that Alma was way ahead of her time), but Oskar was devastated. He took a piece of bloody cloth from Alma at the hospital and proclaimed, "That is my only child, and will always be so." Poor Oskar. He carried that cloth with him for the rest of his life.

From there, things only got worse. That wasn't the only problem. Oskar's mother did not approve of the match—or more likely what the match seemed to be doing to her son, who was now carrying around a bloodied cloth as a kind of security blanket—and wrote to Alma, "If you see Oskar again, I'll shoot you dead." I think you must always accept that there might be some friction with your beloved's family, but when they are vocal about their desire to kill you, that is a good time to take a step back.

That wasn't the only instance where murderousness played a destructive role in their relationship. Alma wrote that Oskar's sexual tastes struck her as a bit . . . offbeat. He was into cross-dressing and liked to wear a bright red nightgown of Alma's around his studio, but that wasn't necessarily what bothered her. She claimed, "Oskar could only love with the most dreadful notions in his head. Since I refused to hit him during our hours of passion, he started to concoct the most horrific images of murder in his head and whisper them quietly to himself."

Alma ended their relationship and, perhaps in light of the death threats and jealousy, felt that Walter Gropius no longer looked so bad. She resumed their romance, while Oskar went off to fight in World War I, in part because Alma had called him a coward. During the war he received a wound to the head, which people have speculated may have impacted his behavior. However, also remember that he'd been known as something of an enfant terrible before then, so what follows doesn't seem completely related to having been wounded. Choose your own interpretation.

Hearing he had been wounded, Alma declined to visit. She noted, "The whole thing doesn't affect me very much. I don't really believe in his injuries. I just don't believe this person at all anymore." She cared much more for Gropius, and not only frantically visited him in Berlin when he was wounded, but married him in 1915. She was over Oskar. Really.

Oskar did not feel the same way. Upon returning to Vienna in 1918 after the war, he was haunted by memories of Alma Mahler. He couldn't stop thinking about her. All of his paintings resembled her (which is especially odd, given that they did not when they were actually a couple). During that year, he not only painted but also wrote the play *Orpheus und Eurydike*, based, unsurprisingly, on the Greek myth about lost love; it was later adapted into an opera in 1921. It seemed clear that Oskar needed some kind of rebound, lest he become one of those sad-eyed people who just keep talking about "the one who got away" for years and years afterward. Most people probably would have rebounded with an actual person, but Oskar was not most people.

He wrote to a doll maker on July 22, 1918, about a very special commission:

I am very curious to see how the stuffing works. On my drawing I have broadly indicated the flat areas, the incipient hollows and wrinkles that are important to me, will the skin— I am really extremely impatient to find out what that will be like and how its texture will vary according to the nature of the part of the body it belongs to—make the whole thing richer, tenderer, more human?

And then on August 20, "Please make it possible that my sense of touch will be able to take pleasure in those parts where the layers of fat and muscle suddenly give way to a sinuous covering of skin."

Oskar wanted to be able to have sex with a doll. But he wanted to court it first. This is the weirdest part, because if I decided to make a doll out of my ex, I'd be really private about it. As someone who stacked three pillows in a roughly human shape to lie alongside in bed after a breakup, I can see some sort of appeal to this. But my main priority would be making sure absolutely no one knew anything about the doll. Every single letter to the doll maker would be prefaced with "please tell no one about this, ever." But Oskar did not hide his beautiful new doll friend away. He began taking her out and showing her a nice time. They went on carriage

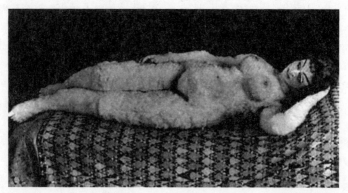

This doll was for sexing. Would you want to sex this doll?

rides. They went to the opera together. They met Oskar's friends at dinner parties. We don't know if she met Oskar's mother, but if so, his mother probably did not hate the doll nearly as much as she hated Alma. He even hired for the doll a special maid *with whom he began having sex*. In his memoirs, Oskar writes, "With a provocative casualness, she said that she simply wanted to take my mind off thoughts of death. Though her duty was only to act as lady's maid to my doll, the destined companion of my life, her sound common sense told her that I would be lacking warmth in my bed."

What's amazing to me is how *nice* everyone was about this special friend. Not just the maid but everyone. People speculated, very understandably, about whether or not Oskar was having sex with the doll. He probably was, because otherwise you don't really need to get so involved in the layers of fat and muscle. And if you just had a dinner party where one of your friends showed up escorting a life-size doll shaped like his ex, this is probably one of the first things you'd wonder about.

But while that was known to be *the* subject of speculation that season in Vienna, nobody actually turned the doll away. When Oskar showed up at parties with his life-size sex doll, people tried to treat it as if he'd brought any lady companion. I'm just going to reiterate that if you are in any way eccentric and possessed of a time machine, early-twentieth-century Vienna would be a great era for you. People were really accepting, so much so that Oskar was made a professor at the Dresden Academy of Fine Arts. And yes, the staff presumably knew about the doll. Everyone knew about the doll.

Sadly, while certainly accepted by everyone, the doll was never up to Oskar's exacting standards. In his last letter to the doll maker, he wrote,

The outer shell is a polar-bear pelt, suitable for a shaggy imitation bedside rug rather than the soft and pliable skin of a woman . . . the result is I cannot even dress the doll, which you knew was my intention, let alone array her in delicate and precious robes. Even attempting to pull on one stocking would be like asking a French dancing master to waltz with a polar bear.

In his defense the doll was kind of lumpy and did not look particularly like Alma Mahler nor Lucrezia Borgia nor the Mona Lisa nor anyone else. It looked like a very large stuffed doll. After all, it's hard to perfectly re-create muscle and flesh and sinew and all the anatomy he was banking on. You know, the lady stuff.

After letting all his friends get to know the doll, Oskar held a large party. It was a top-notch party. There was free-flowing champagne and wine and a lot of merriment. The doll was in its most beautiful dress for the party (helped by the maid who was sleeping with Oskar), and Oskar toasted everyone. As the night progressed, everyone became drunker and the evening more hilarious—until the gaiety ended abruptly when Oskar smashed a bottle of red wine over the doll's head and beheaded it in front of the guests.

Oskar claimed this had been his plan all along. In 1932 he wrote, "Finally, after I had drawn it and painted it over and over again, I decided to do away with it. It had managed to cure me completely of my Passion." Sometimes people just lie. They're embarrassed to admit that they publicly decapitated their life-size doll girlfriend, so they lie. And his "plan" did not cure Oskar of his lifetime obsession with Alma Mahler. On her seventieth birthday, Oskar, who was presumably carrying his bloody cloth at that very moment, asked to see her, claiming, "In *The Bride of the Wind* in Basel we are eternally united!" Alma declined to see him.

As for Alma, while married to Gropius, she had a child with Franz Werfel. He was an Austrian novelist known primarily for *The Song of Bernadette*. Alma had not yet slept with a really famous novelist. I suspect if her life had been longer, she would have eventually made her way to renowned puppeteers. She ultimately married Werfel and remained with him until his death in 1945. At that point, she moved to New York City, where she hung out with people like Leonard Bernstein until her own death in 1964 at age eighty-four.

Alma had, by all accounts, an absolutely spectacular time. She was truly the bride of the wind, and I don't think she ever really wanted to marry anyone, and likely wouldn't have if the convention hadn't demanded it. If you feel sympathy for Oskar, it's easy to write off Alma as a heartbreaker, but she was self-assured and honest about the fact that she didn't want to be married to him. Not everyone needs to get married. Some people just sleep with tons of cool people and have interesting lives.

Meanwhile, Oskar is often remembered as "mad Kokoschka," but I think the really important moments in his life took place after the end of his affair. You know that whole thing about Vienna being a wonderful and accepting place, where you could be a doll fetishist *and* a professor at a respectable university? That ended the moment the Nazis took power. Oskar's work was included in the Nazi Degenerate Art exhibition of 1937. In response, he painted *Self Portrait as a Degenerate Artist*.

Rather than the antic kind of motion you see in many of Oskar's paintings, in this one the subject seems rooted. It's painted in the garden of Olda Palkovská's grandparents. The daughter of a Prague art connoisseur, Olda was a great supporter of Oskar's work. She and Oskar moved to London together at her insistence shortly thereafter. She seemed to be a good influence. How do we know? Well, the content of Oskar's journals changed dramatically around this time. Instead of being utterly dominated by death, they suddenly focus on how Olda made excellent meals, "including rice pudding and Viennese chocolate cake." There was a movie theater near their house, and they apparently enjoyed going to the cinema. They especially liked Fred Astaire and Ginger Rogers movies.

The couple was married in an air-raid shelter during World War II and lived together happily until his death in 1980. Maybe this could be interpreted as some sort of version of Oskar come to epitomize John Hughes's notion that "when you grow up your heart dies." This relationship certainly doesn't seem as dramatic and passionate as his affair with Alma, but I think it was good. You could say that maybe this all felt like a consolation prize, since Oskar loved Alma so much, but that doesn't seem quite true. Certainly, there was always a corner of Oskar's heart that belonged to Alma and remembered that great wild passion. But that's not the kind of relationship that typically has staying power. Oskar needed someone to go to the movies with, and grow old with, and to make him chocolate desserts.

In my favorite picture of them, Oskar is reading a letter while Olda ties his tie for him. (His tie matches her dress.) Both of them look kind of preoccupied. You don't look at this picture, as you might with *Bride of the Wind*, and think, *What an amazing love scene*. But I do not think, in a million years, Oskar and Alma would ever have had that easy, couple-y familiarity. I would also point you to another wonderful picture in which Olda seems to be speaking animatedly and Oskar is watching her, smiling.

These are normal things. They are not as exciting as stormy, passionate affairs, but they are no less meaningful for being normal. Ultimately, I think instead of being swept up in sex doll–beheading fury, most people would choose sitting around and eating rice pudding with someone they love and who loves them in return.

12. Norman Mailer

Adele Morales Mailer

What do you look for in a party? Potato chips? Whiskey? Elegant place settings and conversation? The smell of tobacco? Ball gowns? Noël Coward, someplace? Cole Porter at a piano? No? None of that? How about attempted murder?

Because that's what you'd find at Norman Mailer and Adele Morales's parties.

This sounds a bit like a *Thin Man* comedy, and it shouldn't, because the party they threw in 1960 to announce Mailer's intention to run for mayor of New York City was the opposite of what you would expect from Nick and Nora Charles, *The Thin Man*'s convivial, bantering, unconventional couple. There were no ball gowns and certainly no Cole Porter. Probably tobacco, though, and definitely knives.

No one watches *Thin Man* movies anymore, do they? Maybe you would like to stop reading and watch one. If this book is being distributed in a very unconventional high school history class (*cool* teachers: buy this book for your students!), it would be a good day to let the kids watch any *Thin Man* movie so they know how to develop life skills like drinking martinis and engaging in sparkling repartee.

Regardless of whether you know who Nick and Nora are (though you must remember their dog, Asta, for any future crossword puzzles), you almost certainly know who Norman Mailer was. He wrote some of the great classics of the twentieth century, including *The Armies of the Night* and *The Executioner's Song,* he won two Pulitzers, and he was generally adored by the intelligentsia.

Norris Church Mailer, his sixth and last wife, was once asked, "Would you be with him if he weren't Norman Mailer?" The implication behind the question was that Norman was twenty-six years older than her beauteous self and she might not have been as intrigued were he not a world-famous, Pulitzer Prize–winning author.

Let me say, there is nothing wrong with a younger woman marrying an older man. However, there is definitely something wrong with anyone marrying Norman Mailer. How can the sentiment "Oh, Norman Mailer, he's so *desirable*" square with the fact that Norman Mailer *publicly stabbed his then wife in the heart and the back and left her on the floor to die?*

This is going to be a very different portrait of Norman Mailer than the ones from biographers who fawningly describe how big and blustering and full of life he was. And, man, there are a lot of those. Sometimes it seems as if men who are even a little bit intelligent and "literary" are able to get away with more than human beings should be allowed to get away with. If a female celebrity gets a weird tattoo or haircut or makes the ill-advised decision to turn forty-five, people decide she's crazy, which, as Tina Fey says, is how people describe women they don't want to sleep with anymore. If a male celebrity in the twentieth century tries to murder his wife, people decide he is . . . dashing. Somehow? Like a love pirate?

There is no question that Norman Mailer was a good writer. *The Executioner's Song* is compelling, even if it does seem to owe much to Truman Capote's *In Cold Blood* (of Capote, Mailer claimed, "He's not done anything memorable lately"). *The Armies of the Night* is a great book. Nevertheless, being a talented writer does not make him a good husband or a good person or, for that matter, a good candidate for mayor.

That did not, however, dissuade Mailer from seeking political office, perhaps because he was the kind of person who hailed police cars as though they were taxicabs. He really did do that, and I know what you are thinking. You are thinking, *That is charming. That is the kind of affectation someone might appreciate.* In actuality it was probably a sign that he thought he was a magical person who did not have to abide by any of the laws of human society. He's like an Ayn Rand character come to life.

He also beat up a sailor once because the sailor supposedly questioned the heterosexuality of his dog. Again, this incident has a theatrical element that makes it easy to overlook the fact that beating up a sailor for an imagined insult is a crappy thing to do.

Perhaps, though, the main reason he wasn't necessarily someone you would want as mayor was his 1957 work called *The White Negro: Superficial Reflections on the Hipster.* The book—and there really is no other way to interpret this—glorifies murder. In one passage Mailer comments on two hoodlums beating the elderly owner of *a candy store* to death: "One murders not only a weak, fifty-year-old man but an institution as well, one violates private property, one enters into a new relation with the police and introduces a dangerous element into one's life."

It's a candy store. A store where children buy candy after school (or before school or anytime). What's your favorite kind of candy? That's the kind that old man sold. The delicious kind. A candy store is not a thing that anyone sane feels needs overthrowing. I think even a team of bloodthirsty anarchists would probably leave the little old men who run candy shops alone until the end of their bloody revolution.

People have read that passage and have thought that on some

level Norman Mailer was perhaps joking, in the same way that they might believe Allen Ginsberg joined NAMBLA because he felt every organization needed a voice. It seems more likely, however, that when someone sincerely tells you they believe in something, they actually mean it. We just excuse some people or think they're making some sort of a grander point because we don't want to believe them. We want to like them so we don't have to stop enjoying the works they produce.

Which is, incidentally, unnecessary. Someone can be a terrible person and still produce great works of art that can be enjoyed by many people. Norman Mailer was the worst person, but that doesn't mean many of his books aren't wonderfully written.

Along these same violent lines—and again Mailer was quite serious about this—was his plan to reduce inner-city crime by hosting a series of jousting matches. A lot of his campaign at the time seems to have been about how the sword is a symbol of masculinity. Which, yeah, it is. A sword is a phallic symbol, but that doesn't make Mailer's obsession with swords any less unnerving or helpful in good governance.

He also kicked off the campaign with an open letter to Fidel Castro. In this critique of America, Mailer claimed that the country was not nearly violent enough. As he put it: "In Cuba, hatred runs over into the love of blood; in America, all too few blows are stuck to the flesh. We kill the spirit here, we are experts at that. We use psychic bullets and kill each other cell by cell."

You know some good platforms to base a mayoral campaign upon? Keeping the streets safe. Or plowed during the winter. Or free of garbage. Definitely making sure the streets are safe and plowed and clean. Improving schools is good, too. And if all of those programs seem too complicated, you can just lead with "I believe in this great city!" There are actually campaigns where no particular point is ever established at speaking events beyond "I *goddamn* LOVE this city," and those candidates seem to do quite well.

SWORDS: A SYMBOL OF MASCULINITY is not a campaign slogan. And jousts would be really hard to organize. They would actually be terrible for a city. I know they seem like fun because we think armor and fluttering pennants, but someone is going to break his neck and it's not going to be amusing. There is something to be said for bringing communities together by staging a first-rate spectacular—a large music festival or the Olympics, maybe—but jousts were expensive and deadly in the Middle Ages, and just not an event we ever need to bring back. Except at Medieval Times, and those are not the jousts that Norman Mailer was proposing.

Who am I kidding? I would totally go see jousts. It's the only sporting event I would ever attend. I would get a jousting jersey and wear it to every game. But I'm irresponsible and should never be mayor of anyplace.

Again, all of this was happening in the 1950s and '60s. It was not *that* long ago. None of what is about to happen in this chapter should have occurred or was in any way acceptable.

But, at this point, Norman Mailer running for mayor can be viewed as an interesting "statement." Surely it would be acceptable to attend a candidate's announcement party even if he seemed to be, *must* be joking. To assemble the crowd for his mayoral kick-off party, Norman called his good friend George Plimpton.

My favorite story about Plimpton: In 2003, he was running the *Paris Review* from his New York town house. During the citywide blackout, his staffers began to worry about whether there might be looting. Someone, in the tenor I suppose you can muster only if you are a mildly hysterical young man with a pocket square working at the *Paris Review,* exclaimed, "What if looters break into the building!?" And Plimpton looked over at the prodigious liquor supply and said in his plummy voice, "Well, boys, we'll hope to hell they bring ice!"

So you would *think* a lot of people would show up to any party hosted by George Plimpton. And many did, though not necessarily the people that Mailer wanted. He had been counting on a

Rockefeller. A Rockefeller did not appear because no one in that family would support killing old men who run candy stores. Practically no one but Anthony Burgess characters would support that kind of thing. Nelson Rockefeller was probably off cavorting with his wife, Happy, or collecting art or otherwise doing charitable works—any number of things that would be better than going to one of Norman's frankly scary parties.

The literary crowd went, of course. Allen Ginsberg attended and called Norman Podhoretz "a big dumb fuckhead." It's surprising that Podhoretz showed up at all since he had previously called Mailer's description of the glory of murder in *The White Negro* "one of the most morally gruesome ideas I have ever come across." Maybe he showed up to fight with people? Seems reasonable.

Mailer's second wife, Adele Morales, was of course there as well. Adele and Norman had met in 1951. Though only twenty-eight, he had already published *The Naked and the Dead*, which, along with his blustering man's man personality, had made him very famous. Norman must have seemed irresistible to twenty-six-year-old Adele. Early in life Adele once claimed, "I decided I was going to be that beautiful temptress who ate men alive, flossed her teeth and spit out the bones, wearing an endless supply of costumes by Frederick's of Hollywood." This statement weirdly leads many biographers to write that she was always wearing Frederick's of Hollywood fashions—an interesting choice for daywear.

Not pictured: Norman Mailer, because he doesn't deserve any more attention

Adele lived up to her childhood ambitions. In addition to being a promising painter, by the time

Adele met Norman she had been involved with the writer Jack Kerouac and had been married to the *Village Voice* newspaper cofounder Ed Fancher. She supposedly once threw a piggy bank at Ed, which is spuriously used as evidence that she was maybe the worst shrew who ever lived.

Basically, Adele was a lady who appreciated provocative underwear, and that is enough for me to be on her side. And besides, she seemed like a fine match for Mailer. They were both passionate eccentrics, who enjoyed arguing, affairs, and drama. Fine. All fine.

They were married in 1954 and lived in a walk-up on East Sixty-Fourth Street in Manhattan. They had a ton of orgies. As I think Tolstoy quipped, all orgies are essentially alike except for the one where Norman Mailer had a cigarette extinguished on his butt by a stockbroker. Supposedly, the night Adele gave birth to their first child, Norman left the hospital to sleep with his ex-sister-in-law. It all sounds intensely unpleasant, but I guess it worked for them for a while.

According to the *New York Times*, after Mailer sold the film rights to *The Naked and the Dead* in 1956 to Charles Laughton for $100,000 (equivalent to a billion dollars today if my math is correct), they moved to a farmhouse in Bridgewater, Connecticut. Adele claimed life there was very pleasant. "We had parties, I had a maid, a live-in nanny." She also had her own art studio. But the discreet charms of the bourgeoisie were not for Norman. He went on attempting to hail police cars as though they were taxis, and their drinking habits increased. They returned, probably very sensibly, to New York City, where there were yellow taxis, and where Norman could run for mayor.

Adele claimed the party to announce his candidacy started out OK. In the documentary *Norman Mailer: The American* she recounts, "I had a beautiful velvet dress on. I looked very good and the kids were put to bed, thank God they slept through that whole thing. And the guests began to come. We didn't have any stars, we had really bums."

Castro was probably busy that evening.

Norman Mailer, who was wearing a ruffled bullfighter shirt, grew drunker and drunker, so that midway through the evening he began challenging people, including George Plimpton, to step outside and start fighting. There were actually two fistfights, and the crowd became more full of riffraff until someone claimed, "I couldn't see the furniture for the Beats." Barney Rosset of Grove Press said, "I thought it was the most dangerous evening I'd ever spent in my life."

Adele claimed, "He was down in the street punching people. He didn't know who he was. He didn't know what his name was, he was so out of it. And it wasn't just booze, it was drugs." Apparently, after receiving a black eye, Norman returned to the party and began talking about how he was one of the greatest writers the world had ever known. At which point Adele replied that he was "no Dostoyevsky" and dared him to come at her, shouting, "Aja toro, aja, come on you little faggot, where's your cojones, did your ugly whore of a mistress cut them off, you son of a bitch."

So he grabbed a penknife and stabbed her in the heart. He also stabbed her in the back. One of the wounds was about three inches deep. It was certainly a most Dostoyevsky-like response. As Adele lay on the ground, bleeding, a man reached down to help her. Norman exclaimed, "Get away from her. Let the bitch die."

"That will be seared in my memory forever and ever," Adele later said.

Adele was taken to the apartment of the downstairs neighbor, who called a doctor but not the police. She was then rushed to the hospital—claiming repeatedly that she had slipped on some glass—while Norman was left to "sleep it off." The doctors were, of course, skeptical, since pieces of glass don't often pierce you in the heart and then reach around and stab you in the back. She ultimately admitted what had happened, claiming, "He didn't say anything. He just looked at me. He didn't say a word. He stabbed me."

However, she continued to contend that she and Norman "were perfectly happy together."

The next morning, Norman went to the hospital, where he discussed the probable dimensions of her wounds with Adele's surgeon. If this behavior seems irrational, Adele claimed that Norman also informed her that he'd stabbed her to save her from cancer. He then appeared with Mike Wallace on television, where he talked about how he was campaigning "on an Existentialist ticket" (a ticket that does not exist) and about how you couldn't solve inner-city crime by disarming people. "The knife to a juvenile delinquent is very meaningful. You see, it's his sword—his manhood." He explained his proposal for an annual gangland jousting tournament in Central Park. *TIME* magazine noted that when Wallace noticed the bruise on his cheekbone, Mailer grinned. "Yes." He chuckled. "I got into quite a scrape Saturday night."

Adele didn't press charges—often said at the behest of Norman and his friends, though she contended it was also for the well-being of their two daughters. However, there was the obvious question of whether Norman Mailer should be institutionalized. After a psychological assessment, the magistrate Reuben Levy determined, "Your recent history indicates that you cannot distinguish fiction from reality" and sent him to Bellevue for observation. The medical examiner claimed, "In my opinion Norman Mailer is having an acute paranoid breakdown with delusional thinking and is both homicidal and suicidal. His admission to a hospital is urgently advised."

(Have you seen the television series *Mad Men*? SPOILER AHEAD: read this paragraph only if you have watched the show. There is a character called Ginsberg who has been the token eccentric for a few seasons. He has done all manner of somewhat charming unconventional things like shouting, "I am become death!" And it's all kind of seen as witty high jinks until Ginsberg does something shocking and violent. *What?* you ask. He cuts off his nipple and gives it to his colleague Peggy in a box. At this moment it is immediately understood by all the other characters that Ginsberg is not a delightful eccentric. He is a very mentally unstable man. He is taken away to the hospital in a straitjacket, and the most stoic character on the show cries. It's really sad.)

You would think the threat of institutionalization would be some sort of rock-bottom moment for Mailer, but everybody decided it was no big deal. People wondered if his legal issues were bothering his writing, to which he claimed that he "didn't think about it, except on certain days."

No one much cared about how Adele was doing. *New York* magazine described Norman's treatment by his peers at the time: "Nearly everyone in the know, women included, immediately focused on Norman's fate rather than Adele's. He was One of Us—an intellectual, not a criminal—and after all, he was three sheets to the wind."

Let's play a game where we ask each other questions and raise our hands if the answer is yes. How many of us have gotten three-sheets-to-the-wind drunk at some point? Ah! I see hands! My hand is up! How many of us have successfully tried to stab our spouse not once but twice during that time? A few more than none? OK. Then, if we have done something so awful, how many of us have not expressed contrition? Ah. Almost no hands. A final question for the few with hands still raised: but you do at least privately feel bad about it, right?

As far as anyone can discern, Norman didn't. And he certainly did not want to be declared insane either. "It is important to me not to be sent automatically to some mental institution, because for the rest of my life my work will be considered as the work of a man with a disordered mind. My pride is that as a sane man I can explore areas of experience that other men are afraid of."

He ultimately pleaded guilty to an assault charge and was let go with a suspended sentence.

This leniency was likely in part due to his working productively on his next novel, *An American Dream*. This novel, interestingly, is about a former congressman who writes a book called *The Psychology of the Hangman* and then murders his estranged wife in a drunken rage and attempts to cover it up. Later, a black singer named Shago draws a knife on him (remember, the knife is a symbol of masculinity). He beats Shago, though! In the end the hero takes off, wins some money in Las Vegas, and decides to go to Guatemala. Mailer intended the novel to be a sequel to *An American Tragedy* forty years later, except one in which readers discover that murder is liberating, not tragic. In Dreiser's novel, when the main character murders his pregnant girlfriend he is executed, so that's less upbeat (and likely more realistic).

I have shouted impolite slurs at my exes, words I designed to really hurt their feelings, and felt bad about it for *years* afterward, so it's baffling to me how a guy could stab his spouse twice and not seem to care. But OK, I can accept that there are sociopaths among us. Still, even without the remorse of a Dostoyevsky character, you would think there would be practical consequences. But no. Within a week or two of the crime, Norman described the reception when he walked into a party as being "five degrees less warmth" than he was accustomed to. "Not fifteen degrees less—five."

The critic Irving Howe wrote, "Among uptown intellectuals there was this feeling of shock and dismay, and I don't remember anyone judging him. The feeling was that he'd been driven to this by compulsiveness, by madness. He was seen as a victim."

Some people do not have a clear understanding of the definition of a *victim*.

However, Norman did admit, "If any of us does something like that, people just don't look at them in quite the same way. I think ten years went by before people forgot about it."

Ten whole years. Gosh.

Mailer went on to marry a British heiress, Lady Jeanne Campbell, in 1963. The author Gore Vidal did seem mystified by this and asked her, presumably alluding to the incident with Adele, why

Lady Jeanne had married Norman. She replied, "Because I never slept with a Jew before." It seems that allure wasn't enough to keep them together because they divorced after one year.

And people went on thinking that Norman had been horribly, wrongly accused. Now, there are people who are actually wrongly accused of a crime. We know this from the Bob Dylan song "Hurricane," which is about the imprisonment of the boxer Rubin "Hurricane" Carter. There is no Norman Mailer folk song because he definitely stabbed his wife twice and expressed his wish that she should be left to die. Remarkably, people kept apologizing to Mailer for making the stabbing incident so *inconvenient* for him for the rest of his entire life.

Here is a transcript that may make your stomach turn a bit. Dick Cavett—lovable Dick Cavett, who, to his credit, once told Mailer to stick a piece of paper "where the moon don't shine"— wrote around the time of Norman's death in 2007, "It was at a vividly bad time in Norman Mailer's life that I met him, and a sort of water-treading time in mine. *He had stabbed his wife, and I was a copy boy at* TIME *magazine* [my emphasis]."

We should take a moment to consider whether these conditions are remotely on par, but I guess they were both going through some stuff. Cavett continues:

> TIME had just done a rough piece on Mailer, even publishing a ghastly, wild-eyed picture of him being arraigned at the station house. The magazine's treatment of Mailer had been much protested, as I knew from working at the copy desk and seeing the mail.
>
> One night after work, I emerged wearily from the subway on Central Park West. There was Mailer. My pulse accelerated. He was with three tough-looking guys and he, too, was tough-looking. But I was a big fan and I just had to be able to say to the guys back at the copy desk, "Guess who I met last night."

"Hi, Mr. Mailer. I'd just like to say hello. I can't very well apologize for *TIME* magazine, where I work, but . . ."

He came toward me, exuding the well-known Mailer menace, hands held pugilistically.

"What do they pay you there?" he said, still coming.

"Sixty dollars a week. I'm only a copy boy! But I'm a big fan of yours!"

I'm sure I overstated how bad I really felt about what they had "done" to him. He looked at me with a stare like a drill, said "Get a more respectable job," shook my hand and walked away.

That story is just bizarre. It makes absolutely no sense. Dick Cavett wrote that silly item about how he sniveled and apologized to Mailer for being involved with a news publication that ran an unflattering picture of a man who'd just stabbed his wife. You want a nice picture published? Don't stab your wife. Instead, plant flowers in Central Park. Help the elderly. Do nice stuff for your family. How on *earth* was Mailer able to come out of this looking good?

And it's not just Dick Cavett. Anthony Hayden-Guest, in his obituary of Mailer, kind of, sort of notes that the wife-stabbing thing was unfortunate, but finishes by saying, "It's a joy to know that he was, at the end, as unashamedly, refreshingly unapologetic as when I first met him all those years ago. He will be sorely missed."

Male writers, especially male writers during the 1960s, somehow tricked people into thinking that they were demigods because they had an understanding of *language*. Because they had a grasp on *words*, which (and I am stealing this from playwright Alan Bennett) they always pronounced in a way that sounded peculiarly Welsh. Language and words are important, and so are syllables and even punctuation (as we learned from Timothy Dexter). But being a very good writer is not going to cure Alzheimer's. If someone were going to cure Alzheimer's, maybe I could excuse them stabbing someone in the heart, but I just can't do it for the sake of some well-written stories.

The scandal did not dissuade Norman from his political ambitions because, well, why would it? No one held him accountable. He ran for mayor with the columnist Jimmy Breslin campaigning for city council president in 1969. His platform was that New York City should secede from the rest of the state. According to *The New York Times*, when asked how he would handle snow piling up and blocking traffic during the winter, he said he would melt it by urinating on it. Breslin was aghast at these antics, claiming, "I found out I was running with Ezra Pound." He was alluding not to the fact that Ezra Pound was a great writer but to the fact that Ezra Pound was supposedly schizophrenic.

A few months after stabbing Adele, Norman wrote a poem entitled "Rainy Afternoon with the Wife," which stated, "So long as you use a knife / there is some love left." And in 2007 he appeared at the New York Public Library with Günter Grass and talked about how stabbing his wife had, sadly, probably cost him the Nobel Prize—though he said, "sour and bitter as I could become I can't say I blame [the Nobel Prize committee]," which was . . . big of him. He received a standing ovation.

Admittedly, he regretted the effect "the trouble" had on his children. Moreover, he *was* always sorry about how the incident had stopped his letter to Castro from getting the attention he thought it deserved.

He had no trouble finding women either. There is a story, which may or may not be true, that after entertaining a lady in his bedroom, Mailer would point to a stack of his novels that he kept by his bedroom door and would conclude the session by saying, "I'd be happy to autograph a copy for you on your way out."

At this point you might wonder about this choice for a bad breakup story when Norman did OK and was invited to parties and had women flocking to him. This isn't a bad breakup for Norman Mailer. This is a bad breakup because society decided it was, more or less, essentially cool with something that was *not at all acceptable*. We are supposed to be better than this. We do not live in the sixteenth century. We should not accept violent behavior toward women from people even if they seem charismatic and interesting.

And of course, it was a very bad breakup for Adele, who faded into the background of the literary scene after the incident. She wrote that when she saw her former husband appearing on a TV program, she had a vivid fantasy of "happily scooping out those baby blues like spoonfuls of cantaloupe, slowly slitting his fat, bourbon-soaked liver," and "chopping off his hands, dooming him to write the great American novel with his feet." Unlike Norman, she didn't actually act on those violent impulses.

She descended into relative poverty. The *New York Times* described her as living in later life in a tenement apartment strewn with clutter, a homeless man urinating outside the building. She attributed her poverty to Norman Mailer. "I can't believe I've come to this, and a lot of that is due to him, because Mailer wouldn't help me," she noted in the article, seeming, at age eighty-two, fairly bewildered. "It's the apartment of a depressed person, where I just gave up."

Here is the point of this story: *being unapologetic is not necessarily a good thing*. Remember "Love means never having to say you're sorry"? Being a decent person means when you mess up, you say you are sorry and mean it.

I think—and this is a sense I get from personal interactions—that women ought to apologize for their behavior in relationships a lot less and men should apologize a lot more. When my female friends' relationships end, we go out for a drink, and about halfway through the evening their brains seem to be taken over by some sort of crazed-lunatic hallucinatory virus that causes them to say something like "The problem—the real reason I'm unlovable, basically—is that I can't bake. Because his ex was a really great baker, so I have to take cooking classes tomorrow, while simultaneously losing ten pounds because I am fat, fat, fat and disgusting."

Meanwhile, men often seem to externalize the blame for relationships ending. Whenever one of my male friends has a breakup, we go out for a drink, and at some point he will say, genuinely outraged, "How could she *do* that to me? I was so good to her!" And I could say, "Well, you refused to return her calls for a solid week, and there was that one time you slept with someone else. Remember that? And we agreed 'that didn't count'?" But I just nod and listen, because this venting is healing and could make him feel better. It is not the time to say, "Your reaction exemplifies something interesting to me about how people of different genders behave."

I will not hold my tongue here.

When you have stabbed your wife twice and told bystanders to leave her to die, you have to apologize. A lot. Society can work past it. There are a lot of terrible things that can lead good people to behave in awful ways. But it's the fact that Norman never seemed to view his conduct as anything other than an amusing footnote that kills me. *An apology was owed.*

This is not just a breakup between Norman and Adele. It is a breakup between anyone who has respect for a standard of decency (you and me, for instance) and the great men and women of letters who condone Norman Mailer and his behavior.

I'm resentful. Adele was bitter, too, claiming, "The poorer I get, and he prospers, it just sharpens my anger. The contrast is enormously painful." Which is how Norman dismissed Adele later, when she told her side of the story, as though she were a completely unreasonable harridan, who just wouldn't *be happy* for him.

Well, she and all of us can be bitter together.

As for the value of Norman Mailer's work, if you're one of the people who thinks that great literature excuses this kind of behavior? That all of this was somehow a fascinating literary act? Well, quite frankly, he was no Dostoyevsky.

13. Debbie Reynolds

Eddie Fisher

Elizabeth Taylor

Sometimes, breakups bring together the most unlikely people. That's certainly the case with the story of Debbie Reynolds and Eddie Fisher and Elizabeth Taylor.

You might think this chapter should really be about Elizabeth Taylor and Richard Burton, who married and divorced each other twice, but honestly I don't think they were ever really apart. Burton was writing Taylor love letters the day he died. How does anyone think that's a bad breakup? That's not even a breakup. It's one of those "the past isn't over, it isn't even past" stories.

Taylor and Burton were great together, at least in their own weird way; they were lusty alcoholics who yelled at each other (a lot) and then had sobbing, highly sexual reconciliations. I believe their divorces and subsequent marriages to others were just temporary and that if Burton had lived just one more year they would have reconciled. It worked for them. Dramatically! Insanely! But they fit so well together. Everything I read about Burton and Taylor makes me glad they found each other.

Elizabeth Taylor was absolutely terrible at being married. Though she was great at *getting* married. Her first wedding was in 1950, when she was eighteen years old, to the hotel heir Conrad "Nicky" Hilton Jr. And except for the nine years from 1982 to 1991, between her seventh and eighth marriages, she was always married. Supposedly she wed everyone she slept with, which makes her downright virginal. But that doesn't mean she was a great wife.

My favorite story of Elizabeth Taylor as a wife involves her second husband, Michael Wilding. One day he was working on a crossword puzzle, and she grabbed it out of his hands, screaming, "Go on, hit me! Why don't you!" Michael had no desire to hit her. He told her he didn't go in for feminine hysterics, and Elizabeth wailed, "Oh, God, if only you would! At least that would prove you are flesh and blood instead of a stuffed dummy." And then she tore up his newspaper and threw it into the fire.

Michael was just a nice man who liked puzzles and newspapers, like a lot of people. Suffice it to say, Elizabeth was a woman who liked drama in her relationships. Was such drama necessary? No—not for most people. But she and Richard Burton both wanted to live life on a very large scale with yachts and jewels and epic meltdowns. Can you imagine having that kind of personality and desire if you were paired with a mild-mannered crossword lover? It would be terrible. Burton once referred to Taylor as his "eternal one-night stand," which has a ring of truth to it, insofar as one-night stands are filled with passion, and also some amount of terror that the other person might turn out to be a serial killer. Everyone feels that way about one-night stands, right?

Elizabeth Taylor did not necessarily fit so well with most other people—boring people, crossword-puzzle lovers—but her third husband, producer Mike Todd, was not most people. (Todd has the distinction of being the only husband that Taylor didn't divorce. Much later in life she said that her only true loves had been Mike Todd, Richard Burton, and jewelry.) Todd was known as a cigar-chomping, blustering man's man and a "supercharged little P. T. Barnum." In sixth grade he was expelled for running a game of craps at the school. He never really gave up his gambling habit. Once, Elizabeth reached inside his pocket when they were about to play at a casino and remarked that "there must be ten thousand dollars in there!" He replied that it was vulgar to count money.

He dropped out of high school and worked in construction until he discovered the theater. In 1933 at the Century of Progress Exposition in Chicago, he produced a show called "The Flame Dance." In it, flames burned off the dancer's costume, leaving her naked onstage. Don't worry—she was wearing a flesh-colored asbestos body stocking and ran off unscathed. In 1939 he produced *The Hot Mikado* on Broadway; this version of Gilbert and Sullivan's *The Mikado* featured an African-American cast. He then branched out into cinema, and by 1957 he won the Academy Award for Best Picture for producing *Around the World in 80 Days*. He even showed aplomb when his shows weren't successful. After his play *The Naked Genius*—about a burlesque dancer who writes an autobiography—received terrible reviews in previews, he made its tagline GUARANTEED NOT TO WIN THE PULITZER PRIZE. He also treated his performers nicely; when his shows flopped, he was known to write notes taking all the blame himself.

Mike Todd sounds like an incredibly cool person, and he was a good fit for Elizabeth Taylor. She presumably thought so, too, because they married in 1957, soon after they met. He was forty-seven years old, and she was twenty-four.

It was great! They bought big jewels and flew around the world and drank and had a blast. They fought! Oh my God, they fought. Debbie Reynolds recalls them walloping each other and then kissing passionately. There's also a famous picture of Mike making a rude hand gesture in Elizabeth's direction, to which Elizabeth claimed "some people just can't tell a fight from a family frolic." Elizabeth really did *enjoy* fighting, and she said that she and Mike had "more fun fighting than most people do just making love."

And then he died. In a plane crash, on his plane named *The Lucky Liz*. His last words before boarding were "Ah, c'mon, it's a good, safe plane. I wouldn't let it crash. I'm taking along a picture of Elizabeth, and I wouldn't let anything happen to her." It was a coffin with wings. After the plane went down, Elizabeth sent her children to stay with Mike's best friend, Eddie Fisher, and his wife, Debbie Reynolds, for the next few days. She then made a statement to the press—its theme was "What will I do without Mike?"—and lovingly placed her $10,000 diamond wedding ring on Mike's hand in his casket.

And the answer to "What will I do without Mike?" was, apparently, run off with Eddie Fisher within a matter of weeks. Fisher was a singer who was supposed to be the next Frank Sinatra. He had become a star during his teenage years and by his midtwenties was on the NBC variety television show *Coke Time with Eddie Fisher.* (The title is a handy way to remember that Fisher developed a destructive addiction to cocaine later in life. This tidbit will be helpful . . . probably never, but let's imagine you are going to be quizzed on it. Just remember it, forever.) He was also quite famous at the time. In his memoir he writes, "I had more consecutive hit records than the Beatles or Elvis Presley, I had 65,000 fan clubs and the most widely broadcast program on television and radio."

Debbie Reynolds was an actress who starred as the plucky young ingenue in the 1952 film *Singin' in the Rain.* She was a former Girl Scout and came from a Catholic family who was devoutly religious. When she was young her mother sewed the letters *NN* into her sweaters, which stood for "no necker." She embodied ideal 1950s chaste, Christian womanhood. The postwar years were a puritanical time for everyone.

When Debbie married Eddie in 1955, she was twenty-three and he was twenty-seven. They gave the impression of being greatly in love and were considered a perfect match. Hedda Hopper, the gossip columnist, wrote, "Never have I seen a more patriotic match than these two clean-cut, clean-living youngsters. When I think of them, I see flags flying and hear bands playing." They did this bit when he was onstage, where he would introduce her as "my princess" and she would run up and call him "my handsome prince."

Do they ever sound insufferable. But Debbie Reynolds turns out to be really cool, so withhold judgment for a bit.

Both Debbie and Eddie were very close with Eliz-

I know they seem 100 percent insufferable, but, seriously, Debbie Reynolds is going to get supercool.

abeth Taylor and Mike Todd. Not only did Eddie serve as Mike's best man; Debbie was Elizabeth's bridesmaid. The two women had attended school together and had known each other since they were seventeen. Debbie even washed Elizabeth's hair the night before the wedding. (Question: is this a thing women are doing? I don't bathe with any of my friends or wash their hair, and when I see it on the TV show *Girls* I get confused about how seamlessly it happens because I would definitely see that as a sexual invitation. How do you think Debbie offered to wash Elizabeth's hair in a way that was not fraught with sexual overtones? Discuss.)

And Eddie worshipped Mike. Not only was Debbie and Eddie's son, Todd, named after Mike Todd, but the singer wanted everything Mike had. In *Elizabeth* by J. Randy Taraborrelli, a waiter at Chasen's restaurant in Hollywood recalls, "First the women would order, then Todd, then Fisher. Whatever Todd selected, Fisher would ask for exactly the same. If Todd said steak, medium rare, Eddie wanted steak, medium rare. If Todd wanted sole slightly underdone, Eddie wanted the same thing."

So it's not surprising that Fisher wanted Elizabeth, too.

Shortly after Mike's death, Eddie moved in with Elizabeth, supposedly to comfort her for a few days because that was what big, masculine pop singers did for their friends' widows, I guess. Debbie explained, "He went with my blessing. The four of us were so close, I was sure he could comfort her." He did. He comforted her by having sex with her. Debbie found out about the affair two weeks later when Fisher followed Taylor to a shoot. When Debbie called Elizabeth's suite, Eddie picked up the phone. Debbie could apparently hear Elizabeth saying, "Who is it, darling?" in the background.

At the time, people were seething and shouting, "How could Elizabeth Taylor break up Debbie and Eddie? It was a fine marriage, even if he *is* Jewish!" (Intermarriage of this sort was frowned on by seething people in the 1950s—just wanted to get you in the mind-set of that decade—and the couple had to marry in a Catholic church to appease their fans.) But they would have taken comfort in the fact that the darling marriage of Debbie Reynolds and Eddie Fisher was already on the rocks. Debbie had already tried to file for divorce twice, and according to her autobiography, America's favorite couple almost never had sex. In order to have her second child, Debbie claimed that she had to get Eddie drunk and wrote, "Sure that I was fertile, I was excited about getting my hands on Eddie . . . I soon got Eddie excited too, even though he was half asleep." That's . . . terrible. Clearly, their marriage wasn't great, and they weren't as happy as the magazines wanted them to seem.

When Debbie heard Eddie's voice on the phone, she just said, "Roll over and let me talk to Elizabeth." She wasn't terribly surprised. She later quipped, "Hell, my first husband left me for Elizabeth Taylor. At least that made sense." (Her second and third husbands bankrupted her.) Eddie meanwhile bitterly recounted, "I've often been asked what I learned from that marriage. That's simple: Don't marry Debbie Reynolds."

In his autobiography, Eddie Fisher also claims that Debbie Reynolds drove him to drink because she did not like him playing poker with his friends, and that he never loved her, not even the day he married her. Eddie Fisher comes off as a schmuck.

There are people who, to this day, absolutely love Debbie Reynolds because of how badly they felt she was treated by Eddie Fisher. Including me, kind of! I love her because she seems like a classy lady who very rarely spoke poorly of him in public and probably had a better sense of humor and perspective than she's often given credit for. Composer and comedian Oscar Levant once said that Debbie Reynolds was "about as wistful as an iron foundry," and that does not make her one bit less likable.

Shortly after their affair was discovered, Elizabeth Taylor announced to the press, "Eddie is not in love with Debbie and never has been . . . You can't break up a happy marriage. Debbie and Eddie's never has been." She was later quoted, by the gossip columnist Hedda Hopper, saying, "Mike is dead and I am alive." About Debbie, she told a friend, "She's in show business and didn't get to the top of her profession by being weak-kneed. She must have some inherent strength, like every other dame in this goddamned business."

Debbie retaliated, at the movie studio's insistence, appearing for newspaper reporters as a sad young mother with diaper pins affixed to her sweater. She allegedly asked, "What's a diaper pin?" before her publicist put them on her. And the public was aghast; one newspaper headline read, "Blood Thirsty Widow Liz Vampires Eddie." The actress Shirley MacLaine later recalled the scandal: "I remember the press defining Debbie with a kid on each hip, with bobby pins, pigtails and ribbons in her hair. Her husband had been stolen by the vixen—the scarlet lady. I remember thinking how could Eddie Fisher, this little guy, attract such extraordinary women?"

That was the question that suddenly started occurring to everyone.

The scandal never really hurt the careers of either Elizabeth Taylor or Debbie Reynolds. The latter was thought to be the sweetest woman in America. Seriously, just go watch her being so, so cute in *Singin' in the Rain*. I wish there was a way to embed videos in books so we could all watch it together. Not just a clip, the entire movie. Being a wronged wife—with diaper pins scattered all over her adorable cardigans!—enhanced her darling image. Really, the entire country just felt terrible about what had happened to Debbie. (She was that time's Jennifer Aniston, who, as we all know, lost her husband, Brad Pitt, to Angelina Jolie.) Eddie Fisher furiously said, "Debbie's whole life has been an act . . . When I left her for Elizabeth Taylor, she should have won an Academy Award for her portrayal of the wronged woman."

Elizabeth Taylor was known as a sultry seductress—so much so that after seeing *A Place in the Sun*, which was based on *An American Tragedy*, Hedda Hopper asked, "Elizabeth, where on earth did you ever learn how to make love like that?" Then Eddie added fuel by saying Elizabeth "had the face of an angel and the morals of a truck driver."

Around the same time she was in *Cat on a Hot Tin Roof*, in which, Anne Helen Petersen writes in *Scandals of Classic Hollywood*, "Taylor, playing Maggie 'The Cat,' spends the film wearing a skintight white slip, yelling at Hottest of All Hot Paul Newman, trying to convince him to have sex with her, and conniving to get the family fortune. It's a semi-hysterical perfor-

Interesting fact: Elizabeth Taylor never had a bad hair day in her entire life.

mance, but when Taylor yells, 'Maggie the cat is alive! I'M ALIVE!' it's hard to fault her for using that aliveness on Eddie Fisher."

The only person the affair didn't help was Eddie Fisher. He received about one thousand pieces of hate mail a week and rapidly went from seeming like someone who was on a par with Sinatra to someone who seemed completely, if understandably, in thrall to Elizabeth Taylor. He tried to transition into movies, starring opposite Taylor in *Butterfield 8*, but while he had seemed youthful and cool on television and in concerts, on film he just looked sulky. Everyone seemed to come to the conclusion that maybe they'd never liked Eddie Fisher after all.

The relationship went irredeemably south when Elizabeth Taylor met Richard Burton on the set of *Cleopatra* (1963). By that point there was already a joke circulating that Fisher came third in Taylor's entourage, after her hairdresser, Alexandre de Paris, and her agent, Kurt Frings. And Burton began referring to Fisher as Elizabeth Taylor's "busboy."

Burton was the opposite of Fisher in many ways. The Welsh actor was known mostly for his stage work when he began filming as Antony opposite Taylor's Cleopatra. Despite being married, it was said that he had seduced every single leading lady he had performed with, with the exception of Julie Andrews. I like to think that this is because Julie Andrews is someone who would never sleep with a married man, but it may be that they just didn't get along. In 1967 he griped about how she rose to fame on the strength of "The Horrible Sound of Music" (which is, admittedly, as NPR pointed out, a film where a man sings "you look happy to meet me" to a plant) and that "two years ago she was the darling of America and now she's hardly ever talked about." The only people Richard Burton seemed to really like were himself, Elizabeth Taylor, and, on rare occasions, Humphrey Bogart and Greta Garbo. He was a horrible curmudgeon and pretty crazy. Once at a dinner party, he picked up the Duchess of Windsor and just started swinging her around as though she were a doll. This is both a tribute to the duchess's svelte frame and the fact that Burton was maybe not the ideal gentlemanly dinner guest. He was also an alcoholic and pockmarked all over and would never have made it as a teen idol.

I am irrationally attracted to him. Are you? He would be a fun person to sit with at a stuffy dinner party.

Elizabeth Taylor was not charmed, at least not at first. Perhaps that's because Burton called her fat almost as soon as he met her. For the rest of his life, Burton would have to claim that he'd meant it *as an absurd joke, absurd because Elizabeth was not fat* when it was inevitably brought up by the media every single time he and Elizabeth had a fight.

Eddie Fisher and Elizabeth Taylor were, for a very brief time, united in their mutual antipathy toward Richard Burton. Fisher wrote, "I thought he was an arrogant slob. Elizabeth and I . . . compared him to the great producer of MGM musicals, Arthur Freed, about whom it was said that he could grow orchids under his fingernails." It's worth noting that Eddie was not actually a bad husband to Elizabeth. He nursed her through recovery from a surgical procedure—during which time she won an Oscar for *Butterfield 8* (1960), which famously caused Shirley MacLaine, who had starred in *The Apartment* (1960), to declare, "I lost to a tracheotomy." Debbie Reynolds laughed and said, "Hell, even *I* voted for her!"

The problems with Eddie and Elizabeth's relationship may have lain partly in the fact that, in sharp contrast to his treatment of Debbie, Eddie seemed almost *too* obliging to Elizabeth's needs. Honestly, in the face of Elizabeth Taylor's beauty almost all men turned into agreeable puppy dogs. "Elizabeth was not used to assertive men," said her makeup artist, Ron Berkeley. "Oh they might put on an act for a while, but they nearly all ended up showing love by deference, paying tribute to her beauty. Only one other man had taken her by sheer force of personality. When she met Richard Burton, it must have seemed she had rediscovered Mike Todd."

Eddie was also trying to curb Elizabeth's drinking by not allow-ing the staff at their villa to bring her more than five drinks a day. When Burton came over, he surreptitiously refilled her glass, and she adored him almost instantly. She and Burton began sleeping together in his dressing room on the set of *Cleopatra* shortly afterward; there he told her dirty stories that she found hilarious. He also wrote her some really steamy letters about "the half hostile look in your eyes when you're deep in the rut with your little Welsh stallion." The two went out on the town together, which caused Eddie to issue furious denials to newspapers that Elizabeth and Richard were having an affair. And then in 1962, at a party at Eddie and Elizabeth's villa, Richard turned to her and said, "Elizabeth, who do you love? Who do you love?" She declared, "You."

Let us pause to let bells peal and lovebirds sing. They were both kind of assholes, but they were meant to be.

Moving on.

Eddie is pitiable, here. Fisher fled, and when he called the villa later, Burton picked up the phone. Unlike Debbie, Eddie was surprised and exclaimed, "What the hell are you doing there? What are you doing in my house?"

"What do you think I'm doing?" Richard replied. "I'm fucking your wife."

Look, Richard Burton and Elizabeth Taylor *sort of* tried to stay away from each other. There was enormous pressure for them to end the affair, considering that Elizabeth had just finished breaking up one marriage, and no one thought it would be great for her to end another. And Richard didn't want to leave his wife. But all of that changed when Elizabeth took an overdose of sleeping pills.

Good God, do not do this. It will not make anyone love you.

It was impossible for Burton or Taylor to continue concealing the affair. The *Los Angeles Examiner* declared, "Row Over Actor Ends Liz, Eddie Marriage." Fisher later wrote that he sensed the marriage was nearing an end: "I knew it before she did. Elizabeth desperately needed excitement, and our relationship had settled into a marriage. Comfort wasn't enough for her. She was addicted to drama, to the fights and making up, to breaking down doors."

Poor Eddie became terribly depressed and overdosed on vodka and amphetamines. He had to call a press conference immediately after being let out of the hospital to prove to reporters that he hadn't gone completely mad over the loss of Elizabeth. Although, judging from his future behavior, he wasn't doing all that well.

Decades later, the breaking point in the marriage was recounted in *Vanity Fair*:

> [Elizabeth Taylor] remembered waking up one night in the villa she shared with then husband Eddie Fisher, after news of her affair with Burton broke. A friend of Fisher's had given him a gun and Taylor said she woke to find him watching her, pointing the gun at her head. "Don't worry, Elizabeth," she claims she heard him say. "I'm not going to kill you. You're too beautiful." That's when she fled, gathering up her children and taking them to the rented villa of her confidant and personal secretary, Dick Hanley. (When asked about Elizabeth's account of the incident, the 81-year-old Fisher simply laughed and said, "The past is one son of a bitch.")

In good marriages the whole "not menacing someone in bed at gunpoint" thing is just assumed. It has nothing to do with whether your complexion is looking really rosy that day or how violet your eyes may be. Eddie Fisher kind of proves himself to be an unexpected monster throughout these proceedings. A pitiable, increasingly drug-addled asshole, but a monster nonetheless.

An absolutely nightmarish divorce ensued. Untangling the couple's assets was difficult enough, but it became doubly bitter when Fisher attempted to revive his nightclub act. He started performing a number called "Arrivederci, Roma," which uncomfortably reminded every single person in the world of what had happened between him, Elizabeth, and Richard in Rome. The song contained lyrics like:

> *Save the wedding bells for my returning*
> *Keep my lover's arms outstretched and yearning*
> *Please be sure the flame of love keeps burning*
> *In her heart*

That song, alone, might have been a rather odd choice (and one that was obviously meant as a joke, just not a particularly funny one), but what was really upsetting to everyone with any shred of good taste was that he incorporated a song called "Cleo, the Nympho of the Nile," during which the singer Juliet Prowse slithered onstage and expressed her erotic desires. Elizabeth was absolutely infuriated and tried to bar Fisher from performing it, but it backfired on him more than anyone. He had gone from seeming like a cool pop star to an obsequious cuckold to now a bitter, petty ex.

"Have you ever noticed that he is the only ex-husband I don't talk about?" Elizabeth later said. Probably because of that time *he pointed a gun at her head*. From then on Fisher has been remembered not for his own accomplishments but for being Elizabeth Taylor's fourth husband. Which is a shame, because "Oh! My Pa-Pa" (which reached number one on the U.S. charts in 1953) was probably a good song. I mean, we'll never know unless we Google it, which no one is going to do.

Taylor and Burton married shortly thereafter and tried to put the whole Eddie Fisher thing behind them. Richard later wrote that Elizabeth was "ashamed of herself for having married such an obvious fool. He really is beneath contempt—a gruesome little man and smug as a boot."

Eddie Fisher's career slowed nearly to a halt, possibly because of his now-serious drug use. In his 1999 autobiography, *Been There, Done That,* he wrote:

By the time I was thirty-three years old I'd been married to America's sweetheart and America's femme fatale, and both marriages had ended in scandal; I'd been one of the most popular singers in America and had given up my career for love; I had fathered two children and adopted two children and rarely saw any of them; I was addicted to methamphetamines, and I couldn't sleep at night without a huge dose of Librium. And from all this I had learned one very important lesson: There were no rules for me. I could get away with anything so long as that sound came out of my throat.

No, that was not true. It may have been true for some people—for instance, you can still name a lot of hits by Elvis Presley, even though he came to a pretty bad end. You cannot name an Eddie Fisher song.

Try to hum "Oh! My Pa-Pa." I dare you. (You are making that melody up! You are just humming and bouncing up and down as though you know how to polka.)

By the 1980s he acknowledged, "It was either quit cocaine or quit performing. So much for my career."

So Eddie Fisher was history, but, in a gratifying turn, the women involved in this story moved on with their lives really well. Sometimes disastrous breakups bring people together. I don't just mean Richard Burton and Elizabeth Taylor; I also mean Elizabeth and Debbie Reynolds. Not at once, obviously, but later.

Years after their love triangle imploded, Debbie and Elizabeth met again on a boat. Debbie said, "We got on the same boat to go to Europe—the *Queen Elizabeth*. I sent a note to her and she sent a note to me in passing, and then we had dinner together. She was married to Richard Burton by then. I had been remarried at that point. And we just said, 'Let's call it a day.' And we got smashed. And we had a great evening, and stayed friends since then."

A lot of their friendship seemed based on their common antipathy toward Eddie Fisher. Wow, did they both dislike him. In 2001 they made a movie together called *These Old Broads*, written by Debbie's daughter, Carrie Fisher. Many of the jokes in the film revolve around a character called "Freddie Hunter," who years earlier tore apart the characters played by Elizabeth and Debbie. And when Elizabeth passed away in 2011, Carrie Fisher remarked, "If my father had to divorce my mother for anyone—I'm so grateful that it was Elizabeth."

I suppose you could say that Elizabeth and Debbie were destined to reconcile. After all, they were once close enough to wash each other's hair. And there is something about enduring a breakup with the same man that has the potential to turn women into war buddies.

On September 11, 2001, Debbie Reynolds was staying at the Pierre hotel in New York City. When the news broke about the attacks on the twin towers of the World Trade Center, she received a call from Elizabeth Taylor saying, "Debbie, are you frightened at all?" She replied that she was, because she was there by herself, and it was one of the first times she had ever traveled alone. And Elizabeth said, "Why don't you come over?" They spent the next three days together in Elizabeth's hotel room at the St. Regis, before they found a flight back to Los Angeles. Later Debbie was asked whether she still harbored resentment about the split. She claimed, "These things happen. Best friends should stick together."

I'm pleased that it worked out for those two old broads.

In her will, Elizabeth Taylor left Debbie Reynolds some of her most precious pieces of jewelry. Debbie Reynolds had joked, "Take the husband, leave the jewelry." Given that Elizabeth always claimed that she had only three loves in her life, it's nice to know that Debbie received one of them in the end.

Epilogue

*Y*ou have just read thirteen stories, spanning thousands of years of history, about the spectacular breakups of some very notable people. They searched for love and lost it, and in those breakups displayed behavior that you might only dream of in your most vivid nightmares. Unless you are very bold (or unhinged) in your breakup conduct. In which case, when you wage war against your ex, remember moisturizer to prevent windburn. And if you build a life-size doll, please send photos.

Did these rulers and philosophers, artists and writers, and one (very fortunate) businessman learn from these breakups? Some may have, and for them I am pleased, but we still feel for those who likely didn't, like Anne Boleyn, whose only epiphany may well have been that marrying Henry VIII was, in retrospect, a very poor idea. Not every relationship that ends imparts a life lesson that makes us better people. You don't always "learn something." Relationships aren't fortune cookies; they don't always contain a cool little message for you to carry around after they're done.

Nor do they necessarily leave us better—more confident, more skilled, more interesting—than we were before the relationship ran its course. Occasionally they do, as with Eleanor of Aquitaine and Edith Wharton. But that may take a lot of gumption or patience or very deep inner resources—and more than a little luck.

Still, love does move us in profound and real ways. It may not always take us to a better place, but the act of loving forces our lives into motion. Giving in to love means that your life will change. Maybe that just means that you suddenly have someone to share books with in bed. Or maybe it means you follow your lover to Bali, or you quit your rock band and become an accountant and have four children. Loving and forming relationships with people rarely allows us to keep our lives exactly the same. Loving is powerful because it is the opposite of stasis.

Yes, the saying "a ship in a harbor is safe, but that is not what ships are for" is a cliché, but it is a beautiful one. Our souls are like ships, waiting to be moved by an unstoppable force and launched into dark and unknown waters. What brave little souls we are. I hope that love takes us someplace wonderful—that we are all as fortunate as Timothy Dexter's confoundingly lucky ships—but we can't know that it will. That's what makes the act of loving so courageous. Some of the people in this book were good, and some were horrible, but all of them allowed their lives to be set into motion. When people say that they're "just hanging out" or "keeping things real casual," I always think, *Oh, you coward.* Of course, they're right to be afraid because, as we have seen, love and loss can make people go insane. Still, if you don't love, you condemn yourself to a safe but static life. And that's not enough. On their deathbed, no one says, "Wow, what I regret most is making so many emotional connections with people." We want to be moved. We crave it.

And love doesn't always end badly. Happy endings happen *all the time.* In a world where we can divorce anytime at all (without having to prove your husband was incestuous, the way you might if you were a woman in Victorian England), over 50 percent of people who marry stay with that person *forever*. That's amazing. I go to my parents' house and smell my mother's cooking and see my father watching football, and I marvel that there was ever a time when these people did not know each other. These everyday miracles like family are taken so much for granted that we forget that there was a time when our parents or grandparents or happily coupled friends had to be brave.

I don't like all the people in this book, but at least they tried to love. Many of them were lunatics or evil or very poor judges of character, but they were brave. If you have had your heart broken because you tried to love, well, then you're brave, too. You rejected keeping your life the way it was. You abandoned the comfort of stillness. You set off into uncharted territory. That's very worthy of respect.

If the love ended badly, that's OK. We live longer now than most of the people in this book, and you're likely not in danger of being beheaded anytime soon. You will have more chances. The world is full of many openhearted people and many opportunities. That may be impossible to think about when you're heartbroken, because heartbreak *is* awful, but if you took a chance on love in the first place, you are a courageous soul. There will be a time when you go out and are brave again.

Until then, take comfort. And, as Caroline Lamb wrote, "Peace to the broken hearts."

Sources

1. Nero and Poppaea

Andrews, Evan. "10 Things You May Not Know About Roman Gladiators." *History Lists,* March 4, 2014. http://www.history.com/news/history-lists/10-things-you-may-not-know-about-roman-gladiators.

Champlin, Edward. *Nero.* Boston: Harvard University Press, 2009. Google e-book. http://books.google.com/books?id=30Wa-l9B5IoC&printsec=frontcover&source=gbs_ge_summary_r&cad=0#v=onepage&q&f=false.

Dio, Cassius. *Roman History.* Reproduced by Bill Thayer. Chicago: University of Chicago Press, 2011. Originally published in vol. 8 of the Loeb Classical Library edition, 1925. http://penelope.uchicago.edu/Thayer/E/Roman/Texts/Cassius_Dio/62*.html.

Goldsmith, Sara. "The Rise of the Fork." *Slate,* June 20, 2012. http://www.slate.com/articles/arts/design/2012/06/the_history_of_the_fork_when_we_started_using_forks_and_how_their_design_changed_over_time.html.

Hopkins, Keith. "Murderous Games: Gladiatorial Contests in Ancient Rome." *History Today* 33, no. 6 (June 1983). http://www.historytoday.com/keith-hopkins/murderous-games-gladiatorial-contests-ancient-rome.

Kiefer, Otto. *Sexual Life in Ancient Rome.* New York: Marboro Books, 1990.

Martial. *Epigrams.* Translated by Walter C. A. Ker. London: William Heinemann, 1919.

Plutarch. *Life of Galba and Otho.* Translated by Douglas Little and Christopher Ehrhardt. London: Bristol Classical Press, 1994.

Raia, Ann R., and Judith Lynn Sebesta. "Pseudo Seneca—Octavia—Lines 100–114." *Instruction Companion Worlds*. College of New Rochelle, December 2010. http://www2.cnr.edu/home/araia/seneca_octavia.html.

Seneca the Younger. *Octavia*. Translated by Watson Bradshaw. London: Swan Sonnenschein, 1902.

Suetonius. *The Lives of the Twelve Caesars*. Translated by Alexander Thomson, M.D. Project Gutenberg e-book, 2006. http://www.gutenberg.org/files/6400/6400-h/6400-h.htm.

Tacitus. *Annals (The Annals)*. Translated by A. J. Woodman. Indianapolis: Hackett, 2004.

———. *Historiae (The Histories)*. Translated by William Hamilton Fyfe. Oxford: Clarendon Press, 1912.

Vagi, David L. *Coinage and History of the Roman Empire*. Vol. 1, *History*. Chicago: Fitzroy Dearborn, 2001. Google e-book. http://books.google.com/books?id=WzOGycVVQLEC.

Wright, Clifford A. "History of the Fork." CliffordAWright.com. http://www.cliffordawright.com/caw/food/entries/display.php/topic_id/8/id/108/.

2. Eleanor of Aquitaine and Henry II

Barker, Hugh. "Rosamund's Bower—a Hedge Maze at Woodstock." *Hedge Britannia*, June 8, 2011. http://hedgebritannia.wordpress.com/2011/06/08/rosamonds-bower-a-hedge-maze-at-woodstock/.

Cavendish, Richard. "Eleanor of Aquitaine Marries Henry of Anjou." *History Today* 52, no. 5 (May 2002). http://www.historytoday.com/richard-cavendish/eleanor-aquitaine-marries-henry-anjou.

Chadwick, Elizabeth. *The Summer Queen*. London: Sphere, 2013.

———. *The Winter Crown*. London: Sphere, 2014.

Dickens, Charles. *A Child's History of England*. London: Chapman and Hall, 1880.

Evan, Michael R. *Inventing Eleanor: The Medieval and Post-Medieval Image of Eleanor of Aquitaine*. London: Bloomsbury Academic, 2014.

Matthews, W. H. "The Bower of 'Fair Rosamund.'" Internet Sacred Text Archive. http://www.sacred-texts.com/etc/ml/ml22.htm.

———. *Mazes and Labyrinths*. London: Longmans, Green, 1922. Internet Sacred Text Archive, June 2005. http://www.sacred-texts.com/etc/ml/ml22.htm.

Meade, Marion. *Eleanor of Aquitaine, a Biography*. London: Dutton, 1977.

Reese, Lyn. "Eleanor of Aquitaine—After Returning from the Crusades." *Women in World History Curriculum*, 1996–2013. http://www.womeninworldhistory.com/EofAreturns.html.

Schama, Simon. *A History of Britain*. London: Random House, 2012.

Seward, Desmond. *Eleanor of Aquitaine: The Mother Queen of the Middle Ages*. New York: Pegasus Books, 2014.

Somerville, J. P. "Henry II and Common Law." Lecture notes, Course 123:

English History to 1688. University of Wisconsin, Madison. Accessed Fall 2014. http://faculty.history.wisc.edu/sommerville/123/123%20104%20 Common%20Law.htm.

Vincent, Nicholas. "The Legacy of Henry Plantagenet." *History Today* 54, no. 12 (December 2004). http://www.historytoday.com/nicholas-vincent/legacy -henry-plantagenet.

Warren, W. L. *Henry II*. Berkeley: University of California Press, 1973.

"The Woman in the Bower—A Murder at Woodstock: Fair Rosamund vs Eleanor of Aquitaine." *Sexual Fables*. http://www.sexualfables.com/the_Woman _in_the_bower.php.

3. Lucrezia Borgia and Giovanni Sforza

Aiuto, Russell. "Killers from History—the Borgias." crimelibrary.com. http:// www.crimelibrary.com/serial_killers/history/borgias/4.html.

Black, Annetta, contributor. "Lucrezia Borgia's Love Letters." *Atlas Obscura*. http://www.atlasobscura.com/places/lucrezia-borgias-love-letters.

Bradford, Sarah. *Cesare Borgia: His Life and Times*. London: Phoenix, 2001.

———. *Lucrezia Borgia: Life, Love, and Death in Renaissance Italy*. New York: Penguin, 2004.

Dillon, Charles. *Those Naughty Popes and Their Children*. Lincoln, Neb.: iUniverse, 2004. http://books.google.com/books?id=6Mdz5ogDz0EC&pg=PA140 &lpg=PA140&dq=Giovanni+Sforza+spying&source=bl&ots =zy6mOyLZwA&sig=lTqNIgU2cXqweKZsNzW0LT1MFXg&hl=en&sa=X &ei=GtUTVM-PEbaBsQTFhoLQBg&ved=0CB0Q6AEwADgK#v=onepage &q=Giovanni%20Sforza%20spying&f=false.

Gates, Dr. Larry E. Jr., ed. "The Italian Renaissance." Study notes, Advanced Placement European History. HistoryDoctor.net. http://www.historydoctor .net/Advanced%20Placement%20European%20History/Notes/italian _renaissance.htm.

Gregorovius, Ferdinand. *Lucretia Borgia: According to Original Documents and Correspondence of Her Day*. Translated by John Leslie Garner. Project Gutenberg e-book, 2007. http://www.gutenberg.org/files/20804/20804-h/20804-h .html.

Holcombe, James Philemon. *Literature in Letters: Or, Manners, Art, Criticism, Biography, History, and Morals Illustrated in the Correspondence of Eminent Persons*. New York: D. Appleton, 1866. Google e-book. http://books.google .com/books?id=_liLsTox_REC.

Jensen, Vickie, ed. *Women Criminals: An Encyclopedia of People and Issues*. Vol. 1. Santa Barbara, Calif.: ABC-CLIO, LLC, 2012.

Lewis, Jane Johnson. "Vannozza dei Cattanei, Mother of Borgias." about.com /education. http://womenshistory.about.com/od/medievalitalianwomen/a /Vannoza-dei-Cattanei.htm.

Lucas, Emma. *Lucrezia Borgia*. NewWord City, 2014. e-book. http://www.amazon .com/Lucrezia-Borgia-Emma-Lucas-ebook/dp/B00ON2WGE4.

"Lucrezia Borgia, Duchess of Ferrara Facts." *YourDictionary*. 2010. http://
biography.yourdictionary.com/lucrezia-borgia-duchess-of-ferrara.

Manchester, William. *A World Lit Only by Fire*. Boston: Back Bay Books; Little,
Brown, 1992.

Mills, Patt. *The Golden Thread*. Bloomington, Ind.: AuthorHouse, 2009.

Pinsky, Robert. "Lucrezia Borgia's Hair and Forgotten Names." *Slate*, May 8,
2012.   http://www.slate.com/articles/arts/classic_poems/2012/05/walter
_savage_landor_poems_about_aristocratic_shoplifting_and_senile
_memory_loss_.html.

Sabatini, Rafael. "The Letter to Silvio Savelli." http://www.public-domain-content
.com/books/Life_of_Cesare_Borgia/C21P1.shtml. http://books.google.com
/books?id=Y71MlroFXgkC&pg=PR21&lpg=PR21&dq=lucrezia+borgia
+giovanni+sforza+Plautus+performed&source=bl&ots=G1iUuvEvSu
&sig=09Kfg5ZjEH7vTFVKvBRmuZkrgGs&hl=en&sa=X&ei=76IQ
VKfUCpaNNpGvgYAF&ved=0CEQQ6AEwBA#v=onepage&q=lucrezia%
20borgia%20giovanni%20sforza%20Plautus%20performed&f=false.

———. *The Life of Cesare Borgia*. London: Stanley Paul, 1912. e-book. https://
archive.org/stream/lifeofcesareborg00sabarich#page/n5/mode/2up.

4. Henry VIII and Anne Boleyn and Catherine Howard

Alchin, Linda. "The Tudors Sitemap." The Tudors Web Site. June 2014. http://
www.sixwives.info/the-tudors-sitemap.htm.

Barnes, Julian. *England, England*. New York: Vintage, 1998.

Cohen, Jennie. "Did Blood Cause Henry VIII's Madness and Reproductive
Woes?" history.com, March 4, 2011. http://www.history.com/news/did-blood
-cause-henry-viiis-madness-and-reproductive-woes.

Creamwood, James. "Executions and Horrible Tortures from Olden Times."
Excerpt from Smashwords e-book, 2014. http://free-ebook-samples.com/_/_
/475590/executions-horrible-tortures-from-olden-times.

Henry VIII. *The Love Letters of Henry VIII to Anne Boleyn*. J. O. Phillips, contributor. Rockville, Md.: Wildside Press, 2010.

Ives, Eric. *The Life and Death of Anne Boleyn*. Malden, Mass.: Blackwell,
2004.

Robinson, Hastings, ed. *Original Letters Relative to the English Reformation*.
Cambridge: Cambridge University Press, 1846. Google e-book. http://books
.google.com/books/about/Original_letters_relative_to_the_English.html
?id=3NdhAAAAIAAJ.

Robinson, James Harvey. "Three Sixteenth-Century Dispatches from Venetian
Ambassadors in London." In *Readings in European History*. Boston: Ginn,
1906. Document Discovery Project. http://rbsche.people.wm.edu/H111_doc
_dispacci.html.

Starkey, David. *Six Wives: The Queens of Henry VIII*. London: Chatto and Win-
dus, 2003.

Weir, Alison. *Henry VIII: The King and His Court.* New York: Ballantine Books, 2008.

5. Anna Ivanovna

Anisimov, Evgenii Viktorovich. *Five Empresses: Court Life in Eighteenth-Century Russia.* Westport, Conn.: Praeger, 2004.

"Anna." *The Columbia Electronic Encyclopedia.* 2012. infoplease.com. http://www .infoplease.com/encyclopedia/people/anna-czarina-russia.html.

Batuman, Elif. "The Ice Renaissance." *New Yorker,* May 29, 2006.

Bekorenu, Anna. "Anna Ivanovna." *1906 Jewish Encyclopedia.* http://www .jewishencyclopedia.com/articles/1553-anna-ivanovna.

Bos, Joan. "Ivan V of Russia." *Mad Monarchs Series.* September 12, 2011. http:// madmonarchs.guusbeltman.nl/madmonarchs/ivan5/ivan5_bio.htm.

Curtiss, Mina Kirstein. *A Forgotten Empress: Anna Ivanovna and Her Era, 1730– 1740.* New York: Frederick Ungar, 1974.

Field, Daniel, trans. "The Conditions of Anna Ivanovna's Accession to the Throne, 1730." *Documents in Russian History.* January 6, 2010. http://academic .shu.edu/russianhistory/index.php/The_%22Conditions%22_of_Anna _Ivanovna's_Accession_to_the_Throne,_1730.

Hughes, Lindsey. *Peter the Great, a Biography.* New Haven, Conn.: Yale University Press, 2004.

Laparenok, Leonid. "Prominent Russians: Peter II." russiapedia.rt.com. http:// russiapedia.rt.com/prominent-russians/the-romanov-dynasty/peter-ii/.

Monter, William. *The Rise of the Female Kings in Europe, 1300–1800.* New Haven, Conn.: Yale University Press, 2012.

"Prominent Russians: Anna Ioannovna." russiapedia.rt.com. http://russiapedia.rt .com/prominent-russians/the-romanov-dynasty/anna-ioannovna-empress -of-russia/.

Rhatigan, Joe. *Bizarre History: Strange Happenings, Stupid Misconceptions, Distorted Facts and Uncommon Events.* Bournemouth, England: Imagine, 2011.

Schrad, Mark Lawrence. *Vodka Politics: Alcohol, Autocracy, and the Secret History of the Russian State.* New York: Oxford University Press, 2014.

Shakibi, Zhand P. "Anna Ivanovna." *Encyclopedia of Russian History.* 2004. encyclopedia.com. http://www.encyclopedia.com/topic/Anna_Ivanovna.aspx.

Williams, Henry Smith, ed. *The Historians' History of the World.* London: the Times, 1908. Internet Archive e-book. https://archive.org/details/Historian sHistoryOfTheWorldComprehensiveNarrativeEtc.in25VolumesBy.

6. Timothy Dexter

Cofer, Jim. "Amazing Lives: Timothy Dexter." *History Blog,* April 16, 2013. http:// jimcofer.com/personal/2013/04/16/amazing-lives-timothy-dexter/comment -page-1/.

Currier, John James. *History of Newburyport, Mass: 1764–1905.* Newburyport,

1909. Google e-book. http://books.google.com/books/about/History_of_Newburyport_Mass.html?id=mdA1AAAAIAAJ.

Dexter, Lord Timothy. *A Pickle for the Knowing Ones; Or Plain Truths in a Homespun Dress*. Newburyport, Mass.: Blanchard and Sargent, 1848. Project Gutenberg e-book. http://www.gutenberg.org/ebooks/43453.

"Dexter's Contexture." *Essex Antiquarian* 7 (July 1903). http://www.lordtimothydexter.com/Antiquarian_Transcript.htm.

Knapp, Samuel Lorenzo. *Life of Lord Timothy Dexter: Embracing Sketches of the Eccentric Characters That Composed His Associates*. Boston: G. N. Thomson, 1838. Internet Archive e-book. https://archive.org/details/lifeoftimothydex00knap.

"Noue System of Knollege & Lite." LordTimothyDexter.com. July 2, 2008. http://www.comity.org/lordtimothydexter.com/index.htm.

"*Timothy Dexter Revisited* by John P. Marquand." Book review. *New England Quarterly* 33, no. 4 (December 1960). JSTOR online. http://www.jstor.org/stable/362682.

Todd, William Cleaves. *Timothy Dexter: Known as "Lord Timothy Dexter," of Newburyport, Mass. An Inquiry into His Life and Character*. Charleston, SC: Nabu Press, 2010.

7. Caroline Lamb and Lord Byron

Abbott, Elizabeth. *A History of Mistresses*. Toronto: HarperFlamingo, 2004.

Byron, George Gordon. *Byron's Letters and Journals*. Vol. 3, "*Alas! The Love of Women*," *1813–1814*. Boston: Belknap Press of Harvard University, 1974.

Douglass, Paul. *Lady Caroline Lamb: A Biography*. New York: Palgrave Macmillan, 2004.

Hanson, Marilee. "Lady Caroline Lamb Facts & Information—Lord Byron's Lovers" EnglishHistory.net, June 1997; revised March 7, 2004. http://englishhistory.net/byron/lclamb.html.

Mahan, Elizabeth Kerri. "Mad, Bad and Dangerous to Know: The Life of Lady Caroline Lamb." *Scandalous Women* (blog), October 9, 2007. http://scandalouswoman.blogspot.com/2007/10/mad-bad-and-dangerous-to-know-life-of.html.

Mitchell, L. G. *Lord Melbourne, 1779–1848*. Oxford: Oxford University Press, 1997.

Tallis, Dr. Frank. *Love Sick: Love as a Mental Illness*. New York: Thunder's Mouth Press, 2004.

8. John Ruskin and Effie Gray

Cooper, Suzanne Fagence. *Effie: The Passionate Lives of Effie Gray, John Ruskin and John Everett Millais*. New York: St. Martin's Press, 2010.

Fox, Essie. "Effie Gray's Revenge on John Ruskin." *History Girls* (blog), October 24, 2012. http://the-history-girls.blogspot.com/2012/10/effie-grays-revenge-on-john-ruskin.html.

Hilton, Tim. *John Ruskin*. New Haven, Conn.: Yale University Press, 2000.

Prodger, Michael. "John Ruskin's Marriage: What Really Happened?" theguardian
.com, March 29, 2013. http://www.theguardian.com/books/2013/mar/29
/ruskin-effie-marriage-inconvenience-brownell.

Ruskin, John. *Præterita*. New York: Knopf, 2005.

9. Oscar Wilde and Lord Alfred Douglas

Bentley, Toni. *Sisters of Salome*. Lincoln: Bison Books (University of Nebraska
Press), 2005.

Blake, Sarah. "The Tired Chameleon: A Study in Hues." In *Reading Wilde—
Querying Spaces*. New York University. http://www.nyu.edu/library/bobst
/research/fales/exhibits/wilde/0chamele.htm.

Claudia. "Lord Alfred Douglas." *Oscar Wilde—Standing Ovations*. http://www
.mr-oscar-wilde.de/about/d/douglas.htm.

Daniel, Anne Margaret. "Lost in Translation: Oscar, Bosie and Salome." *Prince-
ton University Library Chronicle*, 2007. http://www.annemargaretdaniel.com
/lost_in_translation__oscar__bosie__and_salome_66169.htm.

Douglas, Alfred. *Oscar Wilde and Myself*. New York: Duffield, 1914. Internet
Archive e-book. http://archive.org/stream/oscarwildemyself00dougrich/oscar
wildemyself00dougrich_djvu.txt.

Ellmann, Richard. *Oscar Wilde*. New York: Vintage, 1988.

Flood, Alison. "Oscar Wilde's Gift to Governor Who Let Him Read in Reading Gaol
Up for Auction." theguardian.com, May 13, 2014. http://www.theguardian
.com/books/2014/may/13/oscar-wilde-gift-governor-reading-gaol-auction.

Gribben, Mark. "Queensbury Rules." *The Trials of Oscar Wilde*. crimelibrary
.com. http://www.crimelibrary.com/gangsters_outlaws/cops_others/oscar
_wilde/4.html.

Harris, Frank. *Oscar Wilde: His Life and Confessions*. New York, Project Gutenberg
e-book, 1916. http://www.gutenberg.org/files/16894/16894-h/16894-h.htm.

"Letters from Oscar Wilde to Lord Alfred Douglas." In *Famous World Trials—The
Trials of Oscar Wilde—A Trial Account*. University of Missouri, Kansas City.
http://law2.umkc.edu/faculty/projects/ftrials/wilde/lettersfromwilde.html.

Lim, Andra. "The Isis, the Spirit Lamp and Male Sexuality: Oscar Wilde and Stu-
dent Journalism at the University of Oxford, 1892–1893." UCLA Library,
1996. http://www.library.ucla.edu/sites/default/files/AndraLim.pdf.

McKenna, Neil. *The Secret Life of Oscar Wilde*. New York: Basic Books, 2005.

Popova, Maria. "Oscar Wilde's Stirring Love Letters to Lord Alfred 'Bosie' Douglas." brainpickings.org. http://www.brainpickings.org/2013/07/15/oscar
-wilde-love-letters-bosie/.

Wilde, Oscar. "The Ballad of Reading Gaol." Project Gutenberg e-book, 2008;
revised, 2013. http://www.gutenberg.org/files/301/301-h/301-h.html.

10. Edith Wharton and Morton Fullerton

Benstock, Shari. *Edith Wharton: No Gift from Chance*. New York: Scribner, 1994.

Crosley, Sloane. *How Did You Get This Number*. New York: Penguin, 2010.

Edel, Leon. *Henry James: A Life*. New York: Harper and Row, 1955.

Erlich, Gloria C. *The Sexual Education of Edith Wharton*. Berkeley: University of California Press, 1992.

Fields, Jennie. *The Age of Desire*. New York: Penguin, 2012.

Franzen, Jonathan. "A Rooting Interest: Edith Wharton and the Problem of Sympathy." *New Yorker*, February 13, 2012. http://www.newyorker.com/magazine/2012/02/13/a-rooting-interest.

Lee, Hermione. *Edith Wharton*. London: Vintage, 2008.

Lee, Robert. "A Female Ulysses." THE (Times Higher Education) Web site, June 5, 1995. http://www.timeshighereducation.co.uk/books/a-female-ulysses/161610.article.

Smith, Joan. "Age of Not So Much Innocence: Edith Wharton—No Gifts from Chance." Book review. *Independent*, October 16, 1994. http://www.independent.co.uk/arts-entertainment/book-review–age-of-not-so-much-innocence-edith-wharton-no-gifts-from-chance-by-shari-benstock-hamish-hamilton-pounds-20-1443210.html.

Tuttleton, James W., Kristin O. Lauer, and Margaret P. Murray, eds. *Edith Wharton: The Contemporary Reviews*. Cambridge: Cambridge University Press, 1992.

Updike, John. "The Changeling—A New Biography of Edith Wharton." *New Yorker*, April 16, 2007. http://www.newyorker.com/magazine/2007/04/16/the-changeling.

Wharton, Edith. "The Fulness of Life." Classic Reader e-book. http://www.classicreader.com/book/1977/1/.

———. "The Life Apart" ("Love Diary"). In *The Heath Anthology of American Literature*, 5th ed. Edited by Paul Lauler. New York: Houghton Mifflin, 2005.

11. Oskar Kokoschka and Alma Mahler

"Alma." *Alma on Tour—History*. http://www.alma-mahler.at/engl/almas_life/almas_life.html.

Connolly, Sarah. "Classical Music: The Alma Problem." theguardian.com, December 2, 2010. http://www.theguardian.com/music/2010/dec/02/alma-schindler-problem-gustav-mahler.

Donatone, Brooke. "Why Millennials Can't Grow Up." *Slate*, December 2, 2013. http://www.slate.com/articles/health_and_science/medical_examiner/2013/12/millennial_narcissism_helicopter_parents_are_college_students_bigger_problem.html#.

Laslocky, Meghan. *The Little Book of Heartbreak*. New York: Penguin/Plume, 2012.

Lukkonen, Petri. "Oskar Kokoschka." *Pegasos*, 2008. http://www.kirjasto.sci.fi/kokos.htm.

Magill, Frank N., ed. *The 20th Century Go-N: Dictionary of World Biography*. Vol. 8. New York: Routledge, 1999.

"Oskar Kokoschka." *Belvedere Collections.* http://www.belvedere.at/en/sammlu ngen/belvedere/expressionismus/kokoschka.

Predota, Georg. "Between Mahler and Gropius: Oskar Kokoschka and the Alma Doll." *Interlude,* July 28, 2014. http://www.interlude.hk/front/between -mahler-and-gropiusoskar-kokoschka-and-the-alma-doll/.

"Silent Partners—Artist and Mannequin from Function to Fetish." *10 Highlight Objects and Context Stories.* Fitzwilliam Museum, Cambridge exhibit. October 14, 2014, to January 25, 2015. http://www.fitzmuseum.cam.ac.uk /documents/20140901SilentPartnersHighlightStories.pdf.

Wallace, David. *Exiles in Hollywood.* Pompton Plains, N.J.: Limelight Editions, 2006.

12. Norman Mailer and Adele Morales Mailer

Bader, Eleanor. "'Norman Mailer: The American': Was He the Most Valiant and the Most Disgusting Patriot of All Time?" *Alternet,* May 25, 2012. http://www .alternet.org/story/155557/'norman_mailer%3A_the_american'%3A_was _he_the_most_valiant_and_most_disgusting_patriot_of_all_time.

Burkeman, Oliver. "Machismo Isn't That Easy to Wear." theguardian.com, February 5, 2002. http://www.theguardian.com/books/2002/feb/05/fiction .oliverburkeman.

Dearborn, Mary V. *Mailer: A Biography.* New York: Houghton Mifflin, 1999.

Gill, John Freeman. "City People: The Woman in the Shadows." *New York Times,* November 18, 2007. http://www.nytimes.com/2007/11/18/nyregion/thecity /18adel.html.

Johnson, Daniel. "Morman Mailer: . . . Or Hate Him." *New York Sun,* November 15, 2007. http://www.nysun.com/opinion/morman-mailer-or-hate-him/66481/.

Kobel, Peter. "Crime and Punishment." EW.com, November 15, 1991. http://www .ew.com/ew/article/0,,316162,00.html.

Lennon, J. Michael. *Norman Mailer: A Double Life.* New York: Simon and Schuster, 2013.

Lord, M. G. "Ancient Evenings." *New York Times,* July 13, 1997. http://www .nytimes.com/books/97/07/13/reviews/970713.13lord.html.

Mailer, Adele. *The Last Party: Scenes from My Life with Norman Mailer.* Fort Lee, N.J.: Barricade Books, 2004.

Mailer, Norman. *Selected Letters of Norman Mailer.* Edited by J. Michael Lennon. New York: Random House, 2014.

———. "The White Negro." *Dissent,* Fall 1979. http://www.dissentmagazine.org /wp-content/files_mf/1353950503Mailer_WhiteNegro.pdf.

Mailer, Norris Church. *A Ticket to the Circus: A Memoir.* New York: Random House, 2010.

McGrath, Thomas. "Norman Mailer: Stabbing Your Wife as an Existential Experiment." dangerousminds.net, June 1, 2013. http://dangerousminds.net /comments/norman_mailer_stabbing_your_wife_as_an_existential _experiment.

"Norman Mailer and the Romance of Crime." *vulgar morality* (blog), November 12, 2007. http://vulgarmorality.wordpress.com/2007/11/12/414/.

Podhoretz, Norman. *The Norman Podhoretz Reader: A Selection of His Writings from the 1950s Through the 1990s.* Edited by Thomas L. Jeffers. New York: Free Press/Simon and Schuster, 2004.

13. Debbie Reynolds and Eddie Fisher and Elizabeth Taylor

Bateman, Christopher. "Liz and Dick: The Ultimate Celebrity Couple." *VF Daily*, June 1, 2010. http://www.vanityfair.com/online/daily/2010/06/liz-and-dick-the-ultimate-celebrity-couple.

"Elizabeth Taylor's Never-Before-Read Love Letters from Richard Burton." *Huff Post Entertainment*, June 1, 2010; updated May 25, 2011. http://www.huffingtonpost.com/2010/06/01/elizabeth-taylor-never-be_n_595960.html.

Fisher, Eddie, with David Fisher. *Been There, Done That.* New York: St. Martin's Press, 1999.

James, Bryan. "Behind the Scenes: The Liz-Eddie-Debbie (& Richard) Scandals." *Classic Films Reloaded.* http://classicfilmsreloaded.com/butterfield8-2.html.

Kashner, Sam, and Nancy Schoenberger. *Furious Love: Elizabeth Taylor, Richard Burton and the Marriage of the Century.* New York: HarperCollins, 2010.

Keck, William. "Scandal's History for 'These Old Broads.'" *Los Angeles Times*, February 12, 2001. http://articles.latimes.com/2001/feb/12/entertainment/ca-24245.

Leafe, David. "The Ultimate Sexual Betrayal—and the Guilt That Haunted Liz Taylor to the Grave." dailymail.com, April 26, 2013; updated April 29, 2013. http://www.dailymail.co.uk/femail/article-2315458/Elizabeth-Taylors-affair-Eddie-Fisher-ultimate-sexual-betrayal-friend-Debbie-Reynolds.html.

Mann, William J. *How to Be a Movie Star: Elizabeth Taylor in Hollywood.* New York: Houghton Mifflin Harcourt, 2009.

Midgley, Neil. "Liz Taylor: Seven husbands, but Eight Marriages." *Telegraph*, March 23, 2011. http://www.telegraph.co.uk/culture/8401053/Liz-Taylor-seven-husbands-but-eight-marriages.html.

Petersen, Anne Helen. "Scandals of Classic Hollywood: Elizabeth Taylor, Black Widow." thehairpin.com, July 25, 2011. http://thehairpin.com/2011/07/scandals-of-classic-hollywood-elizabeth-taylor-black-.

Taraborrelli, J. Randy. *Elizabeth.* New York: Warner Books, 2006.

General
Wikipedia entries were accessed for information on people, places, and things.

Acknowledgments

It doesn't take a lot of people to write a book. It takes one person. But if that person is me, I know that I would have fallen apart psychologically and never actually completed this book without the support from the following people:

My mom, Kathleen Wright, who has been the first person to read every piece I have ever written and the only non-editor who ever reads them before they're published. Thank God she does or the grammar would be completely incoherent. She is brilliant and hilarious and you should look her up if you're in Charleston.

My dad, Tom Wright. I'm 100 percent about to get to work on the novel, for sure, just as soon as I finish this.

Seth Porges, my longtime pal who first introduced me to Timothy Dexter and has listened to me talk enthusiastically about approximately a million other personalities who might have been included in this work.

My amazing editor, Allison Adler, who has held my hand

through a lot of the neurosis and two a.m. anxieties I've experienced as a result of working on this book. There have been *a lot.*

The entire Henry Holt team. What nice, cool people. If you are thinking of publishing a book, you should definitely go with them because they've made this book as good as it can possibly be. I hope it sells lots of copies and we all get rich.

My equally amazing agent, Nicole Tourtelot, who made it possible for me to wake up at 10:30 in the morning and spend all day writing and make a living at it. That is a crazy amazing thing she made possible, and anyone who tells you it isn't is an insane liar.

I should also thank my really nice ex, Davey Volner, who introduced me to Nicole, and who first told me that this was a *great* idea for a book.

Peter Feld, who has been supporting my writing and telling me not to give up since the first day I moved to New York seven years ago. Thank you, especially, for all the potato pancakes.

And the friends from article club, book club, the Junior League, and all the extended family and friends who have listened to me talk about historical personalities and told me it was fun and funny and cool. Thank you all so, so much.

And to my current boyfriend, Daniel Kibblesmith, the funniest man I've ever met, who is also the nicest. You make me so happy and give me faith in a lot of things, including, but not limited to, love.

About the Author

JENNIFER WRIGHT is a contributor to the *New York Observer* and the *New York Post*, covering sex and dating. She was one of the founding editors of TheGloss.com, and her writing regularly appears in such publications as *Cosmopolitan*, *Glamour*, and *Maxim*. Her breakup cure is gin, reruns of *30 Rock*, and historical biographies. She lives and loves very happily in New York City.